Strategy
IN THE
21ˢᵗ Century

Strategy IN THE 21ST Century

*A Practical
Strategic Management
Process*

RANDALL ROLLINSON
EARL YOUNG

LookingGlass Publishing

Strategy in the 21st Century
Copyright © 2010 by Randall Rollinson and Earl Young

International Standard Book Number: 978-0-9841936-0-8
Library of Congress Catalog Number: 2009942788

All rights reserved. No part of this book may be reproduced in any form or by any electronic means, including information storage and retrieval systems, without written permission from the authors, except by a reviewer, who may quote brief passages in a review.

Photographs on pages 70, 434, and the book cover by Richard Faulkner

PRINTED IN THE UNITED STATES OF AMERICA

LOOKINGGLASS PUBLISHING
CHICAGO, ILLINOIS
WWW.LOOKINGGLASSPUBLISHING.COM

Dedication

Our heartfelt dedication of this book goes to the memory of Dr. Gemma Welsch. In 2003, on more than one occasion, Gemma (an associate professor of accounting at DePaul University) said, *"Randy, if you really want to make a lasting impact on the field of strategy, you must write a book."* This challenge has inspired us each and every day since.

And most importantly, we dedicate this book to Diane Rollinson and Yvonne Young, our wives who gave us unfailing support.

Table of Contents

LIST OF FIGURES AND TABLES XV
ACKNOWLEDGEMENTS XIV
PREFACE XXI

Introduction 1
   Chapter 1—Stategic Management: An Overview 3
   Chapter 2—Initiating a Strategic
      Management Program 5
      Step 1: Assess the current strategic direction
         and capabilities 5
      Step 2: Design and organize an appropriate
         startup program based on these assessments 6
   Chapter 3—Stategic Information
      Analysis and Evaluation 6
      Step 3: Conduct external strategic analyses 6
      Step 4: Conduct internal strategic analyses 6
      Step 5: Develop a strategic information system 7
      Step 6: Evaluate results of strategic analysis 7
   Chapter 4—Strategy Formulation 7
      Step 7: Define the strategic direction of the
         organization 8
      Step 8: Compile a comprehensive set of strategies
         for arriving at the desired destination 8

Step 9: Evaluate and select a set of strategies
for inclusion in the strategic plan 8
Chapter 5—Stategic Planning 9
Step 10: Develop a comprehensive strategic plan 9
Step 11: Develop a strategic operating plan (SOP) 9
Chapter 6—Strategy Implementation 10
Step 12: Implement the strategic operating plan 10
Step 13: Strategic management
as an ongoing process 10

Chapter 1 • Strategic Management: An Overview 13

Strategy Defined 13
    Strategy timeline 14
Military Origins of Strategy 16
Strategic Management After World War II 19
    Conceptual foundations are established 21
    SWOT analysis 22
    Strategic management emerges as a
        major business discipline 29
    Contemporary models 29
Strategic Management Competencies 46
    Identifying, articulating, and developing
        a core set of shared values 48
    Visioning 48
    Strategic thinking 49
    Identifying and developing core organizational
        competencies and capabilities 49
    Converting information into strategic intelligence 50
    Identifying, evaluating, and
        selecting strategic alternatives 51
    Team work and team building 51
The Ever-changing Context of
    Strategic Management 53

Globalization... 54
Information technology.. 56
Knowledge management 57
The discipline of strategic management 58
Characteristics of Effective
Strategic Management Systems................................... 59

Chapter 2 • Initiating a Strategic Management System 67

STEP 1: ASSESS THE CURRENT STRATEGIC
   DIRECTION AND CAPABILITIES... 68
   An assessment of the organization's
      current strategic direction.................................... 72
   An assessment of current
      strategy management capabilities.......................... 77
   An assessment of contextual, situational,
      and unique features that will significantly impact
      a strategic management program 81
STEP 2: DESIGN AND ORGANIZE AN APPROPRIATE
   STARTUP PROGRAM BASED ON THESE ASSESSMENTS 85
   Design the program... 85
   Selection of the level and scope of the
      startup program.. 86
   Modify design features 91
   Organize the program 92

Chapter 3 • Strategic Information Analysis and Evaluation 99

STEP 3: CONDUCT EXTERNAL STRATEGIC ANALYSES.......... 101
   Macro-level analysis.. 102
   Micro-level analysis 106
STEP 4: CONDUCT INTERNAL STRATEGIC ANALYSES 110

STEP 5: DEVELOP A STRATEGIC
INFORMATION SYSTEM (SIS) 123
   The rationale for a free-standing SIS 126
   Designing and developing a system versus
      managing within a system 127
   Factors to consider in designing a strategic
      information system... 129
   Basic features of a strategic information system 131

STEP 6: EVALUATE RESULTS OF STRATEGIC ANALYSES......... 137
   Review the external scan carefully............................. 140
   Compile a list of the organization's
      primary market opportunities and threats............ 140
   Agree upon the organization's core
      competencies/competitive advantages................... 141
   Rank the organization's market opportunities and
      threats in light of its core competencies 143
   Review the internal scan carefully.............................. 143
   Compile a list of the organization's primary internal
      strengths and weaknesses 144
   Rank the organization's internal strengths and
      weaknesses in light of its primary
      marketing opportunities 145
   Evaluate the strategic management system................ 145

Chapter 4 • Strategy Formulation 149

STEP 7: DEFINE THE STRATEGIC DIRECTION
OF THE ORGANIZATION.. 150
   Vision 152
   Mission 157
   Values... 159
   Policies 163
   Goals.. 167

Table of Contents

STEP 8: COMPILE A COMPREHENSIVE SET OF STRATEGIES FOR
ARRIVING AT THE DESIRED DESTINATION 173
    Identify activities underway within the
        organization that will impact on strategy 176
    Identify key results areas requiring and/or
        providing opportunities for developing
        new/revised strategies 179
    Develop a framework of key result areas
        with typical strategies 182
    Develop new/revised strategic alternatives 186

STEP 9: EVALUATE AND SELECT A SET OF STRATEGIES FOR
INCLUSION IN THE STRATEGIC PLAN 197
    Provide an overview of strategy evaluation and
        selection processes 198
    Identify and describe core evaluation and
        selection criteria 200
    Identify and describe contextual/situational
        evaluation and selection criteria 202
    Evaluate, select, and modify strategic initiatives
        currently being implemented 210
    Evaluate, classify, and select strategies
        identified/generated in Step 8 212

Chapter 5 • Strategic Planning 233

STEP 10: DEVELOP A COMPREHENSIVE
STRATEGIC PLAN 234
    Compare and contrast strategic thinking and
        strategic planning 235
    Consider strategic planning as
        a two-phase process 236
    Features of effective long-term strategic plans 238
    Features of effective short-term
        strategic plans (strategic operating plans) 243

Identify and evaluate the various types of
    strategic activities currently underway 244
Format new and/or revised strategies 245
Develop a comprehensive planning framework 246
Make provisions for contingency plans 249
Write a summary statement of a
    two-phase strategic plan 249
Obtain management feedback, revisions,
    approval, and authorization to continue 253
Produce an illustrative strategic plan 254

STEP 11: DEVELOP A
STRATEGIC OPERATING PLAN (SOP) 258

Identify implementation planning guidelines 260
Define accountability linkages between the
    longer-term strategic plan and a
    strategic operating plan 264
Identify strategic objectives in core functions............ 269
Develop a strategy deployment map for each goal 271
Identify management roles and responsibilities
    necessary to implement the SOP 273
Develop implementation plans for
    strategic objectives 274
Develop implementation plans for
    strategic objectives in nonproject formats 284
Reconcile requirements of the
    strategic operating plan with available
    implementation capabilities and resources 293
Write a summary implementation budget 294
Obtain management approval and authorization
    for the summary implementation plan
    for the strategic operating plan 295
Distribute and communicate
    the strategic operating plan 296

Table of Contents

Comments on the use of project management tools and concepts 298

Chapter 6 • Strategy Implementation 299

STEP 12: IMPLEMENT THE STRATEGIC OPERATING PLAN 301

Understand the rationale for an organized and disciplined strategy implementation process 303

Identify the key managerial roles, responsibilities, and capabilities required to implement a strategic operating plan 308

Identify key contextual/situational conditions that impact implementation processes 331

Assess the significant contextual and situational conditions that impact the implementation of the strategic operating plan 335

STEP 13: STRATEGIC MANAGEMENT AS AN ONGOING PROCESS 337

Compare and contrast initial implementation processes and ongoing line implementation processes 340

Integrate implementation team roles and responsibilities into line management job descriptions 351

Identify, understand, accept, and prepare to carry out the new implementation responsibilities of the line organization 353

Manage remaining implementation tasks 353

Assess the impact of the strategic operating plan on the organization 354

XIII

Strategy in the 21st Century

Develop a framework for evaluating and continuously improving the current strategic management capability 355

EPILOGUE 359

APPENDIX 1 DISTILLED WISDOM 371
APPENDIX 2 AN ANNOTATED
   BIBLIOGRAPHY OF PUBLICATIONS ABOUT TEAMS 377
APPENDIX 3 INTERNAL ANALYSIS/AUDIT CHECKLIST 389
APPENDIX 4 THE NOMINAL GROUP TECHNIQUE TO
   CLARIFY AND PRIORITIZE AN **OTSW** EVALUATION 397

GLOSSARY OF STRATEGIC MANAGEMENT TERMS 405
BIBLIOGRAPHY 421
INDEX 427

Figures and Tables

Figures

1.1	Strategy Timeline	15
1.2	OTSW Analysis	24
1.3	Ansoff's Grid	27
1.4	The BCG Growth Share Matrix	30
1.5	Porter's Five Forces	32
1.6	Balanced Scorecard	39
1.7	Red Ocean and Blue Ocean Strategy	41
1.8	The Hedgehog Concept	42
2.1	Initial Assessment of the Level of Development of the Current Strategic Direction	76
2.2	Initial Assessment of Current Strategic Management Capabilities	79
2.3	Assessment of Factors Influencing the Nature/Scope of the Strategic Program	83
3.1	Framework for External Analysis	101
3.2	Framework for Environmental Analysis	110
3.3	Framework for Internal Analysis	111
3.4	Strategic Management at Work	124
3.5	OTSW Evaluation	137
3.6	Ansoff's Grid	141
4.1	Shared Vision is a Byproduct of Transparent Communications	156

4.2	Goals Are Directional Themes	171
4.3	Notion of Organizational Building Blocks	179
4.4	Leadership Perceptions of the Likely Impact of Strategies	216
4.5	The Expectation of Goal Achievement	221
4.6	The Linkage/Synergy/Alignment Among Core Functions	226
4.7	Selection of Strategies for Inclusion in the Strategic Plan	230
5.1	Relationship Between Strategic Planning and Strategic Operational Planning	247
5.2	Strategic Plan with Functional Linkages for One Goal	265
5.3	Balanced Scorecard	267
5.4	Deployment Map	272
5.5	Double Loop Learning	275
5.6	Performance Measurement Exercise	278
5.7	Sample Performance Measure	279
6.1	Factors Impacting Implementation Processes	307
6.2	Sample Annual Performance Measurement Calendar	326
6.3	Assessment of Significant and Situational Conditions on the Implementation Process	336
6.4	Framework for Evaluating and Improving Strategic Management	356

Tables

1.1	Kenneth Andrews on Strategy as an Intellectual Process	26
1.2	Criteria for Becoming an Academic Discipline	29
1.3	Balanced Scorecard Perspectives: Types of Measures	38
1.4	Hamel and Prahalad	40

1.5	Misconceptions about Strategic Management	46
1.6	Rationale for Team-based Leadership and Management	52
1.7	Characteristics of Effective Strategic Management Systems	60
2.1	Components of an Initial Assessment	71
2.2	Components of Strategic Direction	73
3.1	Key Dimensions to the Macro-level Environment	103
3.2	Key Dimensions to the Micro-level Environment	107
3.3	Key Components of the Internal Dimension	112
4.1	Components of Strategic Direction	151
4.2	Characteristics of Effective Vision Statements	153
4.3	Examples of Vision Statements	154
4.4	Vision Statement Development Process	155
4.5	Characteristics of Effective Mission Statements	158
4.6	Examples of Mission Statements	160
4.7	Characteristics of Effective Values	161
4.8	Examples of Organizational Values	162
4.9	Examples of Policies	164
4.10	Indirect Impact of Policies on Strategic Direction	165
4.11	Tasks to Complete to Determine Impact of Policies on Strategic Direction	166
4.12	Examples of Effective Goal Statements	168
4.13	Characteristics of Effective Goal Statements	168
4.14	Major Aspects of Goal Setting	169
4.15	Criteria for Evaluating Current Goals	170
4.16	Sample Strategic Direction—National Food Service Association	172
4.17	Benefits to Identifying Activities with Strategic Impact Already Underway	177

4.18	Framework of External Key Result Areas with Sample Strategies	182
4.19	Framework of Internal Key Result Areas with Sample Strategies	183
4.20	Guidelines for Developing Strategic Alternatives	187
5.1	Features of a Long-Term Plan	239
5.2	Suggested Format and Content of the Two-Phase Strategic Plan	250
5.3	Sample Strategic Plan for the National Food Service Association	255
5.4	Effective Implementation Guidelines	261
5.5	Comparison of Balanced Scorecard Model to a Traditional Functional Approach	268
5.6	Questions to Ask and Answer in Translating Strategy into Operational Objectives	269
5.7	Sample Set of Balanced Objectives	270
5.8	Sample Set of KPIs with Targets	280
5.9	Sample Strategic Operating Plan with Projects	283
5.10	Useful Strategic Implementation Formats	285
6.1	Key Premises Executives Ignore Related to Execution (Bossidy and Charan)	304
6.2	Features of the Delta and the Challenges of Change (LaMarsh)	305
6.3	Alternative Implementation Approaches	318
6.4	Key Contextual/Situational Conditions	332
6.5	Dimensions and Challenges of Implementation	341
6.6	Implementation Task Characteristics	344
6.7	Implementation Barriers	346
6.8	Line Management Implementation Skills and Abilities	350
6.9	Implementation Roles and Responsibilities	352

Acknowledgements

Assuming an author has something meaningful to say, it still must be written clearly, organized precisely, and presented effectively from the moment the first word is drafted until the last photograph is taken. We could not have done this project without Richard Faulkner, and we are eternally grateful to him for his friendship, guidance, patience, tenacity, professionalism, and, most importantly, his eraser.

Susan Kroll played an important role in editing an early version of the manuscript. As a dear friend, an experienced planning professional, and an excellent writer, Susan provided most helpful insights and critiques, and we are truly grateful to Sue.

Valerie Hogan also played a significant role. Her skillful desktop publishing support in creating the graphics and doing the page layouts made a timely and tangible contribution to the final product.

Dianne Young made an early contribution to this book with the original design of the OTSW evaluation that appears in the appendices. She is an exceptional consultant, trainer, and professional colleague.

To all these team members we want to express our sincere appreciation.

Preface

When two open-minded and hard-nosed professionals decide to coauthor a book, they have made a life altering commitment. Behind those commitments are two personal "back stories." These stories intersect and then meld, and finally if both parties listen to one another they produce something of unique value. Here are the "back stories" behind our three-year journey in writing this book.

Part 1: Randall Rollinson

My own story begins in St. Louis in 1976. My soon-to-become wife Diane and I had just completed our master's degrees in rehabilitation counseling, and I was working with handicapped adults who were looking to become gainfully employed. My job was to assess the challenges they faced and the capabilities they had to pursue opportunities for work. I listened as each person would describe his or her goals to me. Our program then helped our clients prepare a written plan that helped guide them toward getting what they wanted in the workplace. As in any human endeavor, sometimes the plan worked and other times it did not. Outcome aside, I came to appreciate the synergistic power of listening, teamwork, and planning at the age of 26.

Strategy in the 21st Century

A few years later I became the executive director of a small rehabilitation agency in Chicago. I used my listening and emerging planning skills to help the board and staff build and execute what the management field referred to as a "comprehensive long range plan." Three years and a lot of hard work saw the organization grow to become a respected and valued service provider in the community. The power of working together as a team to ensure success in formulating and executing strategy again hit home with me; only now I had the added the motivation of being entrusted with leading the organization.

In 1980 I became an associate director of a statewide advocacy association representing more than 100 local and regional organizations providing services to people with handicaps. Here my listening skills, team-oriented philosophy, and proven "strategic planning" skills would meld allowing me to help strengthen the capacity and performance of the association and its members. Simultaneously, I pursued an MBA in Management at DePaul University. At DePaul, I dove headlong into studying and understanding what academia was coming to know as the "strategic management discipline."

In the spring of 1985 I was bitten by the entrepreneur bug. Taking on two business partners, we founded the Center for Enterprise Development, an education and training business. Together we designed and developed "applied learning" certificate programs geared to build practical understanding and skills in business administration for two different executive management audiences including nonprofit organizations and for-profit small to mid-sized businesses. *Dr. Earl Young was one of the founding members of the faculty.* Our programs launched as a joint venture with DePaul University's College of Commerce. In 1988 we moved our programs from DePaul to the University of Illinois at Chicago where the for-profit certificate program continues to this day.

Preface

At that core of both programs was a robust and applied module on strategic management named the *Management Through Applied Planning Process*® (MAPP) that we designed and developed and that I taught to approximately 1500 organizations. I then sold my interest in what had become an award-winning curriculum known as the *Certificate in Business Administration Program*. I immediately turned my attention to designing a new certificate program focused exclusively on the discipline of strategic management (www.csmlearning.com).

As a way to fund my continued involvement in education and training initiatives, I hung out a shingle (in 1987) as a strategic management consultant to a wide range of organizations under the name LBL Strategies, Ltd. *(as in Look Before You Leap)*. Numbered among our clients early on were graduates of our certificate programs, and it is the LBL venture we are continuing to grow and develop.

Earlier in 1991 Diane Rollinson and I become business partners. Together we began to create a strategic management software solution to support the MAPP methodology and process. Diane and I had identical academic backgrounds and the same mailing address, but she focused her interest and career in the fields of database design and data architecture. Our first attempt to develop strategic management software ended in failure in the late 1990s. Nonetheless, we learned hugely valuable lessons especially when it comes to the importance of simplicity in design...in all things. After recovering from this decade long development "experiment" and fully armed with lessons learned and new insights, we teamed up with friend and application architect Jobin Ephrem to design and develop a practical web-based strategic management tool that fully complemented our education, training, and consulting services. We successfully launched MAPPware in 2002, and it is fully integrated with our offerings today (www.mappware.com).

Strategy in the 21st Century

Over the years of launching and building entrepreneurial ventures, I remember consciously making and remaking the decision to dedicate the remainder of my career to bringing the power of strategic management to established organizations around the world. In those moments, and in every moment since, I remained inspired by advice given to me in 1978 by Fred McDonald, that is," *Randy, find one thing and become the best at it, and the world will beat a path to your door.*" Fred was CEO of the Lighthouse for the Blind, and his early mentorship of me changed the trajectory of my life.

By early 2003 our team of strategy professionals had worked on approximately 2500 strategic planning and management processes, and we were seeking to gain broader market acceptance of our work. It was at that time that our trusted and respected academic colleague, DePaul University's Gemma Welsch, challenged me to write this book. For several years I contemplated on it, and then, in December 2006, Diane and I made a personal and financial commitment to take it on.

As a first step in the process I recruited my long time friend and professional colleague, Earl Young, to collaborate with me. Earl agreed, and in April 2007 we began a disciplined weekly meeting process that would bring us together 71 times to pour our hearts and souls into the content you now hold in your hands. This was a true team effort between Earl and me and a collaboration that, for me, was an opportunity of a lifetime.

Now 33 years later I can report that it has been quite a journey for me and for our team. We are humbled by what we have learned and experienced along the way. We hope that our passion for the power of strategic management will rub off on those who read this book.

Part 2: Earl Young

We have been friends and colleagues for 25 years. We began collaborating in 1985, when Randy asked me to participate in his newly developed Certificate in Business Administration, which he and his associates were offering through the DePaul University Program for Continuing and Professional Education. At that time, I was teaching several courses at DePaul in operations management, including operations strategy. Previously, I had taught courses in strategic management at the State University of New York at Albany and the Illinois Institute of Technology.

We both had experienced the same challenges in teaching strategic management, since, at the time, the majority of the literature was either a scholar's focus on some dimension of the field or a practitioner's perspective based on his/her experiences with clients. In either case, the result was a rapidly growing body of work that we refer to as the "wisdom" literature. Each new book or article seemed to be "the answer." However, because of its very nature as an integrating management discipline that aligns and focuses all other management disciplines in a given organization, it will probably never have the closure and coherence of, for example, accounting.

At the same time, any teacher committed to the task of giving students an understanding of, and skill in the application of, this key body of knowledge will recognize this challenge. We found this to be the key focal point, mutual interest, and shared challenge in teaching and consulting with respect to strategic management. For the next few years, we dealt with this challenge individually but always with the sense that there "has to be a better way."

During these years Randy enlisted the help of his wife, Diane, an information systems professional. Together they began to develop software that would greatly expand the capabilities of the strategic management team. This made it possible for the team to maintain a strategic management system, based on a continuous flow of the rapidly increasing amounts of information required to formulate and implement a competitive strategy.

His vision and her technical skills proved to be a winning combination as they developed a systematic and easily understood approach to strategic management. Ultimately, their collaboration resulted in the design and development of MAPPware, a software program that provides a forum for multi-individual and/or team inputs to the development of a consensus-driven strategy for an organization.

In 2003 Randy gave a demonstration of the use of MAPPware at the Program for Entrepreneurship at DePaul University to interested faculty and students. After the meeting, Professor Gemma Welsch, a DePaul Professor of Information Systems and Technology, told Randy: "If you really want to make a lasting impact on the field of strategy, you must write a book." The seed was sown in Randy's mind, and it would only be a matter of time before this book would come into being.

A little later that year, Randy asked me to observe one of his graduate courses where he was having students use MAPPware with firms that agreed to use this software to develop new and/or improve upon existing strategies in their organizations. Somewhere along the line in listening to Randy and the students, it dawned on me that it was not about finding another theory, model, principle, or best practice. It was about releasing the creative potential and practical insights and experiences of all the willing participants in an organization and harnessing them in the development of a consensus-based strategy for their organization.

It became increasingly clear to both of us that a book was now the order of the day. The steps that we used in teaching strategic management were essentially the same: analyze, evaluate, determine the strategic direction, identify alternative strategies, select those the team considered the most appropriate, develop a long- and short-term strategic plan, implement the short-term plan, and continuously improve.

What was needed was a book that would incorporate a systematic, process-driven approach based on a comprehensive understanding of the literature. It would also have to capture the innovative and creative aspects of strategic management, as well as the more hard-core dimensions of strategic analysis and planning. We also made an initial assumption that this book would need to be a "stand alone" product that could be used by executives, managers, consultants, and students without supplementary instruction.

As is often said, the "devil is in the details," and these were not easily resolved; in fact, we are still refining and improving on many of these processes, such as identifying strategic alternatives. At the same time, there is enough convergence in our thinking and in the literature to write a book at this time.

Introduction

Beginning in the 1950s *strategic management* emerged as one of the most widely used (and often misused) terms in the business management lexicon. It has been the focus of a constant stream of articles, books, tools, concepts, and software; the primary product/service of many consulting firms; and a required capstone course in most MBA programs. Strategy-focused organizations are increasingly more common, as boards, owners, and executives around the world seek out the advice of the latest crop of consulting gurus. However, the actual practice of strategic management is limited to the innovators and adopters on the cutting edge in developing and applying it as a discipline.

For the overwhelming majority of organizations, including many large, growing, and profitable firms, strategic management is still viewed as an option, even a luxury. For the past 30 plus years management attention has been focused on functional management primarily in marketing and finance, followed by operations, and more recently in information processing and management.

During this time the emphasis has overwhelmingly been on making incremental improvements in systems and processes. The recognition of the need for a strategically-aligned organization capable of responding to disruptive events and accelerating rates of change was not widespread. It remained the province of forward thinking theorists, consultants, and leading edge corporations. The vast majority of organizations had grown accustomed to the incremental and predictable rates of change in a slow-growing economy.

It is not that management in these organizations is unaware of the many benefits attributed to corporate strategy. Executives and managers in these organizations are not averse to change, nor are they unwilling to commit resources to developing new approaches. Their hesitancy is more often based on a healthy skepticism of the steady stream of new conceptual models and theories about strategy and strategic planning with scant consideration for the often more complex processes of strategy implementation.

With these considerations in mind, we designed this book for emerging strategy professionals, owners, and managers that want to accept the challenge of strategic management. They see the need for more effective strategic management processes in their organizations but are understandably confused by the stream of models, theories, and "proven" approaches.

Owners and managers would like to have a basic understanding of strategic management; a practical approach to selecting, developing, and implementing an appropriate strategy; and a means of implementing the strategic management process in their organization. They want to be empowered to take their organization to the highest level of their aspirations, consistent with the resources and capabilities of their organization and its members. Accordingly, this book is organized as outlined below.

Chapter 1—Strategic Management: An Overview

Chapter 1 provides an introduction to the *strategic management process* including:

- Definitions of basic terminology
- An overview of the origin and development of strategic management
- Brief descriptions of selected strategic management models and theories
- A discussion of the emergence of strategic management as a comprehensive management discipline
- A detailed set of core competencies deployed throughout all management levels and functions
- The infrastructure and processes required to develop an effective and sustainable organization strategy
- A presentation of the changing context of strategic management
- Criteria for designing and maintaining effective strategic processes

Two assumptions motivated us to develop Chapter 1. First, there is a need to understand the entire set of processes that are necessary to develop, implement, and maintain an effective organization strategy. Until recently, strategy *formulation* has occupied the attention of academics with little emphasis on strategy *implementation*. This has reinforced the tendency of consultants to focus on strategic *planning*. Who does not know, or know of, a CEO with an expensive, handsomely bound strategic plan gathering dust on his/her credenza? Secondly, the burgeoning literature, whether research-based or practitioner-distilled "wisdom," is quite frankly confusing—even to strategy wonks, much less busy executives.

Consequently, Chapter 1 is intended to be a summary of the key developmental events and trends in the rapidly emerging discipline of strategic management. As such, this chapter provides a framework for analyzing strategic management processes and a guide for executives and managers in the development and management of strategy within their organizations.

The remaining chapters chart 13 steps that, taken together and completed, will move a management team and its organization through the necessary processes to fully analyze, formulate, plan, and implement a strategic management program. It is important to emphasize that these steps, or subprocesses, while presented in a linear, deterministic flow model, present ample opportunity for feedback to any preceding subprocess. Additionally, it is not unusual for a manager or management team to omit or minimize some steps in the overall strategic management process.

While feedback is in most situations an acceptable practice, the same cannot be said for taking shortcuts in the interest of saving time or reaching agreement. Of course, there are always mitigating circumstances in which the processes outlined can and should be modified such as when an organization has a well-established strategic management system in place or when selected subprocesses are functioning effectively and only well-defined changes, modifications, or additions are required. However, not taking into account the outlined processes opens up the possibility of management by idiosyncratic and/or arbitrary guidelines or, even more counterproductive, domination of strategic management processes by a single manager or small group of managers in key positions. A fundamental premise of this book is that a team of leaders will outperform the "all-knowing leader" most every time.

Introduction

This book is primarily written for emerging strategy professionals and management teams yet to employ a strategic approach to management and secondarily for the great number of organizations that have attempted to manage strategically with varying degrees of success. This book can be used in these organizations to review their current strategic management processes and to develop a systematic approach to improving their current processes and initiating those that are missing. Accordingly, we begin as follows.

Chapter 2—Initiating a Strategic Management Program

To manage with a formally stated, integrated, and properly deployed strategy is a major challenge for any organization. To do so without the necessary preparatory steps will in all probability result in wasted time, energy, and misdirected efforts. Even more important, management will be at the disadvantage of attempting the strategic journey without taking into account their current aspirations and plans. To avoid this scenario, two important processes are required:

Step 1: Assess the current strategic direction and capabilities

Before undertaking any significant effort to develop, improve, and/or manage strategy, there needs to be a shared understanding of the scope and depth of the change effort to be undertaken. This, in turn, needs to be grounded in a fact-based assessment of the strategic direction and strategic management capabilities currently in place. This initial assessment, in large measure, will determine the basis for making changes. It is not a full-scope audit; that will come later.

Step 2: Design and organize an approprirate startup program based on these assessments

Once there is an agreement on the scope and level of commitment required, a leadership team must be selected; decisions must be made on its organization and reporting structure; and assignments must be made of organization-wide duties and responsibilities to individual managers.

Chapter 3—Strategic Information Analysis and Evaluation

Chapter 3 builds on Chapter 2's foundation by outlining and describing the process of strategic assessment, the essential prerequisite for the development and implementation of an effective organization strategy. Conducting a comprehensive and thorough assessment at the outset of any significant effort to develop, or simply to improve, organizational strategy or strategic management capabilities is not an option; it is *the* required and fundamental foundation upon which all subsequent strategies are built. Accordingly, Chapter 3 is organized as follows:

Step 3: Conduct external strategic analyses

External analyses focus on the external factors, trends, opportunities, and threats that are, or probably will, affect the direction, scope, and nature of the strategic management program the organization pursues. The sources and types of information that the leadership requires are identified and discussed.

Step 4: Conduct internal strategic analyses

Internal analyses are no less important than external analyses, since they determine the internal factors, strengths, weaknesses, resources, and capabilities available to pursue selected strategic objectives.

Step 5: Develop a strategic information system

From a "best practices" perspective, a strategic management system *must be formulated based on a continuous flow of both internal and external information and data.* Since this is a continuous process, it is most effectively and efficiently maintained using a well-designed data gathering process that meets the needs of the organization. This process assigns management and staff personnel to gather and process these data and information.

Step 5 follows Steps 3 and 4 in order to gain familiarity and experience in working with the concept of collecting and organizing strategic information before attempting to develop a strategic information system.

Step 6: Evaluate results of strategic analysis

The data and information collected and analyzed in Steps 3 and 4 are of little or no use until they have been evaluated in terms of relevance, applicability, and, most importantly, priority to the leadership team and to the strategic management process being developed. The process for conducting an evaluation of information gathered in Steps 3 and 4 is carefully examined.

Chapter 4—Strategy Formulation

Strategy formulation is the key to effective strategic management, since it requires strategic thinking that is rooted in the resources and capabilities of the organization. It also requires an integration of organizational, functional, and project level considerations—all within the dual focus of the long-term vision and the realities of the present situation and contextual factors. This is challenging work. For the strategy formulation process to be successful it must be disaggregated into its component parts. Over the years we have found the following steps to be very useful in guiding this process:

Step 7: Define the strategic direction of the organization

This step more than any other requires a dual focus, that is, on the long-term development of the strategic direction of the organization and on the short-term resources and capabilities available to pursue the chosen direction. This step requires consideration of the five key components of the strategic direction, that is, vision, mission, values, policies, and goals.

Step 8: Compile a comprehensive set of strategies for arriving at the desired destination

Once a strategic direction has been determined, the next challenge is to identify and/or develop a set of desired and feasible strategy alternatives. Close examination of both the strategic direction and the OTSW evaluation is basic to developing a useful set of strategy alternatives. Several illustrative examples are developed.

Step 9: Evaluate and select a set of strategies for inclusion in the strategic plan

The alternatives generated vary with respect to their contribution to achieving strategic goals, the resources that they require, and the time required to implement and reach acceptable levels of efficiency and effectiveness. Those that are selected must meet both functional and organizational evaluation and selection criteria. These processes are discussed and illustrated.

Chapter 5—Strategic Planning

Strategic planning is the process of translating the results of strategy formulation into a prioritized and time-phased program. The output of the strategy formulation process from the preceding chapter contains the content of what will become the strategic plan. However, much needs to be done to translate it into an effective and efficient plan of action. Each strategy must be reviewed to determine its priority, sequencing, and time phasing. The output of these processes is a long-range strategic plan within which is embedded the short-range operating plan for the upcoming year.

Step 10: Develop a comprehensive strategic plan

A comprehensive strategic plan is far more than a prioritizing and scheduling process. It is essentially a refinement of the strategy formulation process that integrates the alternatives in a coherent long-range plan that will be the basis for leading and managing the organization in the future. While always subject to modification, it is the best statement of the goals and aspirations that the leadership team can devise for the foreseeable future.

Step 11: Develop a strategic operating plan (SOP)

Now the strategic plan must be converted into a detailed blueprint for action. The longer-term strategic plan does not provide one. It contains the longer-term strategic direction of the organization and a prioritized set of strategies to achieve the desired future state. There still remains the task of developing the detailed set of operational objectives, performance measures, and projects to move the strategic plan into a coordinated set of actions. This task also includes the assignment of roles and responsibilities for implementation and the commitment of authorized resources.

Chapter 6—Strategy Implementation

Implementation of the strategic operating plan and ongoing management require much more time, commitment, and resources than the planning process ever consumes in planning *per se*. Moreover, the competencies required for implementation and ongoing management are just as complex and demanding as those required for planning; they are simply different. The common error is to value them less and give them less attention, often delegating them to lower management levels. This is not a trivial matter; it remains the single most common reason for faulty and incomplete implementation of strategic plans.

Step 12: Implement the strategic operating plan

It is not uncommon for managers and top executives (in particular) to think that their responsibility for strategic management ends when the plan is completed. In fact, their work has just begun. This is because management processes pertaining to strategy implementation require management's careful attention to delegate responsibilities and diligent oversight to ensure the work gets done.

Step 13: Strategic management as an ongoing process

Implementation is a continuous process. Long after the formal and scheduled process of implementation, that is, the annual operating cycle, has been completed, the processes of imple-

Introduction

mentation continue, at least at the organizational and cultural levels as well as at the individual level as members of the organization make their own personal adjustment to the emerging changes in the strategic direction and changes throughout the organization.

Failure to acknowledge that the implementation processes are long-term and continuous in nature accounts for many of the difficulties encountered in organizations where the changes initiated in previous years are not yet fully integrated and operational, resulting in an understandable resistance to a new wave of strategic thinking and planning.

All 13 steps are summarized in the flow diagram chart below.

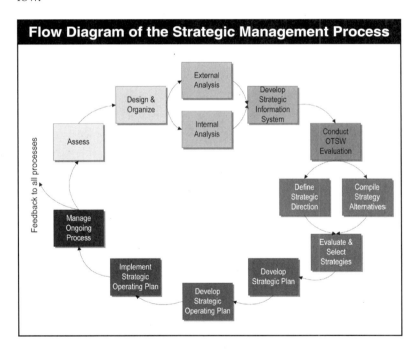

Strategic management, development, and implementation processes are based on the following line of reasoning:

- Implementing major changes in the way an organization plans, organizes, and manages its operations is not usually a well-defined and familiar process in most organizations. This is due to the infrequent need for major changes and to the apprehension and resistance to change inherent in the work force.
- Strategic management is not a separate management process at the operational level. Strategic management duties and responsibilities need to be embedded in the job description of managers at all levels of the organization. Strategic management needs to be made explicit because the overwhelming attention of management at all levels tends to be *operational not strategic.*
- Since many operational processes are urgent, high priority, and time-consuming, it is easy to have a manager's day consumed with attention to these processes with little time or energy to devote to strategy.

Appendices are included on those points that merit additional attention, but they can also be viewed as optional to those seeking an abridged overview of strategic management and an outline of the essential steps in the strategic management process. The bibliography is organized to aid those seeking additional information on various aspects of the strategic management process. A strategic management glossary is included.

In summary, this book is oriented to the needs of emerging strategy professionals and motivated executives and managers starting their first major effort to understand how to develop and manage a strategy-aligned organization.

CHAPTER 1

Strategic Management: An Overview

STRATEGY DEFINED

A *strategy* is defined as a plan of action to achieve a goal or goal set. *Strategic management* is defined as the set of processes required to specify the goals and objectives and develop the initiatives to attain them. To be comprehensive, *strategic management* must undertake the following actions:

- Take into account the external factors that facilitate or inhibit the pursuit of the selected strategy, above and beyond all competitive factors
- Build upon and leverage the unique core competencies of the organization
- Identify, integrate, and formally state the vision, mission, values, polices, and goals of the organization
- Delineate, cascade, prioritize, and time-phase all significant actions required to achieve these goals
- Provide guidelines for the acquisition and allocation of the resources and skills required to execute the strategy at all organizational levels
- Precede and efficiently link with the annual budgeting process
- Provide a program for implementation

- Measure progress and ability for changing the strategy over time

It is not expected that all organizations will develop strategic plans to cover all aspects and actions of the above definition. However, it is important for organizations to have a written strategic plan that meets their needs and aspirations. Many organization managers operate on the assumption that they "have a strategy, although unwritten, and that is all that they need." This avoids answering several important questions, such as:

- How is progress measured?
- How are tasks allocated and responsibilities assigned?
- How is the strategy communicated to key stakeholders?
- How are the management team and staff motivated to take ownership for corporate strategy and its implementation?
- How do you monitor and adjust to changes in the environment?
- How do you move from an authoritarian management structure to a team approach? A fundamental premise of this book is that a team of leaders will outperform the "all-knowing leader" most every time.

In reality, many organizations, owners and managers prefer to operate without a written strategic plan, especially small firms, family-owned businesses, new ventures, and startups. This book is not written for them.

Strategy timeline

In the pages that follow we will present a basic timeline of the principal developments in the study and practice of strategic

Chapter 1

management. As presented in this chapter, a brief overview of the key developments in strategic management over the past 2,300 plus years will prove useful in three ways:

- Gaining a balanced overview of the discipline will offset the tendency to overcommit to just one theory, model, or paradigm.
- Knowing the availability and applicability of strategic management concepts and tools will aid in choosing the appropriate ones for any given situation an executive leadership team may face.
- Developing an interest in the history of strategic management and understanding the scope and depth of the discipline will reveal its necessity in sustaining long-term growth in uncertain and changing environments.

For a comprehensive, albeit brief, review of the primary strategic thinkers and their contributions to the field of strategic management, see Grundy (2003). What follows in Figure 1.1

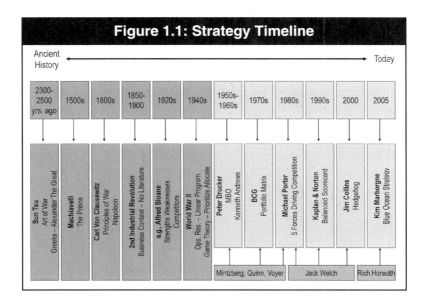

are illustrative of the building blocks of strategic management and their origins from ancient history through today.

MILITARY ORIGINS OF STRATEGY

The primary benefit of studying military strategy is to develop an understanding of the competitive nature of strategic thinking and action. Opposing armies must understand the terrain; gather intelligence regarding their enemy, including estimating their relative strengths and weaknesses and measuring them against their own forces; form a plan of attack; and lead their forces to engage the enemy. Sound familiar? This is strikingly similar to the situation that confronts competing organizations. In fact, it is so similar that it is amazing that it took until the 1980s to realize rich veins of knowledge and experience were there to be mined by studying military history (McNeilly 1996; Michealson 2001; Tracy 2002).

The military origins of strategy predate recorded history. The rivalries between competing tribes; clans; villages; city-states; and, ultimately, nations have been the natural resource for strategic thinking. The origin of the word *strategy* comes from *strategos* or military commander in histories of fifth-century B.C. Greek city-states. The commander's plans for battle and more generally for waging war were the first records of strategic thinking. In the ancient Western world, the city-state was the fundamental political unit of greatest significance. Rome, the most successful city-state of ancient times, developed the art of organized warfare to its highest level until the emergence of Italian city-states beginning in the 12th and 13th centuries.

In the early 16th century the Roman model was reintroduced by Machiavelli in his *Art of War* (Farneworth 2001) as the first model for modern warfare. Enormously popular in the Italian city-states of his day, Machiavelli became the guru on city-state warfare. Many of his precepts and principles, especially on the nature of war, are still incorporated in Western military thinking.

Military strategy continued to evolve incrementally during the next three centuries, but it took the military genius of Napoleon and Clausewitz (Farneworth 2001) to define new paradigms for modern military strategy that were nothing short of a revolution. The result was the emergence of innovations such as conscription; larger independent units that combined infantry, cavalry, and artillery; larger military staffs, both centralized and in military subunits; and, finally, the process of living off the land.

These innovations in both military strategy and structure combined to give commanders many strategic options. These options have continued to have great influence in warfare while becoming the subject of intense interest and study in business and commerce as well. However, for the purposes of this book, the rewards of studying military history lie in understanding military strategy, not military history itself.

Top: Machiavelli
Bottom: Sun Tzu

Western military strategy is but one pillar of the strategic management discipline. Another emerged 2,300 years ago in China when Sun Tzu is credited for having written *The Art of War*, a compilation of essays that might well be described as concentrated essence of wisdom on the conduct of war. There are several important themes developed by Sun Tzu still applied to the strategy challenges we encounter in business and organizational life today (see Appendix 1, *The Art of War*, Sun Tzu).

The study of ancient and medieval military operations is not without its limitations, however. Its primary benefit is to provide an understanding of **strategic thinking** as conceived and carried out by a single military commander, such as a Julius Caesar, Alexander the Great, or Napoleon, with, at most, a few trusted officers. This hardly qualifies as a model for modern strategic management in a large complex organization, or for that matter any organization.

Ironically, it was the introduction of a new method of instruction at the United States Army's military academy, West Point, that ultimately provided the basis for a meta-model of strategic management that could be adapted to any organization operating in any environment. In fact, we know the exact year and the nature of the instructional innovations that laid the foundation for the development of modern strategic management—in both military and nonbusiness organizations. The magnitude and eventual impact of this event on the development of strategic management warrant summarizing here.

In 1817 Sylvanus Thayer, Superintendent of West Point, introduced a revolutionary (at the time) method of running West Point. It was based on a detailed system of writing, examination, grading, and disciplining that covered **all individual and group activities** and maintained detailed permanent performance records.

Graduates immediately began to apply the system in both military and business organizations. Notable examples include the Springfield Armory, where Daniel Taylor, an 1819 graduate, developed single-unit factory management; the Western Railroad, where George Whistler, also an 1819 graduate, introduced a multi-unit system of administration; and the Pennsylvania Railroad, where Herman Haupt, an 1849 graduate,

Chapter 1

developed "a strategic reorganisation, grounded in the collection and analysis of operating statistics and costs, and laid the foundations for the development of country's largest railroad" (Hoskin, Macve, and Stone 1997, 8).

This approach spread during the Civil War with line and staff organizations becoming commonplace, especially in the Northern armies. Following the Civil War this method of managing organizations became widespread in the military and in business.

The key point is that this comprehensive approach to maintaining discipline made it possible for a centralized command to develop and implement a **strategic plan of action** based on a fact-based, continuous record of the performance of an organization and its members.

In the military, logistics became as important as operations, and the objective of winning a final, decisive battle was no longer the goal of an army as it had been throughout history. At the same time, the great military leader (for example, Caesar, Alexander, and Napoleon) was no longer seen as the progenitor of all strategic decisions.

This new system of writing, testing, grading, and disciplining now commonplace in all phases of modern organizations (business, military, government, nonprofit, and academic) does not determine strategic decisions per se but delivers the necessary inputs upon which they rest. There emerged a new power/knowledge relationship and focus on new information experts to maintain this disciplinary system.

STRATEGIC MANAGEMENT AFTER WORLD WAR II

For the most part the development of strategic management following World War II was carried out without particular attention being paid to the military and nonmilitary developments in the previous century at West Point. In essence, the fundamental disciplines of information collection, analysis, and action (based on accounting and statistical data) managed by staff specialists had become second nature and their revolutionary introduction of a century ago long forgotten.

Notwithstanding these early origins of business strategy, it remained to develop more comprehensive and nuanced models of strategic management: models that would take full advantage of the rapidly accelerating collection of organized information and intelligence.

In essence, the foundation for the development of modern strategic management had been established long ago, but as conditions changed rapidly and radically for the postwar pioneers of strategic management, they began to think in terms of sailing toward new horizons.

Before World War II the need for strategic management was not so apparent with a great many unsolved business problems of organization and management still being answered in the military model. In fact, the management literature of the early 20th century is replete with examples of these borrowed concepts, for example: "line and staff," "command and control," "headquarters," "specialization," "functional management (that is, infantry, artillery, cavalry, etc.)." In the absence of new business specific models, military models and concepts were adopted and adapted to cope with the organizational and operational problems of large organizations.

After World War II strategic concepts and tools evolved to become the cornerstones of successful business management thinking and action. As large and complex organizations coped with the challenges of increasingly competitive and changing environments, they faced problems similar to those that had confronted military commanders. Many high-ranking officers left the military to become top managers of large firms. These newly established business leaders found it quite natural to apply the concepts of military strategy to business situations. The use of military-styled organization structures, combined with the infusion of military officers into top private-sector leadership positions, accelerated the focus on strategic management.

In succeeding decades it became clear that neither the military command and control structures *nor* the military models of strategic leadership were well suited to the needs of the private sector. As competition increased and the scope and rate of change accelerated, new paradigms were needed. By the mid-1950s, it was no longer a matter of rebuilding a war-torn world; it was the beginning of a relentless, long-term competitive struggle for profit and market share. Strategic leadership and management were never more necessary, but their concepts needed to be rethought and applied within the situational context of each private sector organization.

A small group of business theorists, teachers, and consultants viewed this as a central management issue. In doing so, they recognized that the fundamental challenge of management was to develop plans of action to deal with a competitive and changing environment and then mobilize their organizations to implement these strategic plans. Half a century later we have a rapidly developing management discipline called strategic management that, in terms of its life cycle, is well into its growth phase gaining momentum beyond startup and introductory stages.

Conceptual foundations are established

Peter Drucker, "the" seminal thinker on management in the last half of the 20th century, wrote about "Management by Objective" (MBO) in his classic *The Practice of Management*

Peter Drucker
Reprinted by permission of the Drucker Institute, Claremont Graduate University

(1954). He further developed his ideas pertaining to strategy in *Management for Results* (1964). This latter work appeared just as strategy as the central organizing concept for planning, structuring, and managing large-scale companies was being developed and taught by leading theorists and scholars of the decade.

Drucker captured many of the ideas that were to be integrated in what has come to be known as "classical strategic management." His essential message was that whatever a company's program may be, the company must decide:

- What opportunities it wants to pursue and what risks it is willing and able to accept.
- What its scope and structure will be and, especially, the right balance between specialization, diversification, and integration.
- How it will balance the use of time and money to attain its goals, especially pertaining to owning versus buying or to sales, mergers, acquisitions, or joint ventures.
- What organizational structure will be most appropriate to the company's economic realities, opportunities, and performance programs.

SWOT analysis

SWOT analysis has its origins and its initial development in two institutions: Stanford Research Institute and the Harvard School of Business. In the former a research study funded by several Fortune 500 firms was conducted by a team of researchers under the direction of Robert F. Stewart from 1960 to 1969 (Humphrey, 2004, pp. 6-9). The study was prompted by the inability of these and other business firms to implement the results of the strategic plans that they had been developing during the previous decade. This research included a 250-item questionnaire completed by more than 5,000 executives in 1,100 companies. Interviews were also conducted during the course of the study. Presumably the results of this study were considered proprietary, at least in part, and therefore not immediately published in books or academic journals.

Parallel to this study, two Harvard Business School professors, George Albert Smith and C. Roland Christensen, were questioning the extent to which a firm's strategy matched its competitive environment. Other professors at Harvard expanded this inquiry at both the organizational and functional level, and several business cases were written and courses developed. The SWOT framework was first described in detail in *Business Policy, Text and Cases* (Learned et al, 1969).

As a consequence of these two major efforts that resulted in the refinement and application of SWOT analysis, and its popularity as a teaching and consulting tool, the continued development and application of SWOT have spread throughout U.S. business firms and other types of organizations. Its use and popularity have spread throughout the world. It continues to be developed as a tool by both consultants and academics, who adapt it to various types of problems and situations.

The essential components of the SWOT framework and approach follow:

- **Strengths (S)** refers to the primary internal strengths the firm has to build on. These attributes are essentially resources the business can draw upon to move the firm forward. Strengths can relate to any of the organization's products or services, or they may emerge from any function or process operating inside the organization.

Strategy in the 21st Century

- **Weaknesses (W)** refers to the primary internal weaknesses the firm has that may interfere with the business moving forward. As with strengths, weaknesses can come from any of the organization's products or services or from the functions and/or processes operating inside the organization.
- **Opportunities (O)** Unlike strengths and weaknesses that are derived from the internal dimension of the firm, opportunities exist in the external dimension, that is, in the market place itself where customers make purchasing decisions. They frequently emerge from changes in industry dynamics, customer buying behavior, new technologies, or from any other change that can give rise to a new business opportunity. Opportunities may exist in the "here and now," or they may relate to some future time frame.
- **Threats (T)** As with opportunities, threats are outside the organization itself. They are essentially storm clouds on the near- term or long-term horizon that may or will stand in the way of the firm moving forward. They can

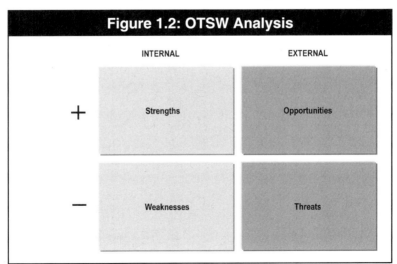

develop as a result of shifting industry trends, competitive actions of other industry players, changing customer buying behavior, and/or a host of other potential sources.

In Figure 1.2 the order in which SWOT is conducted has been changed to be consistent with the order in which the four factors are addressed in this book. Otherwise, the OTSW analysis and SWOT analysis are consistent.

As this technique grew in popularity, it became clear to fully capitalize on this tool organizations should build on those internal strengths that enable it to capitalize on specific high-priority external opportunities. Likewise, businesses learned to eliminate those internal weaknesses that would mitigate against high-priority threats in the external environment.

Other contributors

The concepts of applying strategy to business were further defined and studied in depth at Harvard by Alfred Chandler in *Strategy and Structure* (1962). From his studies of leading corporations, he concluded that strategy is the "determinant of the basic long-term goals of an enterprise, and the adoption of courses of action and the allocation of resources necessary for carrying out these goals" (Mintzberg, Quinn, and Voyer 1995, 2). Quinn noted that many scholars agree this was the first modern definition of business strategy. In 1980 Kenneth Andrews, also at Harvard, elaborated on Chandler's definition in *The Concept of Corporate Strategy*:

> Strategy is the pattern of objectives, purposes, or goals and the major policies and plans for achieving these goals stated in such a way to define what business the company is in or is to be in and the kind of company it is or is to be (ibid., 2).

> **Table 1.1: Kenneth Andrews on Strategy as an Intellectual Process**
>
> - What a company might do in terms of environmental opportunity
> - What it can do in terms of ability and power
> - What the executives of the company want to do
> - What a company should do (ibid., 50-51)

More specifically, he defined *strategy* as the intellectual process of ascertaining what a company can and should do, as summarized in Table 1.1.

Andrews believed these processes must be brought into equilibrium. It is easy to see the military origin of this approach; it is exactly what a military leader does on the field of battle. The Andrews approach to strategy is similar to the other prescriptive approaches, but it differs in that strategy design is not viewed as a delegated and subdivided set of activities. The Andrews approach most often occurs in smaller and mid-sized firms with a strong leader. The manager must:

- Determine what the firm *might do*—assess the firm's external environment for opportunities and threats and identify the key success factors of the industry
- Determine what the firm *can do*—examine the internal environment for strengths and weaknesses and identify distinctive competencies
- Determine what the firm's executives *want to do*
- Determine what the firm *should do*—review the firm's social responsibilities (ibid., 51)

This definition of strategy became popular and spread in business schools throughout the world. It came to be what

Chapter 1

Mintzberg later called the "design approach" to strategy.

The second pillar of the classical school after the Western military strategic discipline is the "planning approach," as developed by Igor Ansoff in *Corporate Strategy: An Analytical Approach to Business Policy for Growth and Expansion* (1965). His view of strategy follows:

> Strategy becomes the rule for making decisions: the "common thread" would have four components—product/market scope; the growth vector (the changes the firm planned to make in its product market scope); competitive advantage; and synergy (a measure of how well the different parts of the firm could work together to achieve more than they could have by each working alone) (ibid., 2).

Figure 1.3: Ansoff's Grid

	CURRENT MARKETS	NEW MARKETS
CURRENT SERVICES / PRODUCTS	Market Penetration	Market Development
NEW SERVICES / PRODUCTS	Service / Product Development	Diversification

Reprinted by permission of *Harvard Business Review*.
From "Strategies for Diversification" by Igor Ansoff, September-October/1957
Copyright © 1957 by the Harvard Business Review; all rights reserved.

Ansoff was a major contributor to the development of the conceptual foundations of strategic management theory and practice. As Grundy (2003, 40 and 45) pointed out, in addition to establishing corporate planning as a formal management process, Ansoff also:

- Popularized SWOT analysis
- Provided us with the Ansoff grid, which helps us to understand the degree of risk involved in diversification strategies
- Developed the ideas of environmental scanning and detecting weak signals of disruptive environmental change
- Repositioned "strategic planning" as "strategic management" as part of a continuing process rather than a once a year (or less frequent) planning process
- Identified "gap" analysis—which looks at the gap between aspirations and the likely outcome of current strategies

Andrew's design approach to strategy and Ansoff's planning approach dominated teaching and research on strategy for an entire generation. These models and all the variations that followed had four elements in common. They are:

1. The firm must follow a set of external conditions. Some conditions are negative (threats) while others are positive (opportunities).
2. The firm's management must perform a situational analysis to determine its posture in the environment and its level of resources. This analysis is often referred to as a SWOT analysis (here OTSW).
3. The firm must establish goals and objectives, the highest level of which is the mission of the firm—a statement of the firm's reason for existence.
4. The firm must plan how to use its resources to achieve its goals and get the best fit possible with its environment.

Chapter 1

Strategic management emerges as a major business discipline

The modern era conceptual foundations of strategic management were established in the 1950s and 1960s. In the decades to follow these concepts were discussed, analyzed, and refined; and strategic management emerged as an accepted business management discipline. It became a recognized academic discipline among scholars and researchers when it met the criteria summarized in Table 1.2.

Table 1.2: Criteria for Becoming an Academic Discipline

- A body of knowledge based on scholarly inquiry and research was established.
- Peer groups exchanged ideas and concepts, thus contributing to the development of this body of knowledge.
- Appropriate research methods were employed to validate propositions and findings.
- Contributors to this body of knowledge included scholars, theorists, researchers, teachers, practitioners, consultants, and the management community.
- The body of knowledge included prescriptive, descriptive, analytic, and research-based knowledge.

Contemporary models

Beginning in the 1970s and continuing through to present day, an increasing number of analytic models, concepts, and tools began to appear in response to the private sector's need for more effective approaches to the accelerating tempo of change

Strategy in the 21st Century

and uncertainty in the environment. Management approaches that could be adapted to specific organizational contexts were required.

The Boston Consulting Group (BCG) growth share matrix

In the early 1970s the Boston Consulting Group (BCG) developed an analytic model for managing a portfolio of different business units (or major product lines). The first use of portfolio analysis, the BCG Growth-Share Matrix, displays the various business units on a graph charting market growth rate versus market share relative to competitors. Resources are allocated to business units based on where they are situated on the grid as follows:

- **Cash Cow**—A business unit that has a large market share in a mature, slow-growing industry. Cash cows require little investment and generate cash that can be used to invest in other business units.

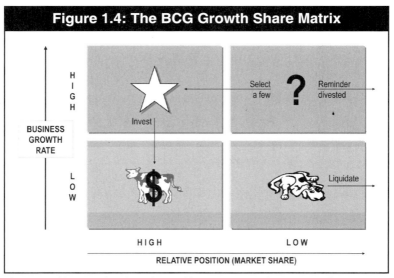

The BCG Portfolio Matrix from the Product Portfolio Matrix, ©1970, The Boston Consulting Group

30

- **Star**—A unit that has a large share in a fast-growing industry. Stars may generate cash, but because the market is growing rapidly they require investment to maintain their lead. If successful, a star will become a cash cow once its industry matures.
- **Question Mark**—A business unit that has a small market share in a high growth market. These business units require resources to grow market share, but whether they will succeed and become stars is unknown.
- **Dog**—A business unit that has a small market share in a mature industry. A dog may not require substantial cash, but it ties up capital that could be better deployed elsewhere. Unless a dog has some strategic purpose, it should be liquidated if there is little prospect for it to gain market share.

BCG's basic strategy recommendation was to maintain a balance between "cash cows" and "stars," while allocating some resources to feed "question marks" (that is, potential stars). The BCG Matrix allows one to compare many business units at a glance. However, the approach has received some negative criticism for the following reasons:

- The link between market share and profitability is questionable because increasing market share can be very expensive.
- The approach may overemphasize growth because it ignores the possibility of declining markets.
- The model assumes market growth. In practice, the organization may not be able to grow the market.

While originally developed as a model for resource allocation among the various business units in a corporation, the

Strategy in the 21st Century

growth-share matrix can also be used for resource allocation among products within a single business unit. Its simplicity is its strength; the relative positions of an organization's entire business portfolio can be displayed in a single diagram.

Porter's Five Forces

In 1980 Michael Porter developed a framework in which he used concepts developed in industrial organization economics to derive five competitive forces that determine the attractiveness of a market. Porter referred to these forces as the microenvironment to contrast it with the more general term macroenvironment. The microenvironment consists of those forces close to an organization that affect its ability to serve its customers and make a profit. A change in any of the forces normally requires an organization to reassess the marketplace.

Four forces—bargaining power of customers, the bargaining power of suppliers, the threat of new entrants, and the threat

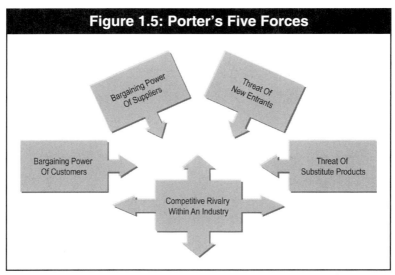

From *Competitive Strategy—Techniques for Analyzing Industries* by Michael E. Porter (copyright © 1980).

of substitute products—combine with other variables to create a fifth force, the level of competition in an industry. Each of these forces has several determinants. Understanding the nature of each of these forces gives organizations the necessary insights to enable them to formulate the appropriate strategies to be successful in their market.

Force 1: Bargaining Power of Customers

Customer power is one of the horizontal forces that influence the appropriation of the value created by an industry. The most important determinants of buyer power are the size and the concentration of customers. Other factors are the extent to which the buyers are informed and the concentration or differentiation of the competitors. Kippenberger (1998) states that it is often useful to distinguish potential buyer power from the buyer's willingness or incentive to use that power, willingness that derives mainly from the "risk of failure" associated with a product's use.

- The risk of failure increases with a few, large players in the market.
- Risk is still present when there are a large number of undifferentiated, small players.
- Risk is low when there is a low cost of switching between suppliers.

Force 2: Bargaining Power of Suppliers

Supplier power is a mirror image of the customer power. As a result, the analysis of supplier power typically focuses first on the relative size and concentration of suppliers relative to industry participants and second on the degree of differentiation in the inputs supplied. The ability to charge customers different prices in line with differences in the value created for each of those buyers usually indicates that the market is characterized by high supplier power as well as by low buyer power (Porter 1998). Supplier bargaining power exists when:

- Switching costs are high (switching from one ISP to another).
- Brand power is high (McDonalds, British Airways, and Harvard).
- There is the possibility of forward integration of suppliers (beer brewer buying a bar).

Force 3: Threat of New Entrants

Both potential and existing competitors influence average industry profitability. The threat of new entrants is usually based on the market entry barriers. They can take diverse forms and are used to prevent an influx of organizations into an industry whenever profits, adjusted for the cost of capital, rise above zero. In contrast, entry barriers also exist whenever it is difficult or not economically feasible for an outsider to replicate the incumbents' position (Porter 1980; Sanderson 1998). The most common forms of entry barriers, except intrinsic physical or legal obstacles, are as follows:

- Economies of scale—benefits associated with bulk purchasing
- Cost of entry—investment in technology
- Distribution channels—ease of access for competitors
- Cost advantages not related to the size of the organization—contacts and expertise
- Government legislations—introduction of new laws that might weaken an organization's competitive position
- Differentiation—certain brand that cannot be copied

Force 4: Threat of Substitute Products

The threat that substitute products pose to an industry's profitability depends on the relative price-to-performance ratios of the different types of products or services to which customers can turn to satisfy the same basic need. The threat of substitution is also affected by switching costs—that is, the costs in areas such as retraining, retooling, and redesigning that are incurred when a customer switches to a different type of product or service. It also involves:

- Product-for-product substitution—based on the substitution of need
- Generic substitution
- Substitution that relates to something that people can do without

Force 5: Competitive Rivalry

The intensity of rivalry, the most obvious of the five forces in an industry, helps determine the extent to which the value created by an industry will be dissipated through head-to-head competition. The most valuable contribution of Porter's five forces framework may be its suggestion that rivalry, while important, is only one of several forces that determine industry attractiveness.

- This force is located at the center of the diagram.
- It is most likely to be high in those industries in which there is a threat of substitute products and existing power of suppliers and buyers in the market.

The nature of competition in an industry is strongly affected by the five forces. The stronger the powers of customers and suppliers and the stronger the threats of entry and substitution, the more intense competition is likely to be within the industry. However, these five factors are not the only ones that determine how organizations in an industry will compete—the structure of the industry itself may play an important role. In concentrated industries, according to this model, organizations would be expected to compete less fiercely and make higher profits than those in fragmented ones. However, the histories and cultures of the firms in the industry also play a very important role in shaping competitive behavior.

Porter's second major contribution to strategic management was his classification of *generic* strategies (ibid., 111–112):

- Differentiation—when you add more value (real or perceived) than your competitors, evidenced by higher prices or discounts avoided
- Cost leadership—when you achieve parity of value at a lower cost than your competitors
- Focus—when you narrow your competitive strategy to concentrate only on your target customers and their specific needs and limit your product range

The attractiveness of the Porter model and analytic approach lies in its usefulness in understanding a specific organizational context by determining the relative impact of the five forces. This requires a certain amount of creativity—within the constraining forces. Porter's five forces model and his generic strategies were developed when there was a need felt for determining how to develop a competitive strategy. The focus was on identifying a competitive advantage. His two major works, that is, *Competitive Strategy* (1980) and *Competitive Advantage* (1985), became immediately popular, both in academia and in major corporations.

While many writers, and researchers (primarily economists) continued to fine-tune, modify, and apply the Porter model, another major trend in strategic management was developing based on the works of such writers and researchers as Peters and Waterman (1982); Senge (1990); Kanter (1983, 1989, 1994); Kaplan and Norton (1992); and Hamel and Prahalad (1989, 1990, 1993, 1994). Taken together they build toward the creative, innovative, and shared roles and responsibilities of management (note: management *not* top management) in formulating and implementing and improving organizational strategy and strategic management processes. Their contributions follow.

Seven S

Tom Peters and Robert Waterman (1982), in their *In Search of Excellence* developed an organizational model called the "Seven S" model that puts strategic management within the context of a complex organizational network.

The model includes:

- Strategy
- Structure
- Staff
- Skills
- Style
- Systems
- Shared values

These seven factors need to be described as currently developed and used within a given organization. However, describing them is only the beginning. Each needs to be properly aligned and balanced to achieve the most effective strategic management system. While the emphasis in this model is internally focused, it does strongly imply that each organization must give adequate attention to both internal and external factors. This was clear to the early strategic thinkers in the 1960s, but the specific factors both externally and internally are being more clearly identified and defined today.

Peter Senge (1990) added to this internal focus by describing the impact of learning on both strategic and operational management. His concept of a learning organization is based on interactive learning and feedback loops. From this perspective, strategic management can be viewed as a formal somewhat bureaucratic process. Organizational and individual learning and the feedback effects on strategic processes modify it.

R. M. Kantor (1989, 1994) had a major impact on strategic management primarily through her concepts of change management that include a major emphasis on empowerment throughout the organization to implement strategy effectively.

Balanced Scorecard

Kaplan and Norton (1992) developed the concept of a "balanced scorecard" that stressed the need to measure and control performance based on measuring and monitoring four types of measure/perspectives.

Table 1.3 summarizes the four types of measures.

The main value of the balanced scorecard model lies in its emphasis on forging a balanced approach to measuring strategic control factors. It remains for each organization to identify its own key strategic measurements. The main assumption un-

Table 1.3: Balanced Scorecard Perspectives: Types of Measures

- Financial performance
- Customer satisfaction
- Operational efficiency
- Learning and growth

Chapter 1

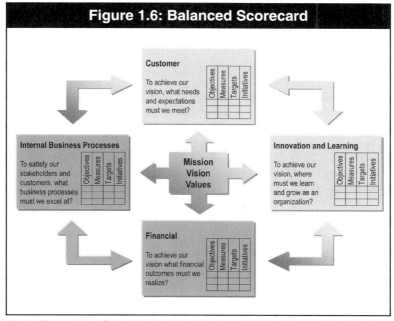

Reprinted by permission of Harvard Business School Press. From *The Balanced Scorecard: Translating Strategy into Action* by Robert S. Kaplan, David S. Norton/Hollis Heimbouch, Carol Franco. Boston, MA 1996, pp 8-9. Copyright © 1996 by the Harvard Business School Publishing Corporation; all rights reserved.

derlying the balanced scorecard, that is, measuring drive performance, should be a prerequisite for any effective strategic management system. It is important to note that the metrics selected can be based on either internal or external factors. It is their emphasis on balanced measures driving performance that makes it an internal consideration, that is, a major determinant of management effectiveness.

Hamel and Prahalad

Hamel and Prahalad (1989, 1990, 1993, and 1994) made several important contributions to the development of the strategic management field. Grundy (2003, 77-78) identifies three of their most famous concepts in Table 1.4.

39

Strategy in the 21st Century

> **Table 1.4: Hamel and Prahalad**
>
> - **Core competencies**—"these are a cluster of skills which either enables us to compete or give us a distinctive way of competing" (more on competencies is included in the following section)
> - **Competing for the future**—they do not see *any* industry as a given; instead they are willing to consider a variety of possibilities
> - **Innovation in strategy**—at the same time they emphasize innovation, they de-emphasize a bureaucratic approach to strategy

Hamel and Prahalad also introduced to the field of strategy the notions of "stretch" *and* "leverage" as means of how one can view what is possible.

Taken together these writers and researchers expand the scope and depth of strategic management to include many internally generated strategies. However, in no case do they deny the impact of external forces on the organization. They counterbalance the tendency to rely too heavily on these forces. They point to the new directions in strategic management that are based on development of the organization's human resources and a supportive infrastructure.

Blue Ocean Strategy

One excellent example of using the concepts of Hamel and Prahalad is demonstrated in the work of W. C. Kim and Renee Mauborgne (2005). They developed an imaginative and creative approach to stretching and leveraging their core competencies so as to gain an advantage in competing for the future.

Figure 1.7: Red Ocean and Blue Ocean Strategy

RED OCEAN STRATEGY	BLUE OCEAN STRATEGY
Complete in existing market space.	Create uncontested market space.
Beat the competition.	Make the competition irrelevant.
Exploit existing demand.	Create and capture new demand.
Make the value/cost trade-off.	Break the value/cost trade-off.
Align the whole system of a company's activities with its strategic choice of differentiation or low cost.	Align the whole system of a company's activities in pursuit of differentiation *and* low cost.

Reprinted by permission of Harvard Business School Press. From *Blue Ocean Strategy: How to Create Uncontested Market Space and Make the Competition Irrelevant* by W.C. Kim and Renee Mauborgne/Melinda Merino. Boston, MA 2005, pp 32. Copyright © 2005 by the Harvard Business School Publishing Corporation; all rights reserved.

Based on a study of 150 strategic moves spanning more than 100 years and 30 industries, Kim and Mauborgne assert that "tomorrow's leading companies will succeed *not* by battling competitors in the 'bloody red ocean' but by creating 'blue oceans' of uncontested market space ripe for growth." See Figure 1.7.

Blue Ocean Strategy (BOS) provides a systematic approach to making the competition irrelevant. Kim and Mauborgne present a tested analytical framework and the tools for successfully creating and capturing blue oceans. BOS highlights six principles that organizations can use to successfully formulate and execute blue ocean strategies. The six principles are reconstruct market boundaries, focus on the big picture, reach beyond existing demand, get the strategic sequence right, overcome organizational hurdles, and build execution into strategy. An effective Blue Ocean Strategy will be one that is about risk minimization, not risk taking.

There are several BOS tools that attempt to make the for-

Strategy in the 21st Century

mulation and execution of BOS as systematic and actionable as competing in the red waters of known market space.

Hedgehog Concept

Emphasis on the creative and imaginative approaches to strategic management continues to receive attention by researchers and practitioners alike. In this regard, it is important to note the work of Jim Collins in developing the Hedgehog Concept. According to Jim Collins in *Good to Great*, the Hedgehog Concept is not a goal to be the best, a strategy to be the best, an intention to be the best, or even a plan to be the best. Rather, it is arriving at a fundamental understanding of what *you can be the best at*. The distinction is absolutely crucial.

In his famous essay "The Hedgehog and the Fox," 20th century philosopher and essayist Isaiah Berlin divided the world into hedgehogs and foxes, based upon an ancient Greek parable: "The fox knows many things, but the hedgehog knows one thing." Those who built good-to-great companies were,

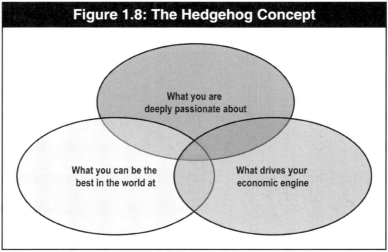

From *Good to Great* by Jim Collins (copyright © 2001).

Chapter 1

to one degree or another, hedgehogs. They used their focused hedgehog nature to succeed. Collins came to call this focused approach to growing a business the Hedgehog Concept. Those who led the comparison businesses tended to be foxes, scattered and inconsistent rather than focused like the hedgehogs.

Collin's study made paired comparisons of for-profit business in 15 industries. The comparison was between two similar companies in each industry, except that in each comparison one company had gone from simply being a "good" company to becoming a "great company." The strategic difference between the good-to-great and comparison companies lies in two fundamental distinctions. First, the good-to-greats founded their strategies on a deep understanding of three key dimensions—what Collins calls the three circles. Second, good-to-greats translated that understanding into a simple concept that guided all their efforts—hence the term Hedgehog Concept.

More precisely, the Hedgehog Concept flows from a deep understanding of three issues illustrated by the following three circles:

- **What can you do best in the world?** (And, equally important, what you cannot do best in the world.) *This goes far beyond core competence.* Just because you possess a core competence does not necessarily mean you can be the best in the world. Conversely, what you can be the best at might not even be something in which you are currently engaged.
- **What drives your economic engine?** All the good-to-great companies attained insight into how to most effectively generate sustained and robust cash flow and profitability. In particular, they discovered the single denominator—profit per x—that had the greatest impact on their economies.

- **About what are you deeply passionate?** The idea here is not to create passion but to discover what makes you passionate.

To have a fully developed Hedgehog Concept, all three circles must be integrated.

This study by Collins and the previously cited one by Kim and Mauborgne bring us full circle to some of the points raised by early theorists, particularly Kenneth Andrews (1980) who first distinguished several issues with which management must grapple to determine strategy for their organization.

- What a company *might do* in terms of environmental opportunity
- What it *can do* in terms of ability and power
- What the executives of the company *want to do*
- What a company *should do*

Today these concepts are still being fleshed out, but the big difference is that organizations now have an extensive body of knowledge and experience from which to draw. Moreover, while the early studies were largely prescriptive in nature, they now include descriptive, analytic, and research-based data as well.

All the preceding approaches to strategic management imply a strategic focus, that is, the deliberate intention to develop and implement an organization strategy. Alternative views of how strategy evolves have been set forth by Quinn and Mintzberg, two respected and well-known scholars that have spent many years studying and researching strategic management issues.

James Brian Quinn (1980) used the expression "logical incrementalism" to express his view of the way strategy and strategic decisions evolve both randomly and logically. Grundy (2004, 116) notes that Quinn's work is very thoroughly researched and that he found ample evidence of logical incrementalism in major U.S. corporations.

Mintzberg's major research (1973, 1979, 1983, and 1994) focused on organization structure and management. He viewed managers as primarily focused on operations activities, with little or no time for thinking about strategy. In short, he viewed strategy as messy and haphazard that could (on occasion) coalesce into an emergent strategy. This does not preclude *intended or deliberate* attempts by an organization to form and implement strategy; rather that the *emergent* strategies merge with and deflect the intended strategies into what he termed *realized* strategies.

Both Mintzberg and Quinn believe that strategic management consists of deliberate processes that can be comprehensively analyzed, designed, planned, and implemented. However, strategic management does not exist without considerable randomness of trial and error and interrupted activity that may bear no relation to orderly strategic management processes.

As we enter a global economy, there will be many new considerations that must be taken into account. Among the more notable are the following:

- Research and analysis on strategic management in other countries made by contributing academics, practitioners, and managers in those countries
- Studies of the cultures, social and economic systems, political systems, and technologies of those countries
- Studies of organizations operating in multicultural settings and having conflicting planning and control issues with the home office wherever it might be
- Studies of the impact of globalization

In essence, not only will strategic management have to grow and cope with the dynamics of growth and development within each organization, but also it will be necessary to consider growth and development in an expanded and increasingly competitive global context.

STRATEGIC MANAGEMENT COMPETENCIES

It is the focus on strategy formulation and implementation that distinguishes strategic management from simply managing ongoing operations. It is not uncommon for the distinction between strategic and operational management to be blurred. When this occurs, it is typically operations management that

Table 1.5: Misconceptions about Strategic Management

- Strategic management does not deserve special attention; good business management automatically includes managing strategy.
- In our organization, we all know the organization strategy—it is our game plan.
- Strategic management is costly and time-consuming, and our energies are better focused on our main objective, that is, making money, satisfying customers, making superior products, and so forth.
- If we all do our jobs, we *are* managing strategy.
- Managing strategy is a top management responsibility. We are only required to do what they tell us to do.
- Strategy development is an academic pursuit. It is too theoretical and does not apply to us.
- If we followed the advice of these academics and consultants we would never get anything done. Even worse, we would go broke in the process.

dominates management thinking and activities, while strategy receives occasional and limited attention. This does not occur from lack of concern about strategy but more often because of misconceptions about strategic management. Table 1.5 summarizes various misconceptions about strategic management.

Unfortunately, believing in these misconceptions about strategic management leads to the very end results they predict and precludes organizations from benefiting from employing a strategic focus and aligning all functions and processes with it.

These misconceptions arise for three primary reasons:

- The need for strategic management is not well-understood.
- The process of strategic management is not understood as distinct from operations management, except that it is a top management responsibility.
- The management competencies required to formulate and implement strategy are not well known or developed in most organizations

Throughout this book, an effort will be made to correct these misconceptions. However, a few comments are in order here to highlight the need to acquire and/or strengthen the basic competencies that are required in order to achieve effective strategic management. These competencies should be placed high on management's list of basic training and development priorities.

While these competencies are necessary for effective strategic management, they are by no means sufficient. There is a much longer list of both general management competencies that all organizations need to address, as well as a list of specific competencies that are necessary to specific types of organizations—in fact, even to specific organizations in given environmental configurations. However, even a brief consideration of this expanded framework of required management competencies is beyond the scope of this book, where the focus will be on required basic strategic management competencies.

Identifying, articulating, and developing a core set of shared values

In part, all shared values evolve as the result of informal group processes. However, every organization needs a formal process that monitors and clarifies the emergence of its core set of shared values because, ultimately, they provide the basis not only for guiding and directing the organization but also for evaluating and rewarding performance.

Arriving at shared values is a significant and revealing process involving the contributions of many individuals. Articulating these values, and communicating them, is the work of a few individuals, usually members of top management and their staff. In any case, arriving at a set of shared values is essential to strategic management as they provide a moral compass for developing the organization's strategic direction and act as the cultural "guideposts" to direct implementation of the strategy and operations of the organization.

Visioning

Developing a clear and accepted vision for the organization is not an easily acquired competency, even among very successful managers. It requires the ability to arrive at a concise statement of a *desired future state* that is *grounded* in the core values of the organization, based on the current capabilities of the organization and its management, and *achievable*, albeit with effort and the improvement and possibly acquisition of new resources and capabilities.

Chapter 1

Strategic thinking

The ability to think strategically has always been essential to developing and implementing new strategies, but only recently has it emerged as an essential skill that managers at all levels can and should acquire. As Rich Horwath describes the process, strategic thinking involves the generation of insights that drives business strategy development. Strategic planning involves the application of strategy (Horwath, 11). Strategic thinking is a combination of skill sets that goes beyond simply generating insights and new directions for the organization. It includes the ability to incorporate these insights in the organization's strategic plan. In short, it is the synthesis of creative and action-oriented thinking applied in a specific organization. Strategic planning, essential for strategy development, requires strategic thinking.

Identifying and developing core organizational competencies and capabilities

With respect to core or distinctive competencies, there is the need to distinguish between doing something new and doing something simply in a different way and, correspondingly, to distinguish between those things currently done and those things at which the organization excels. Unfortunately, it is the last of these competencies that tends to receive the most attention as evidenced by the many attempts to improve quality, cost, and customer service. Sooner or later, this focus on operational excellence will result in widespread standard operational practices, with little lasting strategic advantage.

Consequently, it is immensely important to find those distinguishing and differentiating factors that separate an organization from its competitors. This requires the constant attention of at least some of the top managers and staff personnel in an organization. Constant attention and the realization of the importance of differentiation are the two key drivers in developing this skill. *It is a skill primarily acquired through practice, not education or training.*

Converting information into strategic intelligence

Information gathering is an essential skill. Information cannot be considered either strategic or competitive until it is processed in terms of its utility in developing or applying strategic direction. The process of providing guidelines for sifting information to find its strategic value is primarily, but by no means exclusively, the responsibility of top management. However, the main guidelines derive from the strategic direction that top management provides. Applying these guidelines in processing large amounts of information can be done by staff personnel so long as the results of this process are monitored and evaluated by top management.

The process of converting information into useful strategic intelligence requires the ability to spot trends and events "still on the distant horizon" and to have some notion that they may ultimately be significant. Concentration on a few areas of importance to the organization will enhance the success of such scanning efforts, but, ultimately, success depends on an analytic ability based on tenuous and sometimes far-fetched reasoning. In the discipline of forecasting, this is the ability to foresee third and fourth order effects. To illustrate, monitoring the products and services being generated in areas such as healthcare, agriculture, senior living, education and training, tourism, environmental concerns, technology development, telecommunications, and global trade provides many useful clues for future commercial opportunities. The skills involved include processing large amounts of information, retaining key items of interest, making imaginative and creative connections, and seeing the relevance to the organization and its future development.

Identifying, evaluating, and selecting strategic alternatives

This skill requires an ability to analyze the environment, generate alternatives, evaluate each alternative, and select the most appropriate alternative (or group of alternatives) as the core strategy.

Why then should an individual manager try to acquire this multidimensional competency? Imagination, creativity, evaluation and an action orientation underlie every step of the strategic management process in varying proportions depending on the particular process. Strategic management cannot conveniently be subdivided in the overall management of the organization, although specific strategic management projects can be singled out for development. Even then, projects of this sort are only valuable when integrated into the overall strategic management system of the organization.

In short, strategic management is a holistic process that transcends specialization and expertise as the dominant management skill. Consequently, it behooves any manager, especially those who consider themselves to be upwardly mobile, to build competency in this discipline.

Team work and team building

Strategic management consists of both individual and collective processes. It requires a combination of skills not usually found in a single individual. Hence, the customary solution is

Table 1.6: Rationale for Team-based Leadership and Management

- The challenges facing strategic management are increasingly beyond the scope of an individual, no matter how talented, experienced, or educated. For example:
    - Both internal and external factors are increasing and changing at an accelerating rate.
    - Second, third, and higher order effects need to be taken into account, analyzed, and evaluated.
    - Organizations, management, processes, and technologies are ever more compelling, requiring multiple perspectives to identify and assess their impact and resultant need for innovative improvements and new actions.
- The aforementioned and other challenges facing management are best dealt with in a team format for a variety of reasons. More specifically, teams have a clear advantage over other approaches by:
    - Providing a synergy among individual team members that enhances and magnifies individual contributions;
    - Drawing on each team member's experience, skill, and ideas and incorporating them to develop a shared vision, strategy, and action plan;
    - Providing a multidimensional perspective on problems and issues;
    - Generating alternative courses of action;
    - Giving individuals an opportunity to grow in their commitment, skills, and contributions to the organization.

to break up the process among different individuals, or teams. Every member of an organization will always have individual roles and responsibilities for which he or she is held accountable. However, it is increasingly clear that these roles and responsibilities are being transformed by new paradigms of interdependent and interactive behavior of **teams.**

This has been evident for some time now at the operational level; organizations do not operate effectively without these structures and processes in place. However, with respect to *strategic management* it remains unclear in most organizations that *team work is the primary core competency underlying all other competencies*. This logic, the need to process individual inputs and outputs through collective processes, *especially through teams*, becomes a key organizational/behavioral competency required to develop effective strategic managers. Table 1.6 summarizes the rationale for building a team-based leadership and management culture.

Because teams and effective teamwork are so central to both the design of a strategic management system and to its effective use, Appendix 2, an annotated bibliography of publications about teams outlines the salient features of teams and how to use them effectively. These books were selected to cover the broad range of topics on teams that need to be taken into account in developing an effective team-based approach to strategic management. Additionally, in each section of this book, team functions and responsibilities are identified and explained.

THE EVER-CHANGING CONTEXT OF STRATEGIC MANAGEMENT

The context of strategic management is all-important. The essence of strategic management is to achieve the most effective and productive relationship between an organization's capabilities *and* the environment in which the organization operates or intends to operate in the future—all within the guidelines set forth in the organization's strategic direction. In fact, *the distinguishing characteristics of strategic management are found in paying constant attention to external factors and adjusting strategy accordingly.*

Managers who do not think strategically have no need for concern with constant adaptation to the organization's immediate environment. This mindset is out of touch with best practices in organizational planning, which *should be* strategic but unfortunately is still often done *as if* external factors are not changing significantly, at least not enough to take them into account in organizational planning. Prior to World War II this was the norm in business planning. In fact, beginning in the 1920s and continuing into the 1960s, the capstone course in most MBA programs was titled "Business Policy," and as noted earlier, the term "corporate strategy" did not become widespread until later in the 1960s.

Why this tactical approach persists when a strategic approach is so clearly obvious in well-managed organizations can be attributed to no single source or explanation; rather it is the accumulated impact of several factors that push strategic management into the light of "today" as a universal priority concern for top management. The more important factors are briefly described in this section. Each, in and of itself, could be the subject of a book. Most are familiar because they bombard our lives daily. What is not so clearly evident is their impact on strategic management, which will be highlighted.

Globalization

No phenomenon of this century will impact organizations more than globalization. It began slowly at first, when large

Chapter 1

U.S. firms began to enter overseas markets in the 1960s. It quickly expanded following the fall of the Berlin Wall in 1989 and soon accelerated into today's rush to enter markets on every continent.

Yet even today there is only a handful of organizations that operate on a truly global basis with in-depth experience in many markets. The vast majority of U.S. organizations have only begun to do business globally, primarily to take advantage of cheap labor and lower production costs. The concept of a global strategy is rarely considered by these organizations. The service organizations that follow them usually have even less interest in a global strategy; they are content to follow their clients wherever they are.

Such limited attention to globalization is shortsighted. Today the United States has less than 5 percent of the world population. There are 23 countries with populations of 50,000,000 people or more. By 2050 the world population is expected to grow from six billion people to almost nine billion. This increase of three billion people will include only about 100,000,000 in the United States. In short, it is obvious where the opportunities will be. Progressive and forward-thinking organizations are mindful of these possibilities. Strategic thinking, planning, and operating on a global scale has become a major factor in envisioning the future. Within the next two decades this trend will become commonplace.

A second impact of globalization is one less considered: that is, without intending to enter overseas operations directly to market or produce, many U.S. organizations purchase supplies from overseas companies and thus become international. In this way, many organizations are becoming importers of all kinds of supplies as well as finished products that will be sold in U.S. markets. In short, like it or not, we find ourselves being drawn into operating in a global marketplace. Organizations that choose to ignore these developments will be marginalized, unless they choose to operate in very narrowly defined local markets and then primarily on a service basis.

Information technology

The impact of information technology has already changed the way most organizations operate, even though they may be pursuing the same old strategy. The Internet, computers, and telecommunications equipment tend to be viewed as better ways of achieving the same objectives and with greater convenience, speed, and efficiency. This can hardly be viewed as strategic thinking; it is simply opportunistic operational thinking.

For example, having strategic partners and alliances across the nation or around the world is becoming commonplace. This requires strategic thinking, new organization structures, new lines of communication, and new management systems and styles. These changes require top management decision making and continued involvement, not simply the latest computers and servers. Strategic changes of this nature distinguish an organization from its competitors, who continually buy upgrades to do the same thing that competitors are doing.

In addition to its impact on strategic direction, information technology is having a profound impact on operational systems. More information can be collected, stored, retrieved, and processed faster and less expensively than was possible even a year ago. Gathering and processing information faster is crucial, since it provides management with the ability to make real-time fact-based decisions.

Information technology is also affecting measurement systems, reporting, and record keeping, all used in the process of implementing and managing strategy. Of late, certain strategic management subprocesses are even being computerized. Strategy meetings using computer technology are commonplace. Geographically dispersed organization units can easily be connected using these tools, thus increasing the range and scope of strategic management.

Knowledge management

Knowledge management refers to the identification, generation, collection, transference, and distribution of knowledge for use and reuse. Unfortunately, exactly what constitutes "knowledge" is still the subject of philosophical debates.

In short, knowledge can be viewed, at least in part, as processed information. While knowledge management was first organized and managed as a regular practice in research, engineering, and design activities, it is only since the mid-1990s that *knowledge management* became an established discipline in its own right, studied and taught in universities and well-established in large organizations. With respect to strategy, it is the application of knowledge *management* that is of interest, not what constitutes knowledge per se—the useful definition of knowledge will vary from organization to organization.

Typically, because knowledge management programs are directed at cutting-edge developments that will have significant but not necessarily immediate impacts on the organization, they are monitored closely by top management. Knowledge management can be considered in its traditional forms of on-the-job-training, apprenticeships, formal training programs, and mentoring. Of more recent interest are the development and use of information technology to create knowledge-based expert systems and search engines for general as well as specialized information repositories.

As in the case of information technology, knowledge management affects strategy in two primary ways:

- As a source of knowledge that can directly be applied to developing the strategic direction of the organization
- As a set of tools and concepts that can be used in the strategic management system itself

In both these cases, knowledge management has already become as important to large organizations as think tanks have to government institutions and the military.

The discipline of strategic management

As described earlier in the chapter, strategic management has emerged as a fully developed management discipline, even though it is not yet practiced as such in most organizations. Unfortunately, many managers still perceive it as an experience-based, intuition-driven competency that is relegated to top management. This is not acceptable to younger managers, especially newly-minted MBAs whose graduate programs required strategic management coursework leading them to believe that this is a discipline in which they will participate when hired.

The attitude of younger managers today is reinforced by the new management paradigm that is rapidly taking hold. It is variously characterized as horizontal, flat, team-based, collaborative, cooperative, evolving, and a host of similar terms. The significant point is that management structures such as line and staff and hierarchical are no longer the preferred models, and, as strategies are translated into a portfolio of strategic projects that cascade down and throughout the organization, strategic management is increasingly viewed as an integrated set of management processes requiring the participation of managers at all levels.

However, one fundamental disconnect has not been addressed; the management style accompanying the "almost military" model of organization is still very much alive, reinforcing the perception of strategic management as "strategic command." This generation gap in preferred management styles and structures needs to be addressed as a major contextual challenge in many organizations today.

These are by no means the only trends and events driving management interest in and attention to strategic management, but they are among the more recurrent and long-lasting. There is also another important aspect of the changing context of strategic management that contributes to the need to develop strategic management as a set of core competencies; that is, their combined and interactive impact.

In summary, these and similar dimensions of the context of strategy all point to extensive and continuous emphasis on strategic management to cope with the combined impact of threats and the opportunities that organizations face. Organizations that minimize the importance of strategic management will find it increasingly difficult to compete—regardless of their size and resource base.

CHARACTERISTICS OF EFFECTIVE STRATEGIC MANAGEMENT SYSTEMS

Rapidly changing and hard to predict organizational contexts, especially in business organizations, present executive management with the challenge of developing strategic management processes to cope with them.

Management teams that have accepted this challenge and developed strategy-oriented managers, effective strategic management systems, and strategy-aligned operations exhibit certain recurrent characteristics. For example, Table 1.7 summarizes characteristics of effective strategic management systems.

The extent to which a management team follows these practices is still a matter of choice. However, it will be increasingly difficult to avoid the trend toward ever more formalized and systematized approaches to strategic management. The window for using informal and primarily intuitive approaches is closing—how fast depends on the particular organizational context. These practices should be given careful consideration by those management teams that want to make a significant improvement in strategic management in their organizations.

Table 1.7: Characteristics of Effective Strategic Management Systems	
Process	• Strategic direction and strategic management processes (which includes vision, mission, values, policies, goals, and objectives) are written, distributed, understood, accepted, reviewed, and maintained. • Strategic management processes follow a disciplined approach. • Strategic management is a team-based process. • Strategic management processes are integrated with operating processes to ensure the latter are strategically aligned. • Strategic management performance is measured, monitored, reported, and recorded on a periodic basis. • An internal strategy auditing function covering processes and performance is in place. • A continuous improvement capability covering processes and performance is prioritized.

Table 1.7: Characteristics of Effective Strategic Management Systems (continued)

Executive Leadership	• Strategic management is practiced as a major and continuous executive management responsibility. • Members of the strategic management team understand and accept that managing strategy requires constant attention. • Executive management exhibits proactive leadership in formulating and implementing strategy. • Executive management accepts the primary responsibility for identifying and implementing the organization's strategy and ensuring the provision of resources, that is, people, funds, and equipment. • A chief strategy officer/champion is identified and empowered. • A strategic management advisory board is utilized.
Continuous Learning	• Education and training in strategic management tools and concepts are provided, as necessary. • Strategic management is included as a major topic in the continuous learning activities of the organization. • Opportunities to develop strategic management competencies are provided.

Table 1.7: Characteristics of Effective Strategic Management Systems (continued)

Human Resources	• Managers and professional staff at all levels understand and participate in managing strategy. • Strategic management competencies are specified in job descriptions. • Strategic management roles and responsibilities are identified for all managers and professional staff and included in their job descriptions. • Excellent strategic management performance is required for all managers who advance to higher levels of management responsibility. • Strategic management is a key consideration in succession planning.

In addition, strategic management systems are themselves undergoing significant change to cope with these accelerated, unanticipated, and increasingly complex change patterns. They, too, need to be brought into the 21st century.

One simple example will suffice. Imagine trying to conduct an environmental scan without the use of the Internet, computers, and telecommunications equipment (other than telephone and fax technology). Furthermore, imagine this occurring in a geographically dispersed organization. Fortunately, software tools are being designed specifically for strategic management subprocesses. Examples include the following:

- Consolidating an environmental scan
- Making strategic/competitive analyses
- Prioritizing a OTSW analysis

- Time-phasing strategy
- Conducting performance reviews
- Auditing strategic performance

In addition to software applications, strategic management processes are increasingly being systematized, using features such as the following:

- Virtual managerial and operating processes
- Standardized, transparent, and seamless processes and procedures
- Dashboard displays
- Inputs without attribution
- Geographically dispersed meeting and communication capabilities
- Minimizing the need for face-to-face meetings
- Data and information-based decisions
- Flexible and rapid response capabilities
- Informational inputs, observations, and comments without attribution

Ultimately, effective strategic management processes and support systems require continuous and focused management attention, regardless of the differences in management style and organization culture. Also, regardless of these variations in style and format, there are certain recurrent steps that are found in highly effective strategic management systems.

These steps include the following basic processes:

- **Strategy assessment**

    - Conduct initial assessment
    - Organize the process
    - Conduct external strategic analyses
    - Conduct internal strategic analyses

- Design continuous strategic analysis system
- Evaluate results of strategic analyses.

- **Strategy formulation**
    - Define strategic direction
    - Identify/generate strategic alternatives
    - Evaluate strategic alternatives
    - Select preferred alternative(s)
    - Develop strategic plan for the preferred alternative(s)

- **Strategy implementation**
    - Assemble management to proceed with implementation
    - Determine the implementation objectives, projects and tasks
    - Organize implementation process
    - Direct and coordinate implementation process at the organization level
    - Direct and coordinate implementation process at the functional level
    - Direct and coordinate the implementation process at the project level

- **Ongoing strategic management**
    - Integrate and align implementation processes
    - Measure strategic management performance
    - Evaluate strategic management performance
    - Control and reward strategic management performance
    - Set up continuous improvement processes for strategic management

- Review and evaluate strategic performance and strategic management capabilities

Note: These steps are developed with many variations by different consultants, strategy analysts, and planners. In addition, an organization will often find reasons to make its own changes, modifications, and additions to meet unique situations or to emphasize a particular step that requires expansion and development. This is especially likely to occur in organizations with a great many strategic business units and/or organizations operating in several locations.

With these qualifications in mind, the balance of this book outlines the development of each of the steps incorporating proven models and concepts of strategy where they can be most effectively utilized.

CHAPTER 2

Initiating a Strategic Management Program

Upon the drying of a lake, two frogs were forced to seek water elsewhere.
As they searched they came upon a deep well.
Come, said one frog to the other, let's go in without looking any further.
Said the companion, you believe this fine, but what if the water should fail us here too?
How shall we get out again?

The Moral: 'Tis good advice to look before we leap

—*Aesop's Fables*

All too often organizational leaders move into and through the strategy setting process without building a common information base upon which sound strategic decisions can be made. In a rush to define strategy and approve annual operating budgets, judgments and decisions are made upon an uneven understanding of the strategic environment and its capability to influence the future. This fundamental "knowledge gap" among senior leadership and down through the organization serves to undermine the strategic management process in several important ways by:

- Failing to leverage the existing repository of strategic knowledge available to the planning team via the workforce and via accessible information resources inside and outside the organization
- Decreasing the likelihood an effective strategy will be selected and eventually made operational
- Unintentionally enabling work force resistance to change as the reasons for change are not clearly communicated

Best practices in strategic management point to early emphasis on creating and making available to all strategy team members a *common information base* of facts, perceptions, and attitudes about the external and internal environments faced by the organization. This practice enables leadership teams to better discern the preferred path forward and increases the probability that a desired future state is ultimately realized.

In this chapter we present two prerequisite steps for laying the groundwork for a practical, sustainable, and repeatable strategic management process within an organization. They are:

- **STEP 1:** Assess the current strategic direction and capabilities
- **STEP 2:** Design and organize an appropriate startup program based on these assessments

STEP 1: ASSESS THE CURRENT STRATEGIC DIRECTION AND CAPABILITIES

The prerequisite that ***must be completed*** before attempting to develop a strategy-focused management approach is a comprehensive assessment of an organization's current strategic position and strategy management capabilities. While this may seem obvious and logical, many leadership teams begin by asking where they want to be, might be, or should be—without first making an assessment of the current situation. Such approaches more often than not prove to be inefficient and ineffective and can eventually fall short and lead "back to square one." Management has failed to appreciate the need to have a realistic assessment of the organization's true capabilities, competencies, and resources in order to set realistic and attainable goals and aspirations—and to attain them.

The term *strategic direction* is used here in the broadest sense in that all organizations, whether formally planned, ad hoc, or emergent from ongoing operations, are based on some idea of where they are headed. Later, in Step 7, the process of crafting a formal strategic direction will be outlined in detail. The task, at this point, is to identify the direction the board and/or management have in mind in terms of directing the organization's activities, however uncoordinated and/or disconnected this strategic direction may be stated and pursued.

It is equally important to make an assessment of the strategic management capabilities and the financial and human resources that are and will be available to leadership to pursue its strategic direction and achieve its goals. It will soon become apparent that tangible capabilities and resources will be necessary to initiate and sustain a strategy-based management system. The most critical and influential of these factors are noted below.

In this book, the term *assessment* refers to two equally important and conceptually distinct processes: analysis and evaluation.

Analysis *refers to an examination of data and information to understand its content, meaning, and significance for some purpose, in this case the strategic management of an organization.* The processes of analysis are dependent on the nature of the data and information being analyzed. The information may be qualitative and/or quantitative. It may also include informa-

Strategy in the 21st Century

Taylor and Morgan Rollinson.

tion that is subjective; biased; fragmentary; and, apparently, inconclusive. The important point is that it is recognized as such, and examined in an objective manner.

Evaluation *refers to the process of comparing the information that has been analyzed in terms of some evaluation criteria, whether qualitative or quantitative.* We live in the "information age"; in fact, daily we drown in a sea of information. Evaluation is the process of reducing this literal explosion of information to useful and manageable proportions.

Analysis precedes evaluation and provides a solid information base that can then be evaluated in terms of the needs, expectations, and capabilities of executive leadership and the organization and, subsequently, used for the selection of the most effective organization strategies.

Table 2.1 summarizes the three primary components of an initial assessment.

These assessments are equally important whether the effort to develop strategy and strategic management capabilities is entirely an internal process or includes, to a greater or lesser ex-

> **Table 2.1: Components of an Initial Assessment**
>
> - An assessment of the organization's current strategic direction and strategic management capabilities
> - An assessment of the currently available managerial and organizational capabilities required to develop, implement, improve, or redefine the strategic direction
> - An assessment of the contextual, situational, and unique features that currently exist in the organization

tent, external assistance. Executive leadership must have a realistic assessment of what it takes to carry out a sustained change effort, or it easily becomes another "flavor of the month," soon to become another forgotten initiative.

In those cases where external assistance is used, individuals facilitating this effort will need the results of this assessment to calibrate and align their assistance with the needs of the organization and the organization's leadership team.

The following assessments are most appropriately gathered in direct interviews, facilitated and informal conversations, and direct observations—with board members, executives, top managers, and staff members likely to be included in any effort to initiate a strategy-based management system.

Ideally, one senior manager can be designated who has some knowledge and experience with strategic management processes to coordinate and consolidate the results of these assessments, as well as conduct and/or supervise the interviews and information gathering activities necessary to make these assessments. In those cases where such an individual is not available, the services of a qualified and trusted outside consultant or advisor may be required.

An important caveat: This assessment is an *overview* that will be a major determinant of what the leadership teams ultimately want the organization to become. More detailed information will be gathered in both the external and internal strategic analyses that follow. At this initial stage, the information gathered will be used to determine the level of effort and commitment the leadership team is willing to undertake. Specifically, this means acquiring the following information.

An assessment of the organization's current strategic direction

Strategic direction refers to the organization's vision, mission, values, policies, and goals. It is safe to say that in many organizations these components are not formalized, communicated, or systematically implemented. More often than not they exist as general statements of intentions, not as a basis for leadership decision making and planning.

In any case, a realistic assessment of the current strategic direction will set the tone and provide the basis for defining the scope of the strategic management program. It is an indispensable first order of business. Therefore, it should provide a point of departure by considering questions such as the following:

- What are the shared perceptions about the direction of the organization, its strategy for success, and its priorities?
- Are there any significant differences in these perceptions among senior leadership that need to be addressed?
- Does the board and/or management distinguish between long- and short-term thinking and planning?
- Are the desired outcomes feasible in light of the current level of leadership commitment and organization development?

- What is the probability that the leadership team will have the energy, resources, and willingness to achieve the objectives that they have set?
- Have any problems and/or issues been identified that are likely to sidetrack the leadership team's interest and commitment to this project?
- Are any significant barriers identified that need to be addressed before a viable strategic management process can be launched?

The following components of strategic direction, summarized in Table 2.2, provide a framework for organizing answers to these and similar questions, as well as a basis for analyzing and developing strategy.

Table 2.2: Components of Strategic Direction

- Vision—A statement of where the organization wants to be—a desired future state and the end result of the organization journey
- Mission—A statement of the organization's purpose—the rationale for its existence in pursuit of the vision
- Values—The shared core beliefs that members of the organization hold and that influence their decisions and actions taken in the name of the organization
- Policies—The guidelines, whether formally stated or not, that members of the organization are expected to follow in making decisions and/or taking action
- Goals—The generally stated end results of activities undertaken in pursuit of the organization's vision, aligned with the other components of the strategic vision

The importance of reaching a common understanding of where the organization now stands with respect to these components of strategic direction cannot be overstated. Taken together, these components provide the focus and rationale for all strategic management activities. Every organization has a strategic direction in some state of development. It need not be written to have an impact on members of the organization. Paradoxically, some of its unwritten components are more widely shared and adhered to than those distributed in detailed documents and reports.

However, once an organization embarks on development of a comprehensive strategic management system, it is no longer feasible to treat the components of its strategic direction informally and certainly not haphazardly. Together they are the foundation upon which all strategic management processes ultimately rest. No system can be effectively designed, managed, or maintained without a clearly articulated, widely disseminated, and closely adhered to strategic direction. Consequently, it follows that the leadership team clearly understands where it stands from the outset in order to reach agreement on how to proceed in developing its approach to management.

We have found it useful to assess each of the strategic direction components in terms of its level of development. In those organizations that have not formally designed their strategic direction, these components vary widely in how well they are developed and disseminated throughout the organization.

The level of development is an estimate of the extent of articulation, diffusion, understanding, and adherence to the components of the strategic direction currently existing in the organization. What is required is a realistic estimate of the level of development of each component. In Step 7 in Chapter 4, these components will be discussed in detail with guidance on how to develop a comprehensive statement of strategic direction. At this point, the following definitions of the various levels will provide sufficient guidance for reaching agreement on the level of development for each component:

- **Level 1**—No clear articulation and diffusion of the component, although it may be well understood and used by the leadership to run the organization
- **Level 2**—The component is written and distributed, but is recognized by the workforce as a public relations effort that leadership has little or no intention of using to orient, motivate, or otherwise influence the workforce—except as a passive announcement
- **Level 3**—The component is well documented and distributed, and leadership makes an effort to ensure that all members of the organization understand and accept (hopefully internalize) the component; the level of development of the component still varies considerably from that of other components
- **Level 4**—The component is documented, distributed, and used by leadership to make decisions, plan programs, and develop guidelines in managing all activities and in conducting relationships with customers, suppliers, and employees; the level of development of all components is beginning to approach the same level of articulation and utilization by management
- **Level 5**—All components of the strategic management direction are at the same high level of articulation and utilization and are also integrated and synergistic; the majority of management, staff, and the workforce understands and accepts them and uses them to guide their organizational activities

Estimates of these developmental levels can conveniently be summarized as shown in Figure 2.1.

Strategy in the 21st Century

The entries shown illustrate a typical situation showing uneven development of the various components. Each organization will have its unique set of ratings.

Figure 2.1: Initial Assessment of the Level of Development of the Current Strategic Direction

Level of Development	Vision	Mission	Values	Policies	Goals	Average Level
1		•				
2	•			•		•
3			•			
4					•	
5						

Taken together, these components provide a realistic estimate of the average level of strategic direction development. Management needs to agree on this level since it is the best single indicator of the starting point for designing and developing the strategic management program.

Following this line of reasoning, if the premise of having balanced development is the assumed benchmark, then those components that are above the average level represent aspirations that are probably set too high and therefore beyond current management capabilities to realize. If, however, they are lower than the average, they will likely hold back progress by not providing clearly understood guidelines.

This is easily illustrated in the tendency of organizations to set too many goals without a clear understanding of the time and resources required to achieve them and/or to wax eloquently about the organization's statement of values while not using them to guide behavior or select projects. Finally, in many organizations a clear understanding of the vision and mission is not universally shared/effectively communicated throughout the organization, greatly impeding progress in managing strategically.

An assessment of current strategy management capabilities

Equally important, and complementary to the preceding questions, are the following questions regarding how to pursue a strategic direction in a realistic manner.

They include the following types of questions:

- Does the organization's leadership take into account any of the following distinctions while leading and managing their organization?
    - Working "on" the organization versus "in" the organization
    - Long-run versus short-term thinking and planning
    - Balanced general management versus dominance by one functional discipline
    - In-depth and balanced consideration of both external (opportunities and threats) and internal (strengths and weaknesses)

- To what extent do managers in each of the functional areas take these distinctions into account in managing their areas of responsibility?
- At the corporate level are there policies, procedures, and scheduled activities with the board, staff, and subordinates regarding any strategic management activities?
- What policies, procedures, processes, and/or systems are in place that take into account strategic activities (as opposed to operational activities)?

These and similar questions will be addressed in detail throughout the course of this book. At this juncture, the key objective is to determine the level and scope of the current strategic management capabilities in order to determine the best way to design and organize the strategic management program. Information in these areas may well determine the success or failure of any strategic management effort because of any number of reasons, such as board and management indifference, inadequate management capabilities, lack of resources, competing priorities, and perceived and/or real threats.

The act of listing present management capabilities is pared down to those considered to be the most fundamental determinants of successful strategic management. Of course, many other considerations will be needed to develop and maintain a comprehensive and competitive system. The ones noted here are not only fundamental and required from the very start of any strategic management program, but they are also easily understood at all levels of organization development.

With respect to leadership, there are three levels of critical importance: the board, top management, and the management teams in each major function. Taken together, these three levels will determine the content, format, and timing of the strategic management approach that is ultimately implemented and maintained.

Regarding the processes, the key skill required is an ability to design and develop the new processes that a comprehensive strategic management system requires. Focusing initially on process management has its advantages. Since most strategic processes reside either at the organizational or cross-functional level, they foster the development of teamwork and an organizational perspective—while at the same time focusing on the detail of the processes being developed.

Figure 2.2 provides a format for summarizing this assessment. The entries included here are for illustrative purposes only. Each organization will have its distinct profile of these and similar capabilities.

Figure 2.2: Initial Assessment of Current Strategic Management Capabilities

Leadership & process capabilities	Comments on the current status of the capability	Impact on a successful strategic management program
Board of Directors	Some board members are experienced in strategic management processes	To be effective a common nomenclature and process will need to be defined
Executive Management	Owners and marketing manager closely control all management activities	Executive education in strategic management a top startup prerequisite
Middle Management	Little evidence of teamwork, silo management prevails	All middle management requires functional strategic management education
Financial	Limited to budgeting and accounting duties	Needs to develop financial strategic management capability
Marketing	Dominant and most influential	Needs to limit authority and power in nonmarketing activities
Operations	Focused on new product development, operations management a secondary consideration	Needs direct top management link; currently dominated by marketing
Information Systems	Limited to financial and marketing systems development	Need integration, documentation, control systems

Strategy in the 21st Century

Figure 2.2: Initial Assessment of Current Strategic Management Capabilities (continued)		
Human Resources	Focused on routine personnel processes; no organized training function	Not currently a top management concern. Weakest function. Needs integration in top management thinking.
Process Design and Development (PDD)	No organized capability for strategic PDD; acceptable PDD limited to accounting systems.	PDD capability will be a priority from the beginning

The comments listed above are much too cryptic. However, they are meant to illustrate how the current leadership, management, and process capabilities will impact strategic management processes. The key challenge is to gather sufficient information and insight into the current capabilities in order to develop a realistic plan, followed by gradual development of a competitive and integrated strategic management system that meets the needs of the organization and the aspirations of leadership.

So far this emphasis on the strategic management direction, management, and process design capabilities does not identify those factors that ultimately may be even more critical, that is, the set of contextual, situational, and unique factors that condition and configure the actual strategic management system that will evolve over time. These factors are considered in the next section.

Chapter 2

An assessment of contextual, situational, and unique features that will significantly impact a strategic management program

Managers, consultants, and advisors easily overlook the idiosyncratic factors that constrain, facilitate, or otherwise influence the strategic management decisions and actions of every organization. These are factors only the organization's leadership team can answer, since they alone have the knowledge and experience to develop a program designed to match the aspirations and resources of the organization.

Every leadership team needs to address the following and similar questions that will impact/influence how they go about strategic management in their organization. Obviously, the relevance of these questions will vary greatly, depending on the unique circumstances in each organization. The objective is to find those key factors that will have significant impact.

- To what extent do the board and management understand the need for strategic management, its benefits, and the commitment and resources required to undertake and maintain a strategy-aligned approach to managing their organization?
- Is there a widely shared perception of the need for a strategic management approach in the organization?
- Is there a widely shared desire to initiate a strategic management program, and, if not, what are the major concerns of the naysayers?
- Are there significant strengths and/or weaknesses in either the board, management, or staff skills and capabilities that will facilitate/impede a strategic program?
- Are there immediate or impending performance problems

that must be addressed before any significant changes are made in the managerial system now in place?
- Are there key board members or managers and/or stakeholders (that is,, unions, funders, stockholders, customers) that have the power/influence to facilitate/impede a strategic management development program?
- Has the organization undergone any major changes and/or challenges that will significantly alter the course of a strategic management program, that is, a strike, a merger/acquisition, loss of a key manager or staff member, loss of a key customer, or even loss of a key funding source?
- What organizational features will impact the program, such as multisite locations? A highly centralized/decentralized organization structure, a "one-man show"?
- What is the level of organizational acceptance/resistance to new managerial and organizational changes?
- Are there any impending or anticipated events/trends in the organization's environment that will impact a strategic management program, such as recession, a credit crunch, loss of a major customer, entrance of a new competitor, or loss of a key supplier?
- Are there any high priority problems that have not yet been mentioned that now take leadership's full attention? If so, for how long? Is it a problem that can be leveraged as a starting point for a strategic management program?

Only the significant factors need to be included in a summary manner, as shown in Figure 2.3. The entries included, as in the above assessments, are illustrative and typical. Each organization will have its own unique profile.

Figure 2.3: Assessment of Factors Influencing the Nature/Scope of the Strategic Program

Factors to consider in designing the strategic management program	Comments on the current status	Impact on a successful strategic management program
Management Posture		
Perceptions/ attitudes	Realize must change, not sure of what to do	Requires extensive emphasis on basic management along with strategic management
Skills/ competencies	Seeing new market opportunities	May be able to use this competency to motivate development of other competencies
Performance	Few effective performance measures and controls	A priority that could begin immediately with operational measures and controls
Preferences/ positions	Until recently, satisfied with slow growth and few changes	Need to have specific reasons for each change; need to have examples from other situations
Availability for startup program	No major bottlenecks	Good possibilities of forming the necessary teams
Organization design/ development (ODD)	Recently established a new supplier management program	Need to emphasize horizontal relationships and minimize silo management
Organization culture	Craft unions probably will present resistance to change	Need clear agreement on conditions and rates of change; should have union participation

Figure 2.3: Assessment of Factors Influencing the Nature/Scope of the Strategic Program (continued)

External Factors		
Economic conditions	Sector maturity	Probably will require focus on cost savings, productivity, new products/services/markets
Competitive factors	International competition growing	Explore international opportunities
Supply and service factors	Seeking new supplier	Consider outsourcing and supplier consolidation
Market conditions	Increasing price comp & customer demands	Review customer service systems and processes
Situation-Specific Factors		
High priority problems	Recent manufacturing acquisition focus of top management	May require a rescheduling of a startup program or a scaling back of strategic startup activities
Stakeholder positions	Family owner will stay in control regardless of other changes in management	A major point of consideration; success hinges on how to work with the family without compromising a strategic focus
Financial resources	Solvent but limited funding for new projects	Need to develop strategic alternatives that require low or modest financial requirements; projects must have quantifiable payback

Again, the comments contained in Figure 2.3 are only meant to illustrate how the current leadership and process capabilities will impact strategic management processes. As contextual, situational, and unique factors they will vary in their incidence and impact. At this point, the initial data and information collected, along with the insights and observations made by these individuals, should provide a good estimate of the current status of the organization with respect to the overall strategic direction and the strategic managerial and organizational capability.

The focus now turns to consensus building on the current situation with respect to strategy, strategic management, and organization capabilities. Once consensus is achieved by management regarding these assessments, they will become the basis for determining the scope and extent of the strategic development program to be undertaken, as indicated in Step 2.

STEP 2: DESIGN AND ORGANIZE AN APPROPRIATE STARTUP PROGRAM BASED ON THESE ASSESSMENTS

The results of the preceding assessments and leadership discussions will shape the features of the startup initiative and ongoing activities in the strategic management program. While there is no "standard approach" to kicking off a strategic management program, the assessment work in Step 1 should yield sufficient information to design and organize an effective program configured to meet the needs of a given leadership team and its organization. In all cases the focus should remain on designing a team-based approach to moving the process forward.

Design the program

While the strategic program of each organization will have its unique and distinctive features, it is convenient to first determine the level and scope of the program and then to modify it to meet the needs of the leadership team and the organization.

Balanced growth may be desirable, recommended, and even the most appropriate approach, but it is seldom the result of incremental and/or unplanned growth and development. The usual tendency in most organizations is for some functional area(s) of the organization or a key project to dominate organizational processes—and other functional areas as well.

One dysfunctional outcome of this process of uneven development is the neglect of various processes and at the same time unnecessary commitments of time, energy, and resources to the "overdevelopment" of others. As a consequence of this uneven process development, it is very often necessary to bring strategic management or organizational capability in other functional areas up to a level that is consistent with the dominant processes. What the leadership team is looking for is a consensus among leadership regarding the overall level of performance they consider desirable—and attainable.

Selection of the level and scope of the startup program

The level and scope of the initial program should reflect the best use of management capabilities, available resources and equally important, leadership preferences on how to initiate strategic management activities—regardless of the ultimate level and scope of the strategic management process aspired to and eventually realized. The following three levels describe how most leadership teams initiate the development of their strategic management system.

- At the strategic project level
- At the dominant functional level
- At the organization-wide level

Chapter 2

At the strategic project level

Often a project management approach focused on a high priority strategic project may be the only feasible startup program that leadership is comfortable with and ready to undertake. If so, it should be made clear that this is only a means to initiate strategic thinking and decision making, ultimately the most desirable strategic management system is one that is organization-wide in order to best mobilize and utilize a leadership team and its organization.

It is important to acknowledge that taking a project management approach is in no way a compromise. Once an organization is operating from an organization-wide strategic perspective, projects are often the primary means of undertaking high priority strategies.

One common and often used technique to move to the strategic project level approach is to commit to a "phase one" that can be determined at the outset while reserving judgment about continuing and expanding the strategic management program. The financial commitment made for phase one is based entirely on the organization's financial resources and leadership's perception of the importance of this initial project. In such situations, an initial program of this nature may last three to six months. During this period leadership will have time to become acquainted with the strategic management process so that it can make informed decisions about the scope, content, outcomes, and expectations of continuing to develop a strategy-aligned organization.

In this book, we are only concerned with strategic projects, that is, those that have or will have a significant impact/influence on the strategy of the organization. These projects should have some level of innovation, risk, and uncertainty about how to implement them and about their ultimate impact on the organization. These projects usually require relatively large expenditures over a long term. In essence, these are characteristics of strategic projects.

The aforementioned features maintain close kinship to the original use of the term "project." Such projects are in contrast with what we refer to as "operational projects," that is, replications of or slight variations on previous projects that are executed with little or no risk, with certain outcomes and usually on a much smaller scale than strategic projects.

In recent years management attention has focused on the use of project management design and implementation for both routine and nonroutine management activities. The result is that project management is tending to become the dominant form of management activity. For example, it is not uncommon for a manager to be involved in several projects simultaneously and, as a parallel development, be required to multitask and be a member of several teams and/or committees. This practice often leads to an environment where resources are spread too thinly. Unless this trend is recognized and care given to balancing the selection of projects, an uneven growth and development will occur among the functional areas of the organization. This, in turn, makes a balanced and integrated strategic management approach all but impossible.

At the dominant functional level

An executive leadership team and organization structure that attend to all its functional areas in a balanced and integrated manner based on strategic and operating plans do not evolve naturally in the course of organizational growth and development. Managers do not arrive at the top and suddenly begin to make decisions and take action from an organizational perspective. Often they arrive at the helm of their organizations based on their superior performance in some functional area or areas and naturally begin to manage the organization from this perspective.

Most organizations have one or two functions that are the key to their survival and success. The organization becomes dysfunctional when these functions are allowed to dominate decision making and organization development in other areas. In the long run this unbalanced approach results in unsatisfactory profits, unfulfilled plans, and inefficient processes.

For whatever reasons, a common practice of many business organizations is to rely on the more developed management expertise and experience in a key function or functions. In such cases, it is reasonable to begin the strategic management program from this perspective and then move gradually to an organizational perspective.

In such cases, an effective means of embarking on a strategic management program is to focus primarily on one key functional area, for example, the marketing and sales function. Management is this area must be convinced of the need to broaden their perspective to a balanced organization level; otherwise, it is unlikely that they will fully understand and accept the need to change their dominant functional approach to a more balanced and productive organization-wide strategic approach. In such situations, an initial period may last longer than required for a strategic project approach. The managers in the functional area have a vested interest in keeping their extensive control and influence throughout the organization. In contrast, strategic project managers are usually directing projects that are cross-functional in scope and content—in essence, already an organizational perspective.

As in the case of strategic project management approach, functional management will have time to become acquainted with the strategic management process so that it can make informed decisions about the scope, content, outcomes, and expectations of continuing to develop a strategy-aligned organization.

At the organization-wide level

Any leadership team that makes a serious commitment to a strategy-focused approach and pursues it over the long run will sooner or later confront the challenges—and benefits—of a strategy-focused management approach and decide whether to continue on the strategic management journey. The only relevant question at this point is whether it is desirable and feasible to use this approach *from the outset*. An organization-wide approach is feasible under the following conditions:

- If there is no preference for a strategic project and/or a dominant functional area, the leadership team of the organization or a specific business unit may want to consider a comprehensive development approach. This approach can be used whether the organization has little or no strategic management competencies or a well-developed capability is in place being effectively used to manage the organization.
    - In the former case, it is simply a preference of the management team and the absence of extenuating circumstances that mitigate against this approach.
    - In the latter case, the usual condition is the need to better balance and integrate the various subprocesses of the overall strategic management process. In such circumstances, this is best accomplished by systematically evaluating and adjusting the subprocesses to increase their overall effectiveness and performance levels.

Chapter 2

- Alternatively, the leadership team may want to consider development and/or implementation of selected dimensions of the *strategic direction* and/or *strategic plan* of the organization or business unit, that is, vision statement, mission statement, core values, policies, goals, strategies, and objectives. In programs of this type the primary focus is on the analytic and planning processes with little or no need for development of leadership and organizational capabilities.

Modify design features

Each of these three approaches require further adjustment to the contextual, situational, and unique factors that modify the direction and types of strategies that the organization is able to pursue effectively. Many of the observations and comments made in the assessments above translate directly into design features. Others are implicit in leadership attitudes, preferences, and capabilities.

In all cases, the key task is to determine what the leadership team wants, is capable of, and needs to do in order to launch a strategic management program. The following design modifications are illustrative but certainly not exhaustive:

- Desired level of development
- Desired scope and rate of development
- Development priorities
- Strategy preferences
- Strategy deployment potential at the functional level
- Strategic projects currently underway
- Acceptable risk level of new strategies
- Acceptable scope and rate of change
- Expected benefits and outcomes

- Profile of the initial strategic management team
- Resource requirements and availability of management and staff
- Education and training capabilities and requirements
- Perceived need for outside assistance
- Time horizon
- Initial schedule for the first quarter of the program
- Expanded schedule for the first year of the program
- Key leverage point(s)
- Cost estimates

Organize the program

Step 2 includes several tasks that must be accomplished before an organization can undertake any significant effort to develop strategy as outlined in Step 1. Whereas Step 1 was focused on the assessment process to determine *what* should be included in the program, Step 2 refers to *how* the program should be organized to ensure achieving the desired outcomes. The tasks required to organize the program are the following:

Get commitment from the top

Before effective strategic management can take place, organizational leaders (including the board of directors) must embrace the need for a disciplined approach, *both strategically and operationally*. By accepting this fundamental premise, coupled with the willingness to allocate the resources (time, skills, and money) necessary to clarify the direction of the organization and its implementation, a successful effort can be launched.

Commitment to the effort must come from all levels of leadership and management, since strategic management is an organization-wide responsibility. Before this or any major change program for that matter is undertaken, this commitment must be communicated to all levels of the organization. It is top management who must take the lead, not only in making this commitment but also in ensuring the commitment is understood and prioritized throughout the organization.

Outline how to organize and manage the program

Organizations, even those of the same size that are performing the same functions, vary greatly with respect to organization structures, management authority and responsibilities, degree of specialization, style of managing, and so forth. Therefore, it is only feasible to offer some general guidelines and suggestions to organize and manage in a manner that fits the organization and provides comfort levels and familiar patterns to those involved in the program. It is difficult enough to deal with new tools and concepts without also having to adopt new management styles and systems.

Based on this organization and management approach, it is important to assign responsibility for various aspects of the strategic management program. Obviously, many members of the leadership team will be involved in all parts of the program; however, as the program progresses, new roles and responsibilities will be identified and need to be assigned at that time. At the end of this first phase, the leadership team may choose to adjust the planning team membership to best monitor execution of the plan and refine the strategic management process on an ongoing basis.

At this point, the following assignments should be made:

- **A strategy development champion should be selected.** This is usually the CEO or a senior member of the management team, but it could also be a board member, the owner, the founder, or in some cases an outsider brought in to set a new strategic direction. The title of Chief Strategy Officer has recently been proposed and is being introduced in some organizations. At this point, there is not enough accumulated experience to recommend using this approach.

- **A core strategic management leadership team** should be appointed to provide stakeholder representation, guidance, motivation, and continuous monitoring and evaluation. This working "team-oriented" committee should remain engaged for the duration of the strategy formulation and strategic planning phases of the program. Depending on the nature and culture of the organization, the strategic management leadership team should consist of board members, executive managers, strategic business unit managers, and functional managers, including areas such as marketing, finance, operations, human resource management, and information systems in business organizations. In other types of organizations, such as government agencies, nonprofit organizations, and associations, the main functional areas will be different.

  In all cases, each major functional area should be represented on the strategic management team. This is true even in those cases where few changes in strategy in a given area are contemplated. As members of top management, functional managers have a major responsibility for organization-wide strategic management. Also, at some future date the focus of organization strategy may shift to a functional emphasis.

- **An extended group of committee members or "guests"** can also be included depending on the organization. These extended team members can include the following:

- **Strategy analysts**—Many organizations have staff analysts—perhaps not full-time strategy analysts but nevertheless analysts who can carry out the analyses required in this program. They should be a part of the planning team because they will be better able to conduct studies without a lot of time spent in "getting up to speed." Also, as they gather more information, they become a valuable strategic management resource.
- **Relevant specialists**—At times strategy development requires the expertise of specialists that were not identified or anticipated at the outset. This is especially important in high-tech areas and in making decisions about entering new global markets. These experts can come from within the organization or from the outside. They need not become permanent members of the planning team but only participate so long as their expertise is required.
- **Stakeholders**—Input from individuals and/or organizations that have a significant impact/influence on, or are impacted/influenced by, the organization can also be included in the process. They may include employees, customers, strategic partners, suppliers, major shareholders, investors, and funding bodies. Whether they should be members of the strategic planning team is a judgment call made by each organization.
- **Outside consultants and advisors**—Consultants brought in specifically for this study should become members of the strategic management team.

In all cases it is important to compile a comprehensive set of benefits expected from the process and a list of anticipated concerns to be addressed before the process begins. The team must agree upon and communicate a reasonable work plan and timeline. Throughout the development of the strategic management program, it is vital to maintain top leadership involvement and participation in all phases of the program. This cannot be emphasized too strongly. Determining strategic direction and planning and implementing strategy throughout all functions and at all levels of the organization remains the primary responsibility of top management.

Although it depends on the size of the organization, each unit in those organizations that are divided into strategic business units (SBU) should have its own strategy development and implementation program and follow/adapt the steps as outlined in this book. In addition, there needs to be a relationship between each strategic business unit and the corporate strategic management leadership team. This type of organization is not considered in this book since it involves independent strategy-making groups within the same organization.

Seek outside help, as necessary

Depending on the size of the organization and its internal management and staff experience/expertise in strategic management, it may be necessary/advisable to seek outside assistance. In most cases, this assistance will be that of a seasoned senior facilitator who has had broad experience in strategic management programs in several organizations. This is the only type of assistance that should be sought at this time. Later, as the project evolves, the need for various types of other specialists may be identified. This level of specialization can be necessary for all types of functional expertise and for highly specific expertise, such as gathering competitive intelligence about rapidly changing industries, process improvement, or privately-held businesses.

Careful attention to selecting a team manager/facilitator and to forming the project's oversight team is extremely important, since the composition of its membership will determine the project's scope as well as manage expectations, keeping them realistic and achievable. If key members of the leadership team or the professional staff are omitted, the success of the project may fall short of its deliverables. It is all too easy to make assumptions about a particular function, process, or strategic business unit when its key manager(s) is not on the team.

The magnitude of the changes management and other members of an organization undergo as a result of this work are more than justified. There is simply no comparable set of challenges that a leadership team can commit itself to and try to accomplish. While it may be a truism that all organizations should operate in this manner, very few organizations in any field of endeavor can truly be classified as being managed with an integrated and balanced set of strategic management processes. The effort to complete these prerequisite activities will be well-rewarded from the moment the strategic management program is initiated until it is the shared and continuously improving basis for organizing and managing the organization. In the next chapter, the first strategic management processes are outlined, that is, strategic analysis and evaluation.

CHAPTER 3

Strategic Information Analysis and Evaluation

Once the scope of the strategic management program has been determined, as outlined in Steps 1 and 2, the process of strategic management moves into thoughtful analysis and evaluation of the strategic environment facing the organization.

Effective analysis of the strategic environment is premised on the availability of robust team input and subsequent consolidation of their information regarding the organization's external and internal environments. From a "best practices" perspective this information should be maintained and made available to the planning team via an easy-to-use strategic information system (SIS). However, most leadership teams making a major commitment to strategic management for the first time have neither collected nor consolidated the necessary data to make them useful information. The teams may even lack the understanding about what constitutes strategic information for their organization.

Leadership teams should not begin by building their own SIS. The first step is to discover what constitutes relevant strategic information and then collect and consolidate it as a "first generation" snapshot of the organization's strategic environment. Once this process has been completed, the leadership team will possess a new shared understanding about the nature of strategic information for their organization. Building on this understanding, the team can then develop a practical SIS that will support the next annual cycle of the strategic management process.

Accordingly, four distinct steps are required to effectively and efficiently analyze the environment of any organization. These steps, in order of their initiation, are as follows:

Step 3: Conduct external strategic analyses
Step 4: Conduct internal strategic analyses
Step 5: Develop a strategic information system
Step 6: Evaluate results of strategic analyses

As described in Chapter 2, analysis and evaluation should be maintained as separate processes within a strategic management system, in accordance with the following definitions:

Analysis of strategic information refers to the processing of relevant data and information into useful information of potential relevance in subsequent steps in the strategic management process. There are two primary foci to be considered in analyzing strategic information, that is, external information and internal information. These types of information will be made clear in Steps 3 and 4, respectively.

Evaluation of strategic analyses refers to the process of comparing the information that has been analyzed in terms of some evaluation criteria, whether qualitative or quantitative. In this case, it refers to an evaluation of analyses and classifying the results into external opportunities and threats (Step 3) and internal strengths and weaknesses (Step 4). Further clarification of these bodies of information takes place in Step 6.

Chapter 3

STEP 3: CONDUCT EXTERNAL STRATEGIC ANALYSES

Step 3 focuses exclusively on the gathering and analysis of *external* information. Analysis of *internal* information will be covered in Step 4. This division of the process is based on a fundamental premise of all organizational strategies: they are contextual. That is to say, they seek to make the best fit between an organization and its external environment. Therefore, it is most convenient to mirror this distinction in the classification of information.

There are many external forces, dynamics, and constraints that must be taken into account in arriving at the most desirable and effective strategy, but the analysis begins with a comprehensive understanding of these forces and constraints and

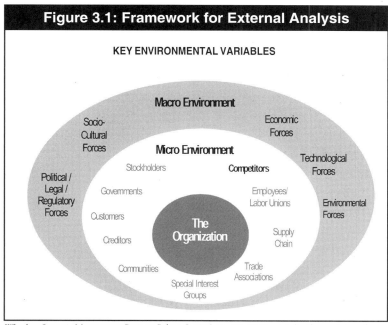

Wheelen; Strategic Management Business Policy; © 1986, pgs. 79, 93. Reprinted with permission of Pearson Education, Inc., Upper Saddle, NJ 07458.

how they interact to enable a particular *strategic direction* to emerge within a specific organizational context.

We begin by breaking the external analysis into two parts, that is, a macro-analysis (global/domestic level) and a micro-analysis (industry/organizational level).

There is no standard format for making these analyses, since organizations vary in the type and level of information that are significant to their needs. However, a number of recurrent dimensions at both levels has been found useful in most organizations.

The following lists will serve as a guide for the macro-level forces. In time, the leadership of each organization will be able to develop a more focused list, adding and deleting forces as they are determined to be relevant. A discussion of micro-level analysis follows this section.

Macro-level analysis

Macro-environment forces can be conveniently considered in terms of global/domestic, broad-based *trends* that impact and/or influence the overall performance of the organization. In this regard it is useful to distinguish between current, short-term, urgent impacts and/or influences and future, longer- or medium-term trends, and cumulative impacts.

Table 3.1 summarizes the five key dimensions to the macro-level environment linked to relevant topics and questions to consider within each dimension.

Each dimension can be analyzed using a combination of *generic* and *specific* questions to drive team thinking and input into the process. Generic questions relate to all or most dimensions, while specific questions pertain to each dimension or subtopic and are best formulated by members of the organization undertaking the strategic analysis. These questions should be developed/reviewed by the manager of the strategic management process. This will focus the task of gathering and presenting the information in a useful format.

Table 3.1: Key Dimensions to the Macro-level Environment

- **Political forces** What political trends are driving change in your organization?
    - Pending home country legislation/regulations
    - International, regional, bilateral agreements
    - Future legislation
    - Government policies, for example, labor, trade, subsidies, safety, health care, immigration, etc.
    - Government funding, grants, and contracts
    - War, terrorism, and international conflict
    - Lobbying and advocacy groups

- **Economic forces** What economic trends are driving change in your organization?
    - Home country economic situation and trends
    - Taxation regulations (general and product specific)
    - Seasonality and climate factors
    - Market, product, and trade cycles
    - Exodus of industries and services
    - Energy issues
    - International economic situation and trends
    - International trade financing and distribution infrastructure
    - Interest and exchange rates
    - Trade and monetary issues

Table 3.1: Key Dimensions to the Macro-level Environment (continued)

- **Social and cultural forces** What social and cultural trends are driving change in your organization?
  - Demographics
  - Generational differences and issues
  - Changing class structure
  - Ethnic and religious factors
  - Enclave cultures within a mainstream culture
  - Necessary versus discretionary spending patterns
  - Shifting lifestyles
  - Changing work patterns, attitudes, and behaviors
  - Regional and local differences in all of the preceding factors
  - Immigration patterns
  - Educational issues
  - Healthcare issues
  - Security and safety issues
  - Ethical issues and corporate social responsibility

- **Technological and scientific forces** What technology and science trends are driving change in your organization?
  - Information and communication technology
  - Commercial uses of the Internet, that is, E-commerce
  - Consumer uses of the Internet
  - Technology licensing and patents
  - Intellectual property issues
  - National research and development expenditures

Table 3.1: Key Dimensions to the Macro-level Environment (continued)

- National rates of innovation and patent production
- Technology legislation
- Manufacturing infrastructure
- Science and engineering manpower issues

• **Environmental forces** What environmental trends are driving change in your organization?

- Impact of global warning
- Changing climate patterns
- Environmental legislation and regulations
- Home country national, regional, state, and local level environmental issues
- International environmental issues
- Public awareness concerning environmental issues
- Industry/sector pollution impact and control
- Pollution control technology
- Energy consumption/environmental impact relationships
- Development patterns versus nature preservation

Examples of generic questions follow.

- How much information is available by soliciting input from core and extended planning team members?
- Which forces (or factors) should receive the greatest attention?
- How sensitive is the organization to changes in a particular force?
- Does it therefore warrant closer scrutiny?

- At the international level, can the focus be narrowed to specific countries of interest?
- What is the rate of change of these forces?
- What is the cost of acquiring this information versus the benefits of its potential use?
- Are there alternative sources for acquiring the information?
- Have the relevant factors been identified within each dimension before beginning the analysis?
- Do any of the forces or factors need to be subdivided or specified in more detail?

Micro-level analysis

It is useful to break the micro-level analysis of forces and trends into two parts: an industry or sector analysis and an organizational environment analysis. Industry analysis can be considered a high-level profile that can be made without considering the organization except as a statistical unit in the industry. An organizational environment analysis is concerned with the specific external relationships of the organization, including those within the industry/sectors that have been profiled.

Table 3.2 summarizes the five key dimensions to the micro-level environment with relevant subtopics and micro-level questions to consider.

Micro-level forces and factors can be analyzed from generic and specific perspectives in the same manner as macro-level concerns. Macro-level generic questions (listed above) can apply equally well to micro-level factors. Also, from the perspective of a given context, questions will always gain in relevance when generated by members of the organization.

As leadership teams become more familiar with the many types and sources of information required for strategic manage-

Table 3.2: Key Dimensions to the Micro-level Environment

- **Industry analysis forces** What is the overall state of your industry and your organization's position relative to competitors and those who influence the industry?
  - Products/services
    - Standardized versus customized products/services
    - Product life cycles
    - Complementary and/or substitute products/services
  - Industry profile (number, size, revenue, location of organizations in the industry)
  - Profile of typical member organizations
  - Profile of leading and/or influential member organizations
  - Government regulations
  - Entry barriers
  - Industry life cycle
  - Patterns of competition (sources, level, intensity, scope)
  - International trends and events pertaining to the industry
  - Interorganizational relationships (mergers/acquisitions/buyouts/joint ventures/alliances/ franchises)
  - Interindustry input-output matrix
  - Offshoring and outsourcing
  - Infrastructure
  - Support services

Table 3.2: Key Dimensions to the Micro-level Environment (continued)

- **Market analysis forces** Which market trends will impact the markets/customers we serve and the needs that we fill?
    - Market segmentation
    - Market niche
    - Market position
    - Market portfolio
    - Market life cycle

- **Customer analysis forces** What is the profile of our customer, and what customer needs do we fill?
    - Usage/consumption/service/buying patterns
    - Demographics
    - Product/service expectations
    - Changing profiles of current customers
    - Potential new customers
    - Organizational versus individual customers

- **Competitor analysis forces** What is the profile of our competitors, and what is our competitive advantage?
    - Competitive factors (price, service, unique product/service features)
    - Level, type, and intensity of competition among industry members
    - Barriers to exit
    - Barrier to entry
    - Profiles of key current competitors

> **Table 3.2: Key Dimensions to the Micro-level Environment (continued)**
>
> - Cross-industry competition
> - New sources of competition
> - Changing competitive forces
> - Proximity to customers
>
> • **Supplier chain analysis forces** What is the nature of our supply chain, and where are the bottlenecks that need to be addressed?
>
> - Suppliers
> - Distributors
> - Strategic partners
> - Transportation
> - Logistics services

ment within their organization, they will be able to combine their ideas and insights in the development of a more comprehensive and systematic approach to information collection and compilation.

Therefore, from the beginning, team members should take note of the types and sources of information they perceive to be relevant to strategic thinking in their organization. This information can then be integrated when developing a systematic and effective strategic information system (see Step 5). The very success of a strategic management system depends on a foundation of comprehensive, current, and accurate flow of information to all members of the leadership team conducting strategic analyses.

Strategy in the 21st Century

STEP 4: CONDUCT INTERNAL STRATEGIC ANALYSES

Step 4 builds on the assessment of strategic direction made in Step 1. It is now time to develop a comprehensive understanding of the internal capabilities of the organization as they relate to the achievement of the strategy. Figure 3.2 is a conceptual model summarizing the placement of internal analysis within the overall environmental scanning and strategy-setting framework.

In all situations it is vitally important to arrive at a chosen strategy based on a clear understanding of which external opportunities and threats mesh with the internal capabilities of the organization. This can be a painful process for many team members, as emotions often run high when the focus of the analysis and subsequent evaluation turn inward. Nevertheless every effort should be made to help the team "confront the

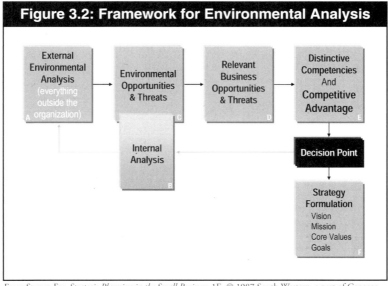

From Stoner, Fry. *Strategic Planning in the Small Business*, 1E. © 1987 South-Western, a part of Cengage Learning, Inc. Reproduced by permission. www.cengage.com/permissions

Chapter 3

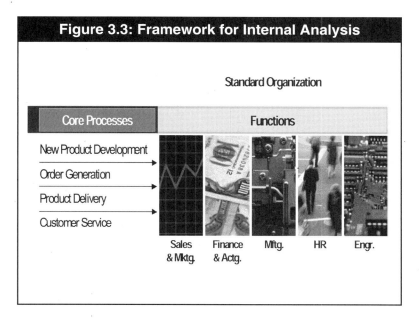

brutal facts" in a professional and productive manner (Jim Collins, *Good to Great,* 2001, 65-70).

In many organizations, the basic "functions" and operational "processes" are inextricably interwoven. Therefore, these organizational "building blocks" should be identified conceptually and used to analyze an organization's internal strategic performance.

An integrated approach to examining the efficiency and effectiveness of core processes and functions results in an objective fact-based analysis of the internal capability of the organization. A robust understanding of these facts enables a leadership team to make modifications and improvements in both organization strategy and strategic management capabilities.

Table 3.3 summarizes the internal dimension and highlights nine sets of issues that, taken together, shape the internal environment and drive organizational capability. (Relevant subtopics and questions to consider are included.)

Table 3.3: Key Components of the Internal Dimension

- **Core competency** What internal capabilities do you have within your own organization that gives you a competitive advantage? What makes you special in the eyes of your customers? Below are typical areas where core competency can be found:

  - Quality of the product or service—high above industry standards
  - Fill a special niche
  - Strong consumer orientation—leading to a high degree of customer intimacy
  - Service levels—high above industry standards
  - Operational efficiency—leading to low cost provider
  - Reputation and brand image—established over many years of outstanding performance
  - Site selection—location, location, location
  - Flexibility and adaptability—needs of customers can change quickly
  - Special and unique technical skills of one or more people on the team

- **Pending issues** What internal issues yet to be dealt with, decided, or settled require the organization's attention? Below are several illustrative examples:

  - Management and board leadership do not agree on how to move the organization forward.
  - The organization does not produce financial statements that accurately track performance.

Table 3.3: Key Components of the Internal Dimension (continued)

- ○ The organization does not know what customers value most.
- ○ A defined marketing and sales process that operates effectively to generate new customers does not exist.
- ○ A defined research and development process does not exist to produce high quality products to meet emerging needs on a consistent basis.
- ○ A process is not in place for leadership development within the ranks of the organization.
- ○ Staff members are not motivated to produce at levels to help the organization reach and exceed its goals.
- ○ A staff development process does not exist to meets the organization's needs across all departments and business units.
- ○ The organization does not recruit and develop the membership of the board of directors to provide visionary leadership.
- ○ One or more senior executives will be leaving the business, and succession planning has not taken place.
- ○ Layoffs have just occurred, and the organization has not adjusted to these painful developments.

- **Culture and general work atmosphere** How would you characterize or describe the culture/general work atmosphere between the board and management, within management, and between management and staff?

Table 3.3: Key Components of the Internal Dimension (continued)

- Culture of mutual respect and honesty exists where staff members feel free to openly discuss their concerns and ideas without fear of reprisal or belief their communications are ignored.
- Skills exist to accomplish the work required.
- Incentives are in place.
- Resources are available in sufficient quantity to succeed.
- Desired actions are taken by the leadership team on a timely basis.
- A history of positive organizational performance exists.

- **New product/service development** What issues within your organization impact your ability to develop and deliver new products and/or services to customers?
    - The entire process is defined, detailed, and communicated to all employees.
    - A baseline of performance is established against which improvement can be measured.
    - Total cycle time is within appropriate limits.
    - The process is consistent, and outputs are regular.
    - Work flows in unison between the external suppliers, the internal providers of the product or service, and the targeted customers.
    - The process can quickly produce work outputs in response to changing customer needs.

Table 3.3: Key Components of the Internal Dimension (continued)

- o The process produces what is needed when it is needed.
- o The process is flexible and responsive and readily accommodates changes while remaining in balance.
- o Problems are identified and eliminated on a systematic basis.
- o Problems identified with the process are solved on the first attempt.
- o Changes to the process are well thought out and carefully implemented.
- o Managers of the process correct problems instead of rationalizing them away or blaming others.
- o Providing value to the customer is the overriding reason for the process.
- o Employees have a thorough understanding of the process and are committed to meeting performance standards.

- **Securing new customers** What issues within your organization impact your ability to grow your customer base?

  - o The entire process is defined, detailed, and communicated to all employees.
  - o A baseline of performance is established against which improvement can be measured.
  - o Total cycle time is within appropriate limits.
  - o The process is consistent, and outputs are regular.

Table 3.3: Key Components of the Internal Dimension (continued)

- Work flows in unison between the external suppliers, the internal providers of the product or service, and the targeted customers.
- The process can quickly produce work outputs in response to changing customer needs.
- The process produces what is needed when it is needed.
- The process is flexible and responsive and readily accommodates changes while remaining in balance.
- Problems are identified and eliminated on a systematic basis.
- Problems identified with the process are solved on the first attempt.
- Changes to the process are well thought out and carefully implemented.
- Managers of the process correct problems instead of rationalizing them away or blaming others.
- Providing value to the customer is the overriding reason for the process.
- Employees have a thorough understanding of the process and are committed to meeting performance standards.

- **Product/service delivery** What issues within your organization impact the quality and timeliness of product and service delivery?
  - The entire process is defined, detailed, and communicated to all employees.

Table 3.3: Key Components of the Internal Dimension (continued)

- A baseline of performance is established against which improvement can be measured.
- Total cycle time is within appropriate limits.
- The process is consistent, and outputs are regular.
- Work flows in unison between the external suppliers, the internal providers of the product or service, and the targeted customers.
- The process can quickly produce work outputs in response to changing customer needs.
- The process produces what is needed when it is needed.
- The process is flexible and responsive and readily accommodates changes while remaining in balance.
- Problems are identified and eliminated on a systematic basis.
- Problems identified with the process are solved on the first attempt.
- Changes to the process are well thought out and carefully implemented.
- Managers of the process correct problems instead of rationalizing them away or blaming others.
- Providing value to the customer is the overriding reason for the process.
- Employees have a thorough understanding of the process and are committed to meeting performance standards.

- **Customer service** What issues within your organization impact your delivery of customer service?

Table 3.3: Key Components of the Internal Dimension (continued)

- The entire process is defined, detailed, and communicated to all employees.
- A baseline of performance is established against which improvement can be measured.
- Total cycle time is within appropriate limits.
- The process is consistent, and outputs are regular.
- Work flows in unison between the external suppliers, the internal providers of the product or service, and the targeted customers.
- The process can quickly produce work outputs in response to changing customer needs.
- The process produces what is needed when it is needed.
- The process is flexible and responsive and readily accommodates changes while remaining in balance.
- Problems are identified and eliminated on a systematic basis.
- Problems identified with the process are solved on the first attempt.
- Changes to the process are well thought out and carefully implemented.
- Managers of the process correct problems instead of rationalizing them away or blaming others.
- Providing value to the customer is the overriding reason for the process.
- Employees have a thorough understanding of the process and are committed to meeting performance standards.

Chapter 3

Table 3.3: Key Components of the Internal Dimension (continued)

- **Location analysis and resource availability** How would you characterize or describe the organization's current location and ability to access required resources?
    - Traffic volumes—street and highway network
    - Financial resources—banks and investors
    - Human resources—employment patterns for management versus staff
    - Physical resources and raw materials
    - Logistic resources—rail and port
    - Professional services—legal and accounting

- **Prerequisites for effective strategic management** How would you characterize your organizations strategic management competencies and overall strategic management system?
    - Our organization is driven by a clearly articulated vision, mission, and core values.
    - Our organization puts the right amount of emphasis on strategic management.
    - Shared perceptions exist about the direction of the organization, its strategy for success, and its priorities.
    - Significant differences in these perceptions exist among senior leadership, which needs to be addressed.
    - The board and/or management distinguish between long- and short-term thinking and planning.

Table 3.3: Key Components of the Internal Dimension (continued)

- Our board and senior leadership regularly review our strategic direction and strategy.
- Our current strategic plan guides the decision making and behavior of managers in this organization.
- Our desired outcomes are feasible in light of the current level of leadership commitment and organization development.
- The probability is high that the leadership team will have the energy, resources, and willingness to achieve the objectives that they have set.
- Problems and/or issues that are likely to sidetrack the leadership team's interest and commitment to this project have been identified.
- Significant barriers have been identified that need to be addressed before a viable strategic management process can be launched.
- We are consistently moving toward achieving our organizational goals.
- We know what the key drivers of our success are, and we know how to measure them.
- We regularly track our performance toward longer-term goals, and our current data show good performance toward achieving our longer-term goals.
- Managers at all levels of the organization clearly understand our strategy.
- We have an information technology structure in place that meets our strategic management needs.

Chapter 3

This approach is limited to an *analysis* of *current* internal functioning and the operating environment of the organization.

The rationale for this approach is simple and straightforward: developing and implementing strategy is an evolving process. To be successful one must first complete the analysis of organization issues and capabilities presently in place. Any attempts to *evaluate* the current strategy—especially in terms of strengths and weaknesses—are premature. Also, efforts to develop a new strategic direction or to formulate alternative strategies are steps that should be avoided at this point in the process. These steps will be addressed in Chapters 4 and 5 of the book.

Providing a sequence of steps is not meant to imply that the strategic management process must and will remain linear but rather that there is a natural order or "linear logic" to formulation preceding implementation and ongoing management.

At the same time feedback loops can occur at any point in the overall process of strategic management. These will arise in response to the combination of intuitive and creative thinking as well as to logical, linear, and systematic analysis. Also, it is a practical matter of presenting a process in an orderly manner while allowing for free flowing feedback.

Developing a strategic focus does not preclude the need for operational analyses to complement strategic analyses. This may occur when a given function, say marketing, is the key focus of an organization strategy. Any given functional area may contain several drivers that are pivotal to executing a new organization strategy, and, therefore, much more information on a particular function is required. With these caveats in mind we can begin the internal analysis.

To facilitate this process a helpful internal analysis checklist is included in Appendix 3—Internal Analysis/Audit Checklist.

As stated in the dimensions for external analysis and now repeated at this point with minor changes and additions, each of these nine internal focused dimensions can be analyzed using a combination of *generic* questions and *specific* questions. Generic questions pertain to all or most dimensions, while specific questions pertain to each dimension and are best formulated by members of the organization undertaking the strategic analysis. These questions should be reviewed and further developed by the strategic management leadership team. This will help to focus the team on the task at hand, that is, gathering and presenting the information in a useful format.

Examples of generic questions follow:

- Do analyses/reports/documents already exist on any of the forces or factors requiring analysis?
- Is each factor strategically significant to the accomplishment of the current organization strategy?
- Has there been a tendency to shift from a strategic to an operational focus?
- Do any of the factors need to be subdivided or specified in more detail?
- Which factors should receive the greatest attention?
- Which factors have the greatest impact on the organization, that is, which ones are driving your organization?
- How sensitive is the organization to changes in a particular factor? Does it therefore warrant closer scrutiny?
- What is the rate of change of these factors?
- What is the cost of acquiring this information versus the benefits of its potential use?
- How much information needs to be collected and for what purpose?
- Are there alternative sources for acquiring the information?

- Are there information services for acquiring and analyzing any of these factors?

Analyzing internal strategic information often proves to be more difficult than analyzing external information. Information about the internal environment of an organization is much more likely to be operational than is external information, and its strategic implications are not always immediately clear. Therefore, in developing a strategic information system, great care has to be exercised to determine exactly what constitutes internal strategic information. For example, many manufacturing firms are, or soon will be, facing a major challenge in attempting to replace an aging workforce. This is an easily identified problem but one that has been neglected in many businesses for years, even decades, and has reached the point of requiring strategic solutions. Does this mean shifting operations overseas? Are there ways to automate processes—assuming that funding is available? Should/can new processes/products/services be developed? These possible "strategic" solutions are very different from short-term operational solutions, such as increasing pay rates to attract new workers, requiring overtime, or training programs and apprenticeships.

STEP 5: DEVELOP A STRATEGIC INFORMATION SYSTEM (SIS)

In best form, strategy setting is a deliberate and disciplined process built upon an accurate, robust and *transparent* set of facts, trends, and perceptions about the environment within which the organization operates. At the beginning of this chapter we discussed the need for building and utilizing a strategic information system (SIS) as the repository for this information. (See Figure 3.4, Strategic Management at Work.)

Strategy in the 21st Century

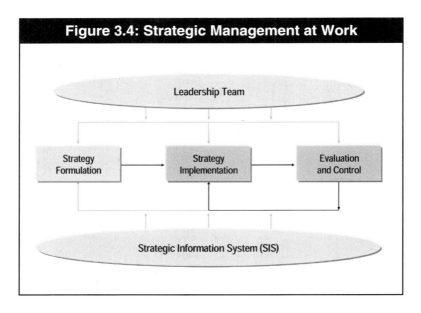

An up-to-date SIS, built by the leadership team, helps them rise above individual perceptions by shining a bright light on the broader perspective of the entire team and the realistic situation faced by the organization. Design, development, and implementation of an SIS are fundamental capabilities a strategy-aligned organization must possess.

Information to include in an SIS can come from a wide range of sources including existing information systems, key stakeholders, planning team members, secondary research findings, and, when necessary, primary research activities. The information consolidated in this system, including the events, trends, capabilities, and relationships external and internal to an organization, helps to close the ever-present organizational "knowledge gap" that exists in most leadership teams. When designed correctly, an SIS enables efficient and insightful assessment of the strategic landscape and causes the leadership team to garner a keen awareness of alternative pathways the organization may consider.

Once the leadership team has completed its first comprehensive strategic analysis, it will have a much better idea of the scope and content of the strategic information that it requires for making analyses in the future. In addition, it will be better positioned to do the following:

- Identify the most useful sources of information
- Understand the most effective ways of collecting and compiling this information
- Assign the roles and responsibilities for the information collection and consolidation
- Determine who will manage these processes
- Understand how to deploy the SIS within the organization

For these reasons the work in Step 5 logically follows the external and internal analyses in Steps 3 and 4, respectively. After the first strategic information collection process is finished and the findings are fresh, the leadership team should begin developing its SIS. The organization, staffing, and scheduling of this project is a matter of management discretion. The one requirement is that the SIS be operational by the time the strategic analysis begins in the next annual strategic management planning cycle.

The purpose of Step 5 is to offer guidelines on the development of an SIS. Accordingly, the following topics are to be considered:

- The rationale for a free-standing SIS
- Designing and developing a system versus managing within a system
- Factors to consider in designing an SIS
- Basic features of an SIS

The rationale for a free-standing SIS

Since the early 1970s the terms *information systems*, *information technology*, and *information management* have been part of the management lexicon. However, the primary focus in the use of these terms has been on *operational information*, that is, the collection and processing of information to coordinate and control day-to-day operations.

This is in sharp contrast to the way most organizations process strategic information; that is, what we define as *strategic information* means information that is of **potential relevance** to the development of a strategy-focused management system and/or the use of that system. Even organizations working through strategy-focused information management systems still tend to consider the collection and compilation of strategic information (prior to analysis) as the responsibility of a key analyst. This is in contrast to a true SIS which is under the control of a more inclusive organization-owned team that carefully manages the process.

This perspective stems from not fully realizing that information processing prior to analysis and evaluation is itself a key determinant of the success of the strategic management system. It is simply too important to be left to an ad hoc approach in which the primary depository of strategic information is in the minds of individual leaders, managers, and staff members.

Employing an ad hoc approach of this kind creates many limitations, including the following:

- The leadership team responsible for analyzing strategic information is forced to rely on the information considered important to individual board members, executives, and managers.

Chapter 3

- Without a team-based consensus understanding on what constitutes strategic information, much time and energy are devoted to processing information that is not strategic and, conversely, to avoiding collecting the types of information that is important to the strategic management team.
- The scope and content of what constitutes strategic information when left to the individual, even as an explicit job requirement, will be impacted by individual perception of how much time and effort should be devoted to this responsibility. Some leaders are quick to see the central importance of this assignment while others view it as a secondary task.
- Lastly, the collection, compilation, and communication of strategic information are processes that can be continually improved. When the primary repository of strategic information is collected and retained by individuals, the opportunities for improving these processes are limited.

These considerations all point to the development of a strategic information system over time using an incremental "lessons learned" continuous improvement approach.

Designing and developing a system versus managing within a system

The development of an SIS illustrates an important management process that is much more encompassing than processing information per se; that is, it is an example of the often neglected concept of working "on the business" rather than "in the business." In the former instance, the focus is on developing the system, and in the latter the focus is on the accomplishment of the task(s) at hand by using the system.

Working on a system can be likened to developing a product or process in which the key activity is designing a system, that is, formalizing, commoditizing, or otherwise systematizing its inputs, throughputs, and outputs so that they can be used repeatedly with little or no change. For example, a data architect is not concerned with the use of the database, except to develop the specifications for its design. In contrast, working within a system is akin to using the database—for whatever purposes the user decides to use it.

To continue this analogy, while this is a simple and obvious distinction, most leaders are database users not data architects. In an organization committed to a strategic management, understanding and acting on this distinction make a world of difference—the difference between average and best-in-class performance.

At no point in the management process is this more applicable than in strategic management systems. The essence of strategic management is to be able to marshal the abilities and competencies of the board, management, and staff and to employ the organization's resources and capabilities in ways that will enhance the long-term survival, growth, and development of the organization in accordance with the strategic direction set by leadership.

Strategy management also requires the ability to be creative and innovative and to make major changes and adaptations in the current organization. This occurs whether the organization is responding to new threats, taking advantage of emerging opportunities, developing new capabilities/competencies, or shoring up managerial and/or organizational weaknesses. In short, there is a continuous need to adjust and adapt the system itself, that is, to work "on" the system.

These observations notwithstanding, some managers/leadership teams simply prefer a more ad hoc intuitive approach to strategic management, while other managers/leadership teams prefer to formalize and move toward a more systems-based and process-formalized approach. Therefore, since management style becomes the final determinant of the extent to which a leadership team sees the need for working "on" the strategic management system, we have elected to strongly recommend the development of an SIS and to allow each organization to determine the extent to which it wants to develop processes and procedures to support it.

Factors to consider in designing a strategic information system

The following factors are illustrative and should be considered guidelines for assisting the leadership team in developing its own SIS.

- **The current information system**—This is the logical starting point for developing an SIS. Some of the information currently being collected and summarized in management reports can be included in the SIS. The management and staff of current management information systems are a valuable in-house resource for the development of the SIS. Once they have a clear understanding of the scope and content of the information required, they can work with the strategic management team to develop the SIS to meet the needs of the organization.
- **Management styles**—Strategic management teams vary widely in their management styles along dimensions that will influence the level of development of the SIS that they prefer, find necessary, and will ultimately use. Organization time, effort, and money can be better employed than in developing an SIS that management will use in a

limited way. It is better to have management guidelines about their strategic information needs established from the outset.
- **Management capabilities**—Managers and management teams also vary widely in their skills, competencies, experience, and expertise. This makes it imperative that an SIS is developed based on a shared concept of at least the key characteristics of what constitutes strategic information. However, current management capabilities can be a constraint on the development of an effective SIS. On the other hand, limited current management capabilities can also provide a motivation to acquire the necessary skills and competencies, either through training, hiring, or outside assistance.
- **Level of process development**—This factor sets an upper limit on the level of development of an SIS with respect not only to information processing capabilities but also to the interpersonal linkages between operational systems. When the level of process development in an organization is at a level 1 or 2 (see Chapter 2, Step 1), management is at a level where interpersonal relations dominate system interactions.
- **Cost of maintaining and operating the SIS**—Cost, whether measured in financial terms, managerial time and commitment, staff time, or resources acquired and/or utilized, is always a key management consideration. Therefore, it is important to have some management guidelines that will give some order of magnitude estimate of the SIS that can be developed and maintained.

Chapter 3

Basic features of a strategic information system

The following features are illustrative and should be considered guidelines for assisting the leadership team in developing its own SIS:

- **Management**—Responsibility for the development and ongoing management of the SIS should be the responsibility of a senior manager or professional staff personnel that serves on the strategic management team. It should not be assigned to a member of the information technology (IT) department, although his or her input into the design and ongoing development of the SIS is important. IT staff can be most helpful in the acquisition and development of any necessary software tools to manage the system.

    The development of an SIS is fundamentally a strategic management responsibility and should be managed by a person that has strategic thinking as a basic competency and organizational responsibility for strategy development. Lastly, except in very large organizations with an advanced strategic management system, management oversight of the SIS is an important but certainly not a full-time assignment. The manager of the SIS should be an active member of the management team intimately involved with the analysis and evaluation of strategic information.
- **Staffing**—The amount of staff time allocated to the SIS is strictly a function of the managerial requirements and budgetary limitations of the organization. The only important guideline regarding staffing is to deploy assignments to skilled staff to ensure proper execution. This will relieve management of the routine administrative func-

tions tied to collecting and organizing information. Once it is clear as to the types and sources of information required, processes can be designed that can be managed by support personnel.

- **Process design**—Strategic analysis is fundamentally an individual intellectual process. As such, it is difficult to separate from other intellectual processes such as evaluation, conjecture, prediction, interpretation, creativity, innovation, and similar modes of thinking. At most, teams can engage in a vigorous exchange of ideas and insights and arrive at a shared consensus in the analysis and evaluation of the information.

The basic processes that need to be developed are as follows:

- **Identify information to be collected**—As a consensus develops and a sense of the strategic direction of the organization begins to emerge, a major portion of the information required will be identified. It is this information that needs to be collected by the SIS. In all cases, team members should be considered as vital sources of valuable strategic information. They understand important industry dynamics, organizational performance, and other unique characteristics.
- **Collect required information**—Prioritize efforts to efficiently and effectively collect and report this information. Data may be both qualitative and quantitative. However, in all cases the process manager should make every effort to ensure that it remains objective and free of his/her biases and assumptions, as covered in Step 1. Perceptions and attitudes of team members are vitally important inputs into the process. Careful listening, timely communication, and nonthreatening

facilitation skills can serve to elicit this important information.

- **Consolidate collected information**—The information collected needs to be assembled, classified, and organized into a useful format for subsequent use. Information in the context of this book refers to the processing of data into a form that makes them understandable to the user and possibly actionable. This role is best performed by the leader of the strategic management team or a designated member of his or her staff.

  It is always a temptation for the consolidator of information to focus on the utility of the information gathered and to turn it into recommendations for the leadership team to consider. This tendency should always be avoided. If not, consolidators of information run the risk of sending their own opinions, interpretations, and evaluations to the team (Steps 3 and 4). The strategic management team has the right to expect that the data and information that they receive from the SIS are accurate, timely, objective, and free of interpretation.

- **Communicate strategic information to appropriate team members**—After the first analysis of strategic information, it will become obvious that all information does not need to be processed in depth by all members of the strategic management team. Some members of the team will be better equipped than others to analyze certain types of information. For example, the significance of new trends in marketing, consumer preferences, and required services may best be identified and analyzed by marketing personnel, while engineering and manufacturing personnel will be in a better position to spot significant new product and process development opportunities.

Assuming that the process manager and/or specific team members have been alerted to monitor these trend and events, they will then have the responsibility of communicating their findings to the appropriate personnel, who, in turn, should submit their analyses to the team at large.

In addition, there will be other bodies of information that should go directly to all members of the strategic management team. Information of this sort is more general in nature and should not be processed beforehand by individual members of the team. Examples include general economic trends, new competitors, new product or service introductions, mergers and acquisitions in the industry or in closely related industries, changes in the board of directors or of top managers in competitive firms, and new government laws and regulations that impact the organization.

- **Identify sources of strategic information**—In time, the strategic management team will identify the most relevant sources of information that they consider strategic. However, this list will always be open-ended and subject to additions and deletions, and the team member responsible for the SIS should always be privy to this list. It will provide guidelines for him/her to pursue. Examples of various sources follow:

  - **Internal information sources**—Internal information sources refer to both organizational and individual sources of information. Organizational sources refer to databases, reports, and documents that are already maintained by the organization for operational purposes, that is, performance records, cost analyses, budgets, and planning records and documents.

- **External information sources**—External information sources pose a far greater challenge for the SIS and provide the best reason for establishing an SIS. The amount of information and the various sources through which it is available grows on a daily basis, and any (ad hoc) attempt to keep abreast of the trends and events relevant to an organization and its growth and development are hopelessly inadequate, even if the leadership team adopts a proactive strategy-focused management system.

  Individuals within the organization each have their own system of monitoring external information sources, but it is not usually done from a strategic perspective. More often this monitoring of external information is to identify those opportunities and threats that impact their domain of interest *within the current strategy*, for example, in professional, industry, and trade journals or from suppliers, customers, and trade shows.

  Until the organization is managed from a strategic perspective, the potential impact of this external information is seldom translated into a new strategic direction or into a systematic process of strategic decision making about the development of new competencies and capabilities.

  In summary, all of these separately collected sources, and the many more that will be identified, need to be monitored and the potentially relevant information collected, compiled, and absorbed by the strategic management team.

- **Primary and secondary sources of information**—Strategic information is collected from either primary or secondary sources. Primary sources refer to information that is collected directly from personal contacts through a variety of techniques, that is, interview, survey, questionnaire, and focus group. The strategic management information system manager should be versed in all of these and other direct contact methods.

Secondary sources refer to information that is collected from the media, whether in books, articles, reports, the Internet, newspapers, trade journals, or professional journals. It is not simply a matter of collecting these sources; they need to be reviewed and the information of potential relevance to the strategic management team retrieved.

- **Provide feedback to the SIS from management and staff**—All members of the strategic management team have a responsibility to maintain an ongoing contact with the manager of the SIS and to convey to him/her their ideas and insights regarding the necessary information they think should be collected and monitored, especially new trends and types of events. Lack of timely and insightful feedback by the team on the information being collected and reported has two significant dysfunctional consequences:

  - Continuing to process unnecessary information
  - Not receiving potentially relevant information that could impact/influence subsequent strategic management processes

- **Ensure continuous improvement of SIS**—It has become a truism to say "continuously improve" this or that system. With respect to an SIS it is important to point out the specific dimensions of improvement, since they differ from operational considerations, such as cost, efficiency, and delivery. SIS systems need continuous improvement in one key respect above all others, that is, the ability to identify strategic information in a timely manner.

STEP 6: EVALUATE RESULTS OF STRATEGIC ANALYSES

In Step 1, an *assessment* was defined as having two components, that is, an *analysis* and then an *evaluation* based on the analysis. So far, the emphasis has been on the analyses occurring in Steps 3 and 4. The objective of these analyses has been to develop a fact-based understanding of the current situation faced by the organization from a strategic perspective. This has included an external environmental scan in Step 3 and an *analysis* of

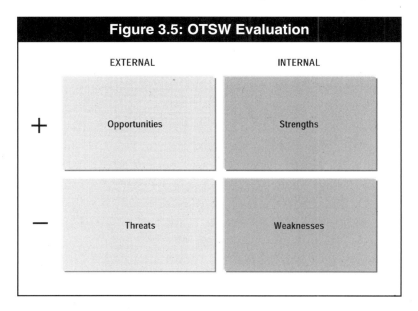

the internal dimensions and dynamics of the organization in Step 4. Step 6 is focused on *evaluation* using this analysis as the primary focus of our attention. The end result should be a comprehensive assessment of the environment from a strategic organizational perspective and its potential for developing and improving strategic management.

To conduct this evaluation we will use the well known approach called SWOT Analysis. From our perspective this tool is better identified as an OTSW Evaluation as we believe opportunities and threats should be determined before strengths and weaknesses (see Figure 3.5). Strategy should be fashioned based on the realities of the current and future market, not the day-to-day operating needs of the organization itself.

This is an extremely effective method for the evaluation of strategic management. SWOT Analysis is an approach that is universally accepted and widely used, providing an excellent starting point for assessing the "current state" environment facing an organization. This is in contrast to Scenario Planning that is a planning technique used to assess alternative "future state" environments a particular organization *may* encounter.

The term *SWOT analysis* has been in use for so long that the term *OTSW evaluation* would probably not be recognized. However, the terms *strengths*, *weaknesses*, *opportunities*, and *threats* are *evaluation criteria*. In organizational settings, there are no absolutes; for example, a strength using one strategy could be recognized as a weakness using a different strategy. In short, these terms are not *assigned inherent* attributes, that is, planning team members must decide if a particular attribute is a strength, weakness, opportunity, or threat.

In using a OTSW approach to evaluate the strategic environment, it is important to remember that it is a general approach that requires careful adaptation to the objectives and the context in which it is used. Strengths, weaknesses, opportunities, and threats are evaluation criteria that have relevance only in terms of the objectives and context in which they are applied. Each organization should consider its own definition of the terms. The OTSW approach has been found useful across a wide variety of applications, including assessing the following:

- Market position
- The current (or anticipated) competitive position
- Method of sales distribution
- Product features
- A new venture
- A strategic option, such as launching a new product
- An opportunity to make an acquisition
- A potential strategic partnership or acquisition
- Changing a supplier
- Outsourcing a service, activity, or resource
- An investment opportunity

During the OTSW evaluation process the planning team works to determine the *potential* for developing and implementing a new/improved/modified organization strategy and for developing the necessary strategic management capability required to implement and maintain it. We refer to this as a "building block" approach. The term *building blocks* is used to identify factors that will, *in most cases*, prove to be useful starting points in the development of strategic management.

Included in Step 6 are eight specific tasks:

- Review the external scan carefully
- Compile a list of the organization's primary market opportunities and threats
- Agree upon the organization's core competencies/competitive advantages
- Rank the organization's market opportunities and threats in light of its core competencies

- Review the internal scan carefully
- Compile a list of the organization's primary internal strengths and weaknesses
- Rank the organization's internal strengths and weaknesses in light of its primary market opportunities
- Evaluate the overall strategic management system

Review the external scan carefully

In all cases the strategic evaluation process is most effective when conducted after completing a thorough external environmental scan and a careful consideration of the findings. The external scan information should be reviewed and discussed by all planning team members. In most situations it is advisable for the team to meet with a skilled facilitator to review and consider the external scan report.

Senior leadership and management's investment of time in this phase of the process serves to "level the strategic playing field" for all team members, enabling the organization to build out its strategy based on a common understanding of the external environment.

Compile a list of the organization's primary market opportunities and threats

Following a thorough review of the external scan, team members should be invited to share anonymously their perspectives in identifying the primary market opportunities and threats facing the organization. Once this information has been collected, it should be consolidated and categorized as necessary.

To maximize effectiveness of the evaluation process, the team facilitator should categorize each market opportunity using the dimensions covered in Ansoff's Grid (see Figure 3.6). In

Chapter 3

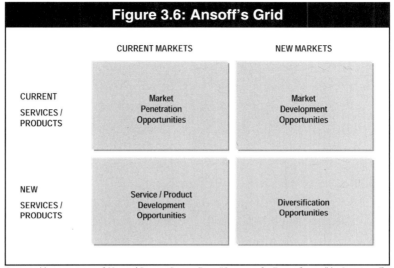

Reprinted by permission of *Harvard Business Review*. From "Strategies for Diversification" by Igor Ansoff, September-October/1957. Copyright © 1957 by the *Harvard Business Review*, all rights reserved.

general, every market opportunity can be categorized as being a market penetration, market development, product/service development, or diversification opportunity.

External threats should be consolidated and categorized as either longer-term, medium-term, short-term, or general if they exist yet defy being cast in one specific time frame.

Agree upon the organization's core competencies /competitive advantages

Before deciding which opportunities are best suited to the organization, it is important to have a clear understanding of the organization's core competencies, that is, those capabilities critical for an organization to achieve in order to maintain a competitive advantage.

The starting point for understanding core competencies is recognizing that competition between organizations is as much a contest for competence mastery as it is for market position and market power (see Figure 3.2).

The main ideas about core competencies were first developed by C. K. Prahalad and Gary Hamel. The central notion behind their work is that, over time, organizations develop key areas of expertise that are distinctive to their business and critical to its long-term growth. These areas of expertise may be in any dimension of the organization but are **most likely to develop in the critical organizational processes where the most value is added to products and/or services**.

Core competencies should not be viewed as fixed; rather they evolve over time in response to the organization's environment. It is possible to develop a competency into a core competency.

Prahalad and Hamel suggest three factors that help to identify core competencies in any business organization:

- Provides access to a wide variety of markets
- Is difficult for competitors to imitate
- Makes a significant contribution to the perceived customer benefits

A core competency must be "competitively unique." In many industries, most skills can be considered a prerequisite for participation and do not provide any significant competitive differentiation. To qualify as a core competency, a competency must be an attribute that is valued by the customer and that competitors wish they had within their own organization. A competency that is central to the organization's operations (yet not exceptional in some way) should not be considered a core competency since it does not differentiate the organization from its competitors.

Rank the organization's market opportunities and threats in light of its core competencies

The goal of the ranking process is to *select* those market opportunities that best leverage the core competencies of the organization and therefore enhance its overall competitive advantage.

One approach to prioritizing market opportunities and threats is to use the *nominal group technique*. This is a very structured process that involves full participation by the entire planning team. This nonthreatening method provides anonymity for all and ensures a broad based input into the evaluation process. A complete set of instructions and scoring sheets are included in Appendix 4: The Nominal Group Technique.

Review the internal scan carefully

As with the external scan, the strategic evaluation process is most effective when conducted following completion of a thorough internal environmental scan and a careful consideration of the findings. The internal scan information should be reviewed and discussed by all planning team members. In most situations it is advisable for the team to meet with a skilled facilitator to review and consider the internal scan report.

Senior leadership and management's investment of time in this phase of the process will serve to "level the strategic playing field" for all team members and enable the organization to build out a common understanding of the internal environment.

Strategy in the 21st Century

Compile a list of the organization's primary internal strengths and weaknesses

Following a thorough review of the internal scan team members should be invited to share anonymously their perspectives regarding the internal strengths and weaknesses of the organization. This is a critical stage in the process, one that allows team members opportunity to communicate their unvarnished insights into the operational capabilities and limitations of the organization. This information is then consolidated and categorized as necessary by the strategy manager or a designated team member.

We recommend an organization-wide assessment of the type that the *Malcolm Baldrige Quality Award for Performance Excellence* provides. In general, every organizational strength or weakness can be categorized into one of the following dimensions:

- Leadership
- Strategic management
- Customer and market focus
- Measurement, analysis, and knowledge management
- Work force
- Process management
- Outcomes and results

In some cases leadership teams may prefer a more traditional approach to categorizing their strengths and weaknesses, that is, by function and/or core process (see Figure 3.3).

By function:

- Board of directors
- Management
- Marketing

- Finance
- Operations
- Human resources management
- Information technology

Alternatively by process:

- Governance
- Order generation
- New product development
- Order fulfillment
- Customer service

Rank the organization's internal strengths and weaknesses in light of its primary marketing opportunities

The same process is used for ranking strengths and weakness as for ranking opportunities and threats. A complete set of instructions and scoring sheets are included in Appendix 4: The Nominal Group Technique.

Evaluate the strategic management system

Finally, the team should evaluate the strengths and weaknesses of the organization's ability to manage its strategy. Effective strategic management does not require a separate management system. Quite the contrary, the most effective strategic management systems are embedded in a holistic integrated management system—one with well-articulated and linked strategic and operational processes. This is due to the nature of strategic management itself. It is intended to direct and activate all systems and processes as well as motivate, coordinate, and direct management and staff.

For those organizations that are embarking on their first significant effort to develop a strategic management system it is helpful to consider questions such as the following:

- Is the strategic management process well designed?
- Is it being managed effectively?
- How can it be improved with respect to flow, variability, and documentation?
- Do board members, management, and/or staff need training in its operation?
- Are there effective performance measures in place?
- Do these performance measures include measures of strategic management performance?
- Is performance being measured with respect to operations? With respect to personnel responsible for the process? With respect to operating staff personnel?

In addition, the planning team should separately evaluate the strengths and weaknesses of the following strategic management processes:

- Analysis and evaluation
- Planning
- Implementation
- Performance measurement
- Ongoing management
- Project management
- Process design and improvement
- Change management
- Developmental learning organization
- Benchmarking

In making these evaluations, keep in mind the terms *strength* and *weakness* are both general and relative; that is, they only have meaning within a given organization. As mentioned, they are building blocks. A rating of strength also implies that the strategic management processes (listed above) are well developed processes. A rating of weakness implies that a particular process needs further development to manage the organization strategically in an effective manner.

It is important to remember that these are not technical evaluations; rather, they are intended to provide an understanding of the existing system from a strategic perspective in order to better direct and design subsequent efforts to improve organization strategy and strategic management capabilities.

CHAPTER 4

Strategy Formulation

The processes of strategy formulation are set in motion based on the analyses and evaluations of Chapter 3. These processes, once executed, deliver a comprehensive strategic plan for the organization (Chapter 5) and lay the groundwork for complex change management processes often required in implementing the strategic operating plan (Chapter 6).

Strategy formulation covers the processes necessary to articulate the overall strategic direction of the organization as well as the high-level strategies an organization pursues to arrive at the desired destination. From a team-based perspective, the importance of building and managing strategy, in tandem with the resulting change management process, is vital in the strategy formulation phase. This is the point at which overall direction and core strategies are defined. To do this effectively and arrive at a consensus regarding these plans, the team must carry out the following steps:

- Step 7: Define the strategic direction of the organization
- Step 8: Compile a comprehensive set of strategies for arriving at the desired destination
- Step 9: Evaluate and select a set of strategies for inclusion in the strategic plan

Strategy in the 21st Century

Many top managers are accustomed to setting the strategic direction of their organization and carrying out the above steps in an intuitive and subjective manner. Their intent may be simply to craft a strategic plan. However, the central premise of this book is that strategic planning, as one in a number of strategic management processes, is most effectively executed using a team-based approach. Therefore, these steps define an orderly process that should include a number of team members.

While these strategy formulation steps are presented in a linear sequence, this does not preclude feedback loops and repetition of previous steps. For example, the organization's strategic direction should not be inflexible and nonresponsive to changing events. Having a clearly stated strategic direction in place does not preclude making adjustments when a new opportunity is identified so long as the requisite capabilities, resources, and competencies exist.

Similarly, adjustments should be made when a new or existing threat appears or intensifies. Any strategic management process should continuously seek new opportunities, monitor threats, and then adjust the organization's strategies accordingly. This can only be done within a system designed with enough flexibility to make adjustments and changes whenever desired or required.

STEP 7: DEFINE THE STRATEGIC DIRECTION OF THE ORGANIZATION

In Steps 1 and 6 the current elements of the strategic direction of the organization were assessed to determine relative strengths or weaknesses and the extent to which they could be used as strategic building blocks in development of new ones. By extrapolating from these evaluations, the leadership team begins the the strategic planning process with the assumption

Chapter 4

that the leadership team is going to convert the current strategic direction into a new or refined strategic direction and plan including well-crafted guidelines for strategy formulation and implementation.

Step 7 has two primary objectives:

- Provide an understanding of the components of the strategic direction
- Provide guidelines as to how a leadership team can formulate these components to establish strategic direction

The primary function of a strategic direction is to set a course that is sufficiently explicit to guide and motivate the board of directors, management, and staff of an organization, while at the same time sufficiently general to identify and consider alternative strategies consistent with this strategic direction. In effect, the strategic direction acts as a primary selection filter removing from consideration strategic alternatives that do not meet leadership's consensus thinking, thereby eliminating search, analysis, and evaluation work in considering alternatives that do not fit the direction and the intended growth path of the organization.

Table 4.1 summarizes the components of strategic direction that must be examined and defined.

Table 4.1: Components of Strategic Direction

- Vision—destination
- Mission—purpose
- Values—beliefs
- Policies—guidelines
- Goals—directional themes

The components are interdependent, and every effort should be made to identify and record each as an integral piece to the composite strategic direction. The order in which the components are listed and defined can certainly be changed, but the order in which they are being presented here is a useful sequence to follow.

Vision

A vision statement is central to an organization's strategic direction. It is not created simply to dress up the annual report or to display at the annual stockholders' meeting. It is a concise, thoughtful, and inclusive statement of where the organization is going and what it looks like when it reaches the desired destination.

In essence, it is a "change management tool" that describes a desired future state—the broadest statement of direction. It projects what the organization will look like and where it will be in the accepted long-range planning horizon of the organization. It identifies and seeks to align the organization's actions and operations in the pursuit of its vision. It is a team development tool of the highest order, as it communicates a sense of being comprehensive, integrated, and sustainable, while allowing for change, development, and innovation.

In developing a well-crafted vision statement, it is best discerned and then defined after building a common information base as outlined in Steps 1 to 6. It grows out of a set of shared values and beliefs of the members of the organization, a common understanding of marketplace needs, and a belief that organizational capabilities can successfully align behind meeting those needs.

If the current vision statement is essentially that of the founder, leader, president, or some key stakeholder, it should be transformed into a shared and accepted vision statement.

> **Table 4.2: Characteristics of Effective Vision Statements**
>
> - Are presented as what the organization can realistically expect to achieve, based in part on past experience and also with provision for "stretching" to new levels of achievement
> - Are presented as sustainable and the basis for continuous expansion and advancement
> - Are written in terms that will clearly communicate to all stakeholders how achieving the vision will benefit them
> - Are written in present tense and in a style that will energize and mobilize the various units of an organization and give the board, management, and staff a sense of purpose and direction
> - Are written in terms that are clear, concise, distinctive, and easy to remember

The most effective vision statements are developed by a team, with all team members contributing.

Table 4.2 summarizes characteristics of effective vision statements.

Table 4.3 presents generic examples of "externally oriented" and broadly defined vision statements.

For "internal" communication purposes we recommend supplementing a concise vision statement with a separate and more descriptive paragraph, which provides added detail on the destination and stakeholder benefits. The advantage of a more descriptive statement, written in present tense, is that it conveys the scope of the gap between the actual present state and the desired future state. It further conveys a sense of stra-

Table 4.3: Examples of Vision Statements

- A globally competitive consulting enterprise being number one or number two in market share in every country we serve
- A recognized middle market provider of innovative financial products and professional services
- A premier supplier of reliable, high-quality, complex military defense systems and commercial aerospace products

tegic intent to focus available resources on attainment of the desired future state and, in turn, is the basis for designing and developing actionable programs. The following is an example from one disguised organization:

> The National Food Services Association enables an educated and trained workforce with leadership bench strength for the future.
>
> The NFSA has grown to become the industry leader in education solutions for food safety, responsible alcohol consumption, and workforce development, generating $80M annually. We leverage an extensive network of industry relationships to outdistance all competitors and have extended our reach to multiple international locations. The NFSA makes a real difference by delivering meaningful products and services meeting the highest quality standards. Adherence to core values has resulted in outstanding employee satisfaction, customer satisfaction, and profitability.

Producing an effective vision statement is a matter of great interest—primarily because of the imperative that it be a shared vision, that is, the product of a team-based development and decision-making effort. Arriving at a shared decision of this magnitude can be a challenge especially for organizations emerging from command and control cultures with a strict top-down management philosophy.

Table 4.4 summarizes an effective process to overcome these challenges.

Table 4.4: Vision Statement Development Process

- Begin with a group of five to ten members—fewer is not representative, more can result in difficulties in communication and domination by the more vocal unless carefully facilitated.
- Develop ground rules on process and meeting frequency, record-keeping, agenda preparation, individual assignments, and use of existing organization documents and reports.
- Collect the key ideas and phrases the organization is currently using and finds effective.
- Have individuals or subgroups give input into a "straw man" statement for consideration by the team as a whole before drafting a shared vision.
- Have the process facilitator then use the team's input to draft a small set of vision statements for the team to review.
- Have team members then critique the initial draft(s) and note suggestions for improvement.
- Ask the process facilitator to redraft *a* vision statement for further team consideration.
- Distribute the "final" draft for review, refinement, and approval by senior leadership or the board of directors depending on the organization type.

Strategy in the 21st Century

The process we have outlined is a practical approach to developing a shared vision statement. Variations to it can easily be adapted to fit the specific needs of the organization depending on its experience with teamwork and other forms of small group exercises. Regardless of the subtleties of execution, the focus should be squarely on the vision statement's development—the end result of this effort.

The value of having an effective well-crafted vision statement cannot be overstated. Its development can, at times, be frustrating and time consuming, especially if an organization has never made an effort to do it in the past. In such instances, it is important to remember that the process of strategic management requires formulating a clear vision as a precursor to the development of the remaining components of strategic direction.

The first time all the components of an organization's strategic direction are identified and documented, the task can be arduous and time consuming. However, because of its fundamental importance in the strategic management process, the

Figure 4.1: Shared Vision is a Byproduct of Transparent Communications

value of time and energy spent in identifying the components cannot be overestimated. In short, *a substantial investment is required here.*

Mission

A mission statement defines an organization's purpose and reason for its existence. It describes who an organization is, what it does, and how (in general terms) it does it. It is the operations-focused melding of invested resources and leadership commitment to mobilize the organization in accordance with its reason for being. While a vision alludes to the future, the mission statement deals with the here and now—what the organization currently does. However, the two are not unrelated. A mission statement should describe activities that will lead to the fulfillment of the organization's vision.

A second, and very important, difference between mission and vision is that a vision statement can be revised and refocused with comparatively little effort, since it lives in the future. A mission statement cannot, for it serves to communicate the organization's purpose "here and now" and provide high-level direction to its intended actions.

A mission statement's content development benefits from the vision statement. Articulating a mission statement is challenging to leaders who spend much of their time immersed in the micro-detail of managing day-to-day activities of the organization. It becomes a case of "not seeing the forest for the trees," and therein lays the challenge. Having the vision statement already in place helps provide a framework for thinking about and subsequently developing the mission statement at a "strategy-focused" level.

Regardless of the reason, every organization needs to clearly state its mission, linking its human capital, systems, and processes to keep the organization from straying from its shared commitment. A process analogous to the formation of a vision statement (see Table 4.4) can be employed to identify and write a mission statement. From the start, the focus should be to seek consensus on who the organization is, what it does, and, in very general terms, how it does it. Do not be surprised if a consensus is not arrived at easily in the first meeting. It is much more likely to emerge from several informal discussions and inputs from members of the strategic management team as ideas are shared and developed in group meetings.

As in the case of writing a vision statement, it can be effective to have a facilitator or a small group of two or three team members write the agreed upon key components of the mission statement. Copies of the drafts of the mission statement should

Table 4.5: Characteristics of Effective Mission Statements

- Communicate a sense of purpose
- State clearly the area of interest, that is, what the organization does
- Identify, in general terms, how the organization pursues its mission
- Establish boundaries within which the organization operates
- Affirm the direction set forth in the vision statement
- Avoid broad statements that are of little use to leadership in guiding the organization
- State as action oriented, to the point, and easily remembered
- Divide into functional mission statements, as necessary

then be circulated to the entire strategic management team for review, refinement, and eventual approval by senior leadership. The consequences of a poorly conceived or incomplete mission statement can be a major barrier to the achievement of effective strategic management. Conversely, a well-crafted mission statement serves to energize and focus the team while providing a major reference point for making longer-term strategic decisions.

A useful and effective mission statement is not "cast in concrete" since missions change over time as organizations grow, evolve, and respond to changes in their environment. A good example of this is found in the petroleum industry where oil companies now include the finding and developing of "alternative" sources of energy as part of their mission.

Leadership teams should recognize the characteristics of good mission statements and use them for reference/guidance in crafting their own mission statement.

Table 4.5 summarizes characteristics of effective mission statements.

Table 4.6 presents mission statements that illustrate how some organizations have crafted their mission statements.

Values

Organizational values are the fundamental beliefs or philosophies that guide the action of an organization's leaders. They are the qualities that directors, managers, and staff strive to incorporate into their production of goods and delivery of services.

Values play an important role in determining the strategic direction of an organization. In large measure, this is a result of more inclusive managerial styles and organizational structures and operating processes. A corollary of a "flat organization" is the need to include a wide variety of ideas, opinions, and val-

Table 4.6: Examples of Mission Statements

- Our mission is to generate electricity, deliver electricity, and distribute natural gas in a safe reliable, efficient, and environmentally sound manner.

   —Ameren

- Our purpose is to enable individuals and businesses to manage financial risk. We provide insurance products and services tailored to meet the specific and ever-changing financial risk exposure facing our customers. We build value for our investors through the strength of our customers' satisfaction and by consistently producing superior operation results.

   —American Financial Group, Inc.

- The mission of CSC is to be a global leader in providing technology-enabled business solutions and services.

   —Computer Sciences Corporation

- Our mission is to be the leading global innovator, developer, and provider of cleaning, sanitation and maintenance products, systems, and services. As a team we will achieve aggressive growth and fair return for our shareholders. We will accomplish this by exceeding the expectations of our customers while conserving resources and preserving the quality of the environment.

   —Ecolab INC

ues. If organizations are not just giving lip service to inclusive management systems, they sooner or later need to include diverse views. The process of arriving at a consensus is perhaps more difficult, but the results are a set of widely shared values that form a solid foundation for strategic management.

To be major factors in determining strategic direction, values must share several common characteristics.

Table 4.7 summarizes these important characteristics.

Values are the foundation of strategic direction, providing stability to the selection process of core strategies. For example, if "protecting the environment" and "conserving energy" are held as organization values, they should figure heavily into the consideration and decision-making process for developing strategies and deploying tactics.

Table 4.7: Characteristics of Effective Values

- Represent organizationally relevant core beliefs
- Are held over the long-term and subject only to slow, incremental changes
- Are shared widely among members of the organization
- Are believed to be central to the development and maintenance of corporate culture
- Are defined as substantive beliefs, not slogans, soundbites, or superficial statements made for promotional or public relations purposes or to enhance the organization's image
- Are developed to be sufficiently specific to translate into actions and transactions
- Are incorporated in the way the organization acts and reacts with its stakeholders

Strategy in the 21st Century

The objective is to articulate the (shared) values that the directors, managers, and staff will proactively commit time and resources to implement. However, these values should not be so narrowly stated as to preclude considering new strategic options and opportunities before making a final decision on the strategies to pursue.

Identifying core values helps to determine a strategic direction consistent with the highest aspirations of the organization and to define an ideal state and reinforce the vision statement. At the same time core values must have the capacity to translate into meaningful actions, processes, services, and products.

Regardless of what values an organization identifies as its core values, the key is to identify only those held as "shared" values impacting the strategic direction of the organization.

Table 4.8 illustrates examples of what values organizations identify as core values.

Most organizations have a fairly clear sense of what they believe are the values governing their collective thinking and ac-

---

Table 4.8: Examples of Organizational Values

- Ethical behavior/integrity
- Commitment to customers, employees, shareholders, and community
- Teamwork and trust
- Openness
- Accountability
- Social responsibility/corporate citizenship
- Innovativeness/entrepreneurship
- Environmental responsibility
- Commitment to diversity

tion. They may not have stated these values for publication, but they can pull together these values after some discussion. The new values that find their way into leadership thinking are the ones that need to be identified and articulated.

Over the course of a few group meetings in which discussing organization values is one of the agenda items, the core values that are deeply held and shared by the board of directors, management, and staff should begin to emerge. Each value statement should be succinct, well defined, and resonate with the employees of the organization. Values become little more than "window dressing" and easily dismissed if there is no demonstrated commitment to them by leadership.

Policies

Policies are guidelines an organization develops to influence/instruct/specify how members of the organization should act in given circumstances. Policies are also key components of strategic direction. However, the role policies play in strategic management is often not considered.

This lack of consideration can be traced, in part, to two primary factors. First, many of the most important policies of an organization have been a part of the organization's culture for so long that they are taken for granted. And second, most policies govern the design and use of operations, processes, systems, and procedures—not strategies. Thus, it becomes easy to omit consideration of policies as components of strategic direction.

Consider the following illustrative policies. When they were initially conceived and put into effect, it was seldom with the explicit recognition of the impact/influence that they would have on facilitating or constraining the future strategic direction the organization might pursue. These policies are cited as real policies that have been used in organizations. Many are

Strategy in the 21st Century

common and easily recognized; others are more recent and less known. However, in no case are these policies being cited as examples of "good" or "bad" policies.

Table 4.9 presents examples of policies that impact/influence an organization's strategy.

These policies may be facilitative and expansive or, conversely, limiting—even severely limiting. However, in all cases they

---

Table 4.9: Examples of Policies

- We will always promote from within our organization.
- We will pursue international opportunities only when in support of our domestic customers.
- Our debt to equity ratio will never be lower than .5 or greater than 1.5.
- Our policy on retained earnings versus dividends will be determined by the executive committee on an annual basis.
- Our family will always retain control of the organization.
- We will outsource whenever possible.
- Our professional staff must make partner in three years or leave the firm.
- "All our businesses must be number one or two in the industries in which they operate."

    —Jack Welch, former President of General Electric

- "You can have any color you want as long as it is black."

    —Henry Ford regarding the Model T

must be recognized and taken into account to set a realistic strategic direction for the organization.

Table 4.10 presents the indirect impact of policies on strategic direction.

With respect to strategic direction, the aim is to identify all the policies, written and unwritten, that will have an impact on formulating a strategic plan of action. Some of these policies are inviolate and simply need to be identified and taken into account. Others may well be due for a review by leadership.

Table 4.10: Indirect Impact of Policies on Strategic Direction

- The debt to equity constraint may limit the investment in new equipment required to enter a new market.
- Having family members run the business can impose major constraints on the scope and nature of growth, funds available for expansion, R&D, or the willingness to assume risks inherent in new opportunities.
- Outsourcing whenever possible will require new competencies and capabilities in order to increase the scope and level of outsourcing. New management systems may be required, as well as new cash flow limits. In short, this could lead the firm into a new or modified strategic direction.
- Some policies outlive their usefulness, such as Henry Ford's famous quote about the color of his Model Ts. Eventually, he had to shut down for an entire year (1927) to become competitive with General Motors that introduced a variety of colors and other model changes annually!

> **Table 4.11: Tasks to Complete to Determine Impact of Policies on Strategic Direction**
>
> - Identify all the current written policies that have an impact on formulating the strategic direction of the organization. Since impacts are not always direct and easily identified, this task will not be easy the first time it is done. However, because these policies impact both the organization's strategy and strategic direction, it needs to be done carefully and thoroughly.
> - Review and re-assess the identified policies to determine whether they should still be retained in light of the new/revised strategic direction that may be emerging.
> - Identify unwritten policies, assess their strategic impact, and, if still accepted, put them in writing and distribute them to the organization.
> - Develop new policies consistent with the new strategic direction and existing policies.

Table 4.11 summarizes the four primary tasks necessary to determine the impact of policies on strategic direction.

All told, the final result of work done here should be a list of agreed upon policies with strategic impact. If policy creation is being done for the first time, a finalized list may not be complete, but the value of assessing the impact of current policies and establishing new ones will be evident as soon as a strategy is implemented. The need for policies follows from the need for guidelines and directions on how to go about the implementation and ongoing management processes. The primary function of a policy is as a guideline for action.

Once policies have been reviewed, assessed for strategic impact, documented and put into effect, there remains the need to establish a process for the periodic review of these policies. As organizations evolve, grow, and mature, policies will become more or less relevant, requiring periodic assessment. It is more effective and less disruptive if this is done on a consistent and systematic basis, rather than reactively in crisis situations.

Goals

Goals are defined while developing the organization's vision and mission statements. They are the long-range, generally-stated directional themes or aims to be achieved in accordance with the organization's vision and mission. Goal statements serve to energize and motivate the board of directors, management, and staff. Goal statements are more narrowly focused than either vision or mission statements. In fact, lower-level managers and staff often find it easier to focus their efforts on goals than on the more generally-stated vision and mission statements.

In this book, the term *goal* is distinctly separate from the term *objective*. There are no hard and fast rules governing the use of these terms related to strategy, which has led to a major source of confusion in management literature. In fact, many authors use the terms interchangeably. However, in this book they arise from two different development processes serving two very different purposes.

Goal setting is included as part of the process of setting the strategic direction of an organization. Goals may or may not be derived from the previously discussed components of strategic direction, that is, vision, mission, values, and policies. However, if the resources and capabilities of the organization are to be focused on the central thrust of the strategic direction, goals must be consistent with the other components of the strategic direction.

> **Table 4.12: Examples of Effective Goal Statements**
>
> - Stabilize and increase yield while improving production efficiency and the environment.
> - Facilitate a culture of innovation and collaboration across the region and throughout the country and focus on aligning resources to achieve environmental outcomes.
> - Utilize all tools available to achieve and enhance compliance with environmental laws.
> - Protect and grow the core business.
> - Position and invest for the future.

In contrast, objective setting is a part of the process of strategy implementation. Objectives are established when specific initiatives, processes, and projects are being designed, integrated into an overall operating plan, and then implemented. Suf-

> **Table 4.13: Characteristics of Effective Goal Statements**
>
> - Are not sufficiently encompassing to be the organization's vision or mission statement
> - Are consistent with the organization's values but are not value statements per se
> - Are not policies that guide action; they are the actions
> - Imply a completion date at some point in the future but not defined at this point
> - Can be divided into milestones that, in turn, can be translated into achievable, assignable, and measurable objectives

fice it to say that objectives are set after a specific strategy has been selected. They are achievable, assignable outcomes and used to manage ongoing operations.

Table 4.12 presents examples of effective and useful goal statements.

These aforementioned examples incorporate many of the more important features of effective goal setting. Table 4.13 presents features of effective goals.

Table 4.14 presents four major aspects of the goal-setting process that need separate consideration.

It is important to realize that because of the predominant focus on objectives and ongoing operations in most organizations, goals are not explicitly stated, updated, and reviewed periodically from a strategic perspective. This is a result of the now outdated practice of top manager's setting organization goals but not communicating them to other members of the organization or educating colleagues on their significance to the future growth and development of the organization.

Table 4.14: Major Aspects of Goal Setting

- Reviewing and evaluating existing goals and the desirability and feasibility of continuing to include them as part of the new strategic direction
- Making revisions to current goals in light of the new and/or modified strategic direction being formulated
- Identifying new goals that should be pursued to realize the vision, fulfill the mission, and activate the values and policies of the organization
- Limiting the number of goal statements to provide focus and enhance alignment

An effective review process should begin by identifying current goals, regardless of their state of acceptance, utility, or attainment. Once assembled, each should be subject to close scrutiny.

Table 4.15 presents a series of questions to ask to evaluate current goals.

The results of this process should be a very small set of organizational goals that are consistent with the shared vision statement being pursued by the organization forming and are the basis for a coherent organization strategy.

Table 4.15: Criteria for Evaluating Current Goals

- Is this goal consistent with the new strategic direction being developed?
- Specifically, how does this goal reinforce, enhance, or otherwise contribute to the new vision mission, values and policies?
- Is this goal widely shared?
- Do the benefits of pursuing the goal significantly outweigh its costs?
- Is this goal in conflict with other goals (current or new)? If so, how?
- Is this goal synergistic with other goals (current or new)?
- What will be the impact of eliminating this goal?
- Do we have the resources to pursue this goal effectively and efficiently?
- What results can be realized as a result of pursuing this goal?
- Has this goal been translated into achievable objectives? If so, with what results?

Chapter 4

Figure 4.2: Goals Are Directional Themes

Modifying current goals is a relatively straightforward process. In fact, the questions listed above can be used to examine extensions and modifications of current goals. This approach to goal setting should never be overlooked, since current goals are usually in leadership's "comfort zone" and are more easily modified to set a new strategic direction.

The downside to this approach is that it may prove to be too easy, that is, leadership may feel that it has made some changes—enough to avoid the more difficult process of setting new goals to define the strategic direction in a sufficiently challenging manner.

When it comes to setting new goals, the process is not easily defined. An organization is often entering new terrain with little or no experience to guide it. A useful approach is to examine each of the preceding components of strategic direction, that is, vision, mission, values, and policies, and derive a targeted set of goals that will fulfill them.

The goal-setting process will vary depending on the leadership style, organization structure, and the organizational context. However, as with the other components of the process of setting strategy direction, the processes that were outlined for developing vision statements can also be used to develop organizational goals. The number of organization-level goals should not become a "laundry list"; only a very small number of the most important strategic goals should be selected. In many cases one or two goal statements are recommended.

Before continuing to the next step, each component of the strategy-setting process should be set forth in writing and formally approved but not in a cursory fashion. The task of formulating strategy is directly dependent on the care and attention given to the process of setting the strategic direction.

In essence, the strategic direction is the core of the strategic plan. Certainly there may be necessary changes in its component parts as the process of strategy formulation unfolds, but this first draft serves as the line in the sand from which to embark on the process of developing a new/revised strategy.

Table 4.16 presents a sample strategic direction summary for the hypothetical National Food Service Association.

Table 4.16: Sample Strategic Direction—National Food Service Association	
Vision	The National Food Service Association enables an educated and trained workforce with management bench strength for the future.
	The NFSA has grown to become the industry leader in education solutions for food safety, responsible alcohol, and workforce development, generating $80M annually. We leverage an extensive network of industry relationships to outdistance all competitors and have extended our reach to multiple international locations. Adherence to core values has resulted in outstanding employee satisfaction, operational efficiency, customer satisfaction, and profitability.

Table 4.16: Sample Strategic Direction—National Food Service Association (continued)

Mission	Advance the food service industry through workforce development certification and training
Values	We exist to serve the food service industry and, in doing so, hold to and are guided by the following values: • Our Team—Committed to each other, passionate about our mission, celebrating our successes, and balanced between work and life • The Way We Work—Professionalism and mutual respect for each other • Ethics—Honesty, integrity and a strong belief in doing what's right lead us to intelligently and constructively disagree • Customer Satisfaction—Listening, understanding, and striving to meet their needs • Financial Viability—We make and keep our commitments toward growth and self-sustainability
Policies	We will pursue international opportunities in support of our domestic customers.
Preliminary Goals	• Protect and grow the core business • Become a global leader • Grow nontraditional membership • Position and invest for the future

STEP 8: COMPILE A COMPREHENSIVE SET OF STRATEGIES FOR ARRIVING AT THE DESIRED DESTINATION

Once the components of the strategic direction have been constructed, the next step is to identify a set of strategies for achieving this direction that leverage the organization's strengths and exploit available opportunities. In order to ensure the best deployment of resources to achieve the vision and overall intent of the strategic direction, every effort should be made to identify a comprehensive set of alternatives consistent with the external and internal dimensions of the organization.

The output of this step is a set of potentially actionable strategies developed by the strategic leadership team. It is a pivotal accomplishment requiring both analytic and creative thinking to arrive at a comprehensive set of strategic alternatives. Analytically, this step requires the identification of alternatives that flow from a study of the strategic direction and the capabilities and resources of the organization to achieve them. Creatively, it requires the development of new alternatives that will best, or at least counter, the competition with innovative and, if possible, unique strategies.

The two processes, inextricably entwined in the human mind, can be difficult to separate. Yet for the best results they can and should be separated during team-based exercises. More than in any other part of the strategic management process, this step focuses on developing alternative strategies and demonstrates the benefits of a team approach to strategic management.

Ultimately, a well functioning leadership team is able to discern the best strategies to implement as part of their ongoing strategic thinking and communication processes. These processes should flow from their collective and ongoing study of the environment rather than from a set of linear activities and requirements to be followed.

To become a well functioning leadership team is no easy task. Leadership teams become effective in identifying and creating effective and sustainable competitive strategies by incorporating rigorous disciplined thinking with open inquiry, team discussions, regular feedback, and interaction.

In contrast to a team-based approach, strategies based only on the perceptions of an "all knowing leader" severely limit the development of optional approaches to moving forward and—more important—the opportunity to build a multilevel strategic leadership team. It is no longer effective for top leadership to formulate strategy and relegate lower levels of leadership to simply implement strategy. Consequently, we strongly advocate that all levels of leadership be involved continuously throughout the process. In short, all tasks identified in the strategy process outlined below are most effective when carried out as a team.

Using a team approach helps to ensure that strategy formulation and implementation are more likely to be incremental processes that build on the existing capabilities and current strategic direction. Thus, deciding on a small number of carefully selected areas in which to develop and implement strategic change is usually more effective than attempts to make sweeping changes.

The essence of team-based strategic thinking consists of developing multiple options for realizing the vision and a repertoire of feasible responses to deal with the ever-changing environment and unexpected events. Developing a set of strategy alternatives, even if several are not selected for current implementation, can be viewed as pragmatic contingency planning. Using a team approach not only increases the number of feasible options to consider, it also increases the level of commitment and the effort of team members responsible for strategic management.

Accordingly, in this step we offer suggestions and considerations that have been found useful in using a team approach to identify, create, and develop strategic alternatives. More specifically, the objectives of this step are as follows:

- Identify activities already underway within the organization that will impact on strategy

Strategy in the 21st Century

- Identify *key result areas* requiring and/or providing opportunities for new/revised strategies
- Develop a framework of key result areas with typical strategies
- Develop new/revised alternative strategies for consideration

Identify activities underway within the organization that will impact on strategy

An organization does not need to have a well-developed strategic management system in place to engage in strategic thinking and action. Exhibiting these behaviors is basic and natural to individual and organizational problem solving. Both behaviors have their roots in the universal need to act and react under competitive conditions to seek out competitive advantage.

Consistent with this view many leadership teams rely on their operational managerial abilities as their primary modus operandi. It is only since World War II that more comprehensive strategic management models and approaches have been defined, developed, and adopted to eliminate/reduce the need for this stop-gap approach (see Chapter 1). Unfortunately, the widespread diffusion of these models and more comprehensive approaches has yet to occur.

In any case, whether an organization has a well-developed strategic management system or still operates on an ad hoc basis, a basic strategy formulation task remains for identifying activities underway that currently have or will have an impact at the strategic level.

Table 4.17 presents three primary benefits to identifying activities underway that have strategic impact.

There are two major tasks to identifying the current activities that are likely to have an impact on the organization's strategic

> **Table 4.17: Benefits to Identifying Activities with Strategic Impact Already Underway**
>
> - They indicate where leadership is now placing its time energy and resources with respect to strategy.
> - They provide leadership with a realistic assessment of the level of strategic management capabilities presently being employed within the organization.
> - They provide a starting point and a platform for making changes and additions to strategy that are based on a realistic understanding of the baseline situation.

direction, proposed strategy, or subsequent strategic planning and implementation.

- **Task 1** is to identify all *high impact activities* currently underway that may or may not have resulted from a previous strategy formulation process. Many of these activities evolve incrementally over time, and even the initiators of the strategy may not recognize them as "strategic." This is important, since these strategies can be a double-edged sword. They may be the basis of a new and rewarding approach or be counterproductive to the newly agreed upon strategic direction. The key at this stage of the strategy formulation process is to highlight and recognize these strategies and activities and then begin to monitor and evaluate them to determine their place in the strategic plan.
- **Task 2** is to identify the *strategy support processes*, that is, operational capabilities that are essential systems and/or processes that need to be in place before a given strategic alternative can be executed. These prerequisite processes

are dictated by the strategies selected for implementation and will vary depending on the organization and its capabilities, resources, and competitive conditions.

More than one organization has been burned by entering a new market or offering a new service only to discover it was unqualified to compete. Having the necessary prerequisite processes in place is of fundamental importance, and they require serious consideration in the strategy formulation process. For example, penetrating a particular market may be desired but not possible unless the organization's product development process incorporates customer expectations with respect to quality, delivery, price, or competitive value. Achieving competitive performance levels in any one of these areas may not be possible or be in the best strategic interests of the organization to pursue until the required skills and capabilities are in place and functioning at the required level.

On the other hand, the prerequisite processes may eventually be honed to such a high level of performance that they themselves become strategies for success, for example, the Japanese automobile industry used quality as a primary strategic advantage when they took the United States market by storm. A downside of this type of strategy is that eventually competitors adopt these same strategies, and the innovator loses his initial competitive advantage.

At this point, it is not necessary to catalog all the prerequisite processes, but it is important to identify those that are known and obvious to the leadership team. Later, if a strategy is selected for inclusion in the organization's strategic plan, specific prerequisite processes can be developed in more detail as part of the strategic plan.

Chapter 4

Identify key results areas requiring and/or providing opportunities for developing new/revised strategies

Before beginning the process of identifying strategy alternatives, it is important to define the components of the organization where explicit strategy statements are needed. We liken these components to the notion of being organizational building blocks. When put together they form a cohesive infrastructure around which strategy statements can be thoughtfully articulated to achieve the organization's vision, mission, and goals.

In this book we refer to organizational building blocks as "key result areas." A key result area is an explicitly stated component or dimension of the organization where tangible results must be realized in order for the shared vision, mission, and goals to be realized. Key result areas can be external or internal in their focus. For example, an externally-focused key result

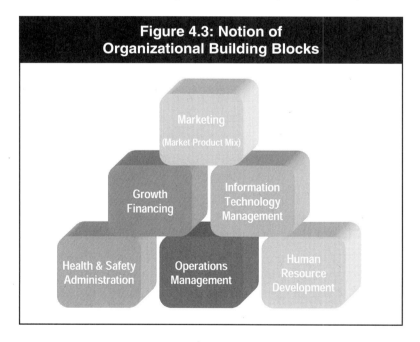

179

area can be the *market/product mix* the organization chooses to prioritize, while an internal counterpart would be the effective and efficient *operations* of the business to deliver the products and services to the chosen market(s).

A key result area may be more narrowly defined. For example, customer relations is a dimension of marketing, and it may be considered a key result area for the organization. Defining key result areas focuses leadership attention on those high-priority dimensions of the organization where there is a consensus that modifications and revisions in strategies are required.

Even in organizations that do not have a strategic management process in place, the top leadership has its priorities that receive the most attention and interest. However, this experienced-based approach often overlooks or minimizes the amount of attention other areas could and/or should receive. For example, one of the great shortcomings of many business organizations is a preoccupation with financial performance. When reinforced by a short-term focus on the measurement of same, it serves to limit the development of more encompassing and equally relevant considerations.

It follows that the immediate task at hand is to identify critically important key result areas for the organization, ones that should receive priority attention. The basis for identifying key result areas is grounded in the experience and judgment of the leadership team and in consideration of the outputs of the strategic management process completed to this point. There is no standard set of key result areas to include. This work remains a contextual process based on the needs, structure, resources, capabilities, and strategic direction of a particular organization.

Later in the process the team will agree upon strategies for the most important areas, as every key result area is not equally essential. Even more important, as a practical consideration, only a few areas can be considered for major strategic implementation in any one planning period. Nevertheless, it may be necessary to include areas and initiate strategies requiring a long period of incubation, as for example, the cultural changes in attitudes and values required to operate within other countries. Hence, no key result area should be ignored, since it may require a long period of preparation.

External key results areas

In the final analysis, strategy is driven by choices leaders make in terms of the particular product and service mix they offer to chosen markets or market segments. Other strategies impact the effectiveness of these choices, but the target market offerings are primary drivers of strategy. Below are five examples of external key results areas:

- Market/product mix
- Competitive forces
- Customers
- Suppliers
- Technology

Internal key results areas

Looking inward, feasible strategies should be identified for the organization itself, that is, internally-focused strategies that support and enable the chosen external market-facing strategies to be successful. Below are eight examples of key result areas for the internal dimension:

- Organization structure and governance
- Leadership development
- Core competencies
- Human resource development/people alignment
- Operations

- Marketing
- Finance
- Information systems

Develop a framework of key result areas with typical strategies

Alternative groupings of similar key result areas may emerge as suggested strategies are sorted and classified. In organizations in which the leadership teams are already applying the tools and concepts of strategic management, there will be a limited number of groupings since the strategic focus has already been determined. This step is primarily useful in organizations embarking on a major commitment to managing their organizations strategically.

Taken together, Tables 4.18 and 4.19 review the framework of key result areas and provides example strategies. Organizations can add and/or subtract key result areas that are unique and significant in their organizations.

Table 4.18: Framework of External Key Result Areas with Sample Strategies	
Market / product mix	Feasible strategies can be grouped into four generic categories: • Go deeper into current markets with the current mix of products and services, that is, pursue a "market penetration" strategy • Leverage current mix of products and services into new markets, that is, pursue a "market development" strategy • Create new value in the current market by adding new products and services, that is, pursue a "product development" strategy • Offer new products and services to new markets, that is, pursue a "diversification" strategy

Table 4.18: Framework of External Key Result Areas with Sample Strategies (continued)

Competitive forces	• Compete within the chosen markets by lowering costs • Compete within the chosen markets by differentiating • Compete by lowering costs and differentiating, that is, a "Blue Ocean Strategy"
Customers	• Focus on high profile customers • Focus on mid-tier customers • Focus on price sensitive customers
Suppliers	• Partner with suppliers to add value and lower costs • Consolidate supplier base to achieve the lowest cost • Vertically integrate—acquire supplier
Technology	• Invest in leading edge technology to lower costs and improve customer satisfaction • Integrate proven technologies only when a clear ROI can be realized • Leverage core technologies into a new global industry

Table 4.19: Framework of Internal Key Result Areas with Sample Strategies

Organization structure and governance	• Remain completely autonomous—go it alone • Spin off the ABC unit as a separate organization • Merge with XYZ and leverage their network • Acquire another organization • Form strategic alliances

Table 4.19: Framework of Internal Key Result Areas with Sample Strategies (continued)

Leadership development	• Build future leaders by investing inside the organization • Supplement existing leadership team by recruiting outside the organization • Pursue a blended approach
Core competencies	• Take to the next level without major investment • Invest heavily in order to build a stronger competitive position • Build new core competency
Human resource development / people alignment	• Invest in and develop staff • Reorganize roles and responsibilities to better support the strategy • Bring in new staff resources to complement existing capabilities • Develop a multicultural organization to go global • Emphasize the link between accountability and incentives
Operations	Order generation • Focus on organic growth via existing marketing and sales capabilities • Outsource lead generation and/or sales • Pursue a blended approach Product development • Maximize use of internal resources • Outsource product development • Pursue a blended approach Order fulfillment • Centralize and leverage internal resources • Outsource • Pursue a blended approach

Table 4.19: Framework of Internal Key Result Areas with Sample Strategies (continued)

Operations (continued)	Customer service • Optimize and streamline internal processes • Outsource • Pursue a blended approach
Marketing	Product/Service • Invest heavily in research and development • Personalize existing products • Further differentiate through a commitment to quality at all levels of the organization • Bundle services with products • Improve customer service Price • Be the low cost provider • Offer competitive pricing • Offer premium pricing Promotion • Leverage the web • Become a leader in the primary industry associations • Focus on publicity and public relations Place • Build a robust distribution network • Form a strategic alliance for distribution • Leverage the Web to distribute products and services
Finance	• Downsize and reallocate resources • Invest retained earnings • Reinvest operating margins • Sell assets to raise capital

Strategy in the 21st Century

Table 4.19: Framework of Internal Key Result Areas with Sample Strategies (continued)

Finance (continued)	• Share risk and return • Incur debt • Seek governmental and/or private sector grants • Seek sponsors and donations
Information Systems	• Leverage Microsoft platforms • Leverage software-as-a-service • Build proprietary systems • Outsource IT support • Create state-of-the-art internal IT capabilities

Develop new/revised strategic alternatives

At this point, the team is ready to develop new and/or revised strategies for the key result areas it has selected. All the necessary analytic and evaluative steps have been completed. Let us recapitulate the main steps briefly:

- Scan the external and internal dimensions of the organization (Steps 3 and 4).
- Conduct an OTSW evaluation (Step 6).
- Set the strategic direction (Step 7).
- Identify activities now underway that have an impact on strategy (Step 8).
- Identify support processes required to execute high priority strategic alternatives (Step 8).
- Create a framework of key result areas and typical strategies (Step 8).

Long before these steps are completed, most leadership teams have begun to identify new strategic alternatives. While this is

Table 4.20: Guidelines for Developing Strategic Alternatives

- Include and involve all members of the strategic leadership team, particularly in team meetings and exercises.
- Understand the many attributes of a well-conceived and executed strategy. The following are attributes to consider:
  - A platform for maintaining the strategic direction
  - Deployable and actionable strategies that will facilitate achieving the strategic direction
  - Strategies based on a thorough external and internal environmental assessment
  - Strategies that build on the organization's strengths and opportunities
  - Strategies that shore up weaknesses and counter threats to the organization
  - A means of linking strategy to operations
  - A challenge to the current state of the organization's strategic management capabilities.
- Ensure that all strategic alternatives are formulated based on two basic components—an "end" (the goal—what to do) and a "means" (the strategy—how to do it). This is very important, since there is a widespread tendency to omit considering the "how." If the "how" is omitted, then the "what" simply stands alone as a goal. If the "what" is omitted, the "how" will simply exist as a means lacking an end—a capability without a direction.

entirely natural and should even be encouraged, the most effective time to create new and/or revised alternatives is after completing the foregoing steps. Taken together, they constitute "total immersion" in the situation that will ultimately lead to creative thinking. Several exercises, such as brainstorming and its many variations, scenario planning, and the nominal group ranking technique can and should be employed to stimulate the creative processes that lead to new and innovative ways for the organization to respond.

In any case, Table 4.20 contains three primary guidelines in developing strategic alternatives that should be followed to get the most comprehensive and useful set of alternatives.

The process of developing new and/or revised alternatives depends on the level of development and depth of experience of the strategic management team. Therefore, expect a wide range in the number and quality of the alternatives identified. In the initial annual cycle of the strategic management process, the number and feasibility of the alternatives are not issues since, in Step 9, all alternatives identified or generated will be evaluated and only the most promising will be selected for potential inclusion in the strategic plan. Over time the team will become increasingly skilled in identifying and developing new and creative strategies.

Some additional guidelines for developing strategies deserve leadership attention. They are the evaluation criteria that will be considered in more detail in the evaluation and selection of strategies in Step 9. It is important to be aware of these criteria as they will form the basis for evaluation and selection to identify the strategies that will help realize the strategic vision, mission, and goals and to frame a balanced and comprehensive set of options. Therefore, it is useful to review them at the outset of the process of identifying feasible strategies. They include:

Criterion 1: Consistency with leadership perceptions

One of the key determinants for identifying potential strategy alternatives is the set of perceptions the executive team has about its abilities and managerial skills and the capabilities and resources of the organization. With respect to strategic management there are three critical perceptions:

- The perceived **need to change** any of the current strategies of the organization or to adopt new/revised strategies. The origin, focus, and urgency of this perceived need all enter into the process of each leader and guide his/her decision making. However, no matter how nuanced or provisional the decision, each executive, and collectively the leadership team, will adopt or reject a strategy based on perceived need. The level of satisfaction (or dissatisfaction) with the current situation will be a key determinant of this perception. Questions that must be addressed are: Do we need to undertake this alternative? If so, how urgently?
- The **willingness to change** any of the current strategies or to adopt new/revised strategies. This perception has its roots in a set of complex factors, among the more important of these are leadership's assessment of risks, costs, benefits, impact on the organization, competitive threats, and other similar factors. The strategic management team must ask: Are we willing to undertake this alternative?
- The perceived **feasibility of changing** any of the current strategies or of adopting new/revised strategies. In a similar manner, the perception of feasibility of a given alternative is rooted in a number of factors such as those listed above, but ultimately leadership is governed by its own estimate of just how feasible it will be to undertake a given alternative. No matter how much the team may be willing to undertake an alternative or to determine that

it is urgently needed, the team is governed by a third set of factors expressed in a perception of feasibility. The key question is: Can the organization undertake and implement this alternative successfully?

Criterion 2: Expectation of goal achievement

Goals, in effect, are the summary statements of leadership expectations. They encapsulate the best expression of what leadership expects to accomplish during their tenure. It follows that if a strategy is viewed as having a significant impact on achieving a goal (or goals), it will be a strong candidate for inclusion in the strategic plan.

Keeping this criterion in mind, while identifying and generating strategic alternatives, will make the process more effective and efficient. Even though the expectation of goal achievement is only one evaluation and selection criterion, it is one of the most important that leadership has at its disposal.

Criterion 3: Linkage/synergy/impact across core functions

This criterion differs from the two preceding criteria in a significant way; it does not originate with leadership perceptions or preferences. Also, it is not immediately obvious. It has its basis in the characteristics of one of the most effective types of organizational strategy, that is, strategies that require significant and balanced contributions from across the organization, including finance, marketing, operations, information technology, and human resource management.

Initially, identifying and/or creating strategic alternatives may seem to be a deceptively easy process. After all, it is the chief purpose of a leadership team to set the strategic course and to pursue it effectively. While this is certainly true, that does not make it simple. Becoming an effective strategy-focused leadership team that can successfully chart and follow a new course of action is no easy matter.

The points that follow describe a process for refining the organization's strategic thinking. These considerations build on Steps 4, 5, 6, 7 and 8 and facilitate the identification of strategies for realizing the vision, mission, and goals. They should be adapted to fit the needs of the organization. Only those processes that are of obvious relevance in stimulating the formulation of potential strategic "pathways" should be used. For example, organizations that have a formal strategic management process in place may not find it necessary to go through some of the considerations outlined below.

However, we have found five "refined strategic thinking" considerations to be very useful in a variety of organizations, especially those in which the leadership team is making a serious commitment to strategic management for the first time. There is no set pattern or sequence as to how each leadership team will identify its own set of feasible strategy alternatives to be considered for inclusion in the strategic plan. Every consideration may not be applicable, but all are worthy of at least cursory attention, since they may stimulate new and innovative approaches.

Consideration 1: Identify major market opportunities that will drive the strategy

The various opportunities that were identified in Step 4 and evaluated in Step 6 need to be considered from two additional perspectives:

- How will exploiting the prioritized opportunities help us to follow our strategic direction and fulfill our vision and mission?

- How will pursuing these opportunities allow us to use our capabilities, resources, and competencies to our best advantage?

Exploiting opportunities can often be a time-consuming process. The process is also uncertain because we frequently do not know the extent or type of competition that we will meet in the marketplace, nor can we count on the needs, wants, and preferences of our customers to remain unchanged. Therefore, the selection of specific opportunities or the search for certain types of opportunities must be done with the utmost care.

Below are several questions that will facilitate selection of opportunities to pursue as part of the new/revised/improved strategy.

- Does pursuing this opportunity stretch our current capabilities and help us to reach new levels of organizational maturity?
- What capabilities, resources, and competencies are required to pursue this opportunity?
- What is the time horizon for the life cycle of products and/or services required to pursue this market?
- What are the advantages of pursuing this opportunity as opposed to others?
- What is the likely response of competitors with respect to pursuing this opportunity?
- What will be the consequences of not pursuing this opportunity?

Consideration 2: Identify significant external threats that must be managed

Threats should be classified according to how and when they will have an impact on the formulation of strategy. Every threat in today's environmental scan does not grow into one of tomorrow's major problem areas, but in hindsight we are usually able to identity a few micro-trends we wish we had considered more seriously. Questions such as the following need to be addressed:

- Are we able to detect any threats that will require us to change the strategic growth path that we have selected?
- Are there any emerging threats that will eventually impact/influence our strategic plans?
- Should we monitor this threat and continue to gather more information regarding any changes in the impact or in its nature?
- Are other organizations dealing with this threat at the strategic level? If so, how?

Consideration 3: Identify primary internal strengths or competencies to emphasize

Even the most successful and profitable organizations derive much of their success from a few areas of strength. It requires constant attention and effort to acquire, improve, and maintain the basic skills and resources required to remain competitive, let alone try to achieve a sustainable competitive advantage.

We are searching for the strategic option(s) that will allow the organization to build on its current strengths and move forward in accordance with the strategic direction that is to be pursued. This is the point in the strategic management process where the team exercises both imagination and judgment to identify which of its capabilities and competencies can be any of the following:

- Platforms for future growth
- Taken to the next level of development without major investment

- The basis for a new line of products or services
- A new and competitive image
- The basis of growth and development
- In the growth phase of their life cycle
- Difficult to replicate
- A basis for entering new markets
- Protection of the core business

Consideration 4: Identify critical internal weaknesses that must be addressed

Weaknesses are often overlooked in the process of strategy formulation. This is a major mistake. Formulating strategy that first recognizes critical weaknesses and then assesses them competitively avoids the considerable difficulty that results from ignoring them. A few illustrative questions follow:

- Is this a weakness that will impede or severely limit our ability to pursue any new strategic alternative until we have addressed the weakness satisfactorily?
- Which strategic alternatives allow us to accept the impact of this weakness without putting forth a major effort to deal with it?
- Is this a weakness that we can accept in the short term, provided that we gradually minimize or overcome it?
- Which of our weaknesses require major leadership time and continued close attention before pursuing a given strategy?
- Is this a weakness that will gradually become less/more important in time?
- What are the strategic costs and disadvantages (or benefits and advantages) to overcoming this weakness?

Chapter 4

Consideration 5: Confirm the key challenges the team faces currently and in the future

At any given time, the leadership team is dealing with a variety of challenging questions, problems, and issues. However, not all of them are of strategic significance. Usually the great majority of leadership concerns are "day to day," focused on operational problems and issues that demand attention now.

The task is to identify issues, problems, and concerns the leadership team is currently dealing with so that they can be incorporated into the strategic plan. They may even be of such a magnitude as to become the major strategic focus until the challenge has been met successfully.

In short, strategic management is a dynamic and continuous process. Dealing with current problems and issues that have a long-term impact is the essence of strategic management. In fact J.B. Quinn's notion of "logical incrementalism" (1980) is aptly put. Strategy is emergent with its root system deep in the accomplishment of operational considerations on a daily basis.

As an outcome of this refined strategic thinking process, new strategic alternatives will be identified and should be entered into the key result area framework. New strategy alternatives are not always easily classified in the existing framework. It may be that a new key result area must be added or that a particular strategic alternative may drive performance in more than one area. However, in most situations there is an area in which a strategy has its primary impact and impetus, even when its implementation requires changes in other functional areas of the organization. It is these strategic alternatives that end up having the greatest impact on the organization. They are strategies that transform into organization-wide strategies. In Step 11, the development and application of cross-functional linkages will be explained and illustrated in detail in the formation of strategy implementation plans.

The process of creating new and innovative strategies seldom results in the development of a comprehensive set of strategies for each key result area. The creative process is not driven by filling out a list. The strategic thinking process is innovative, serendipitous, circular, iterative, and stochastic—as well as deductively driven. However, once each key result area contains the strategies that the leadership is able to identify and/or create in a reasonable length of time, it is desirable to examine each area in more detail. In so doing the emphasis is on ensuring that each key result area contains a reasonably comprehensive set of alternatives. This is both a creative and analytic process with no specific end point, other than a team consensus that the point of diminishing returns for further discussion has been reached.

Since the process of formulating a comprehensive set of strategic alternatives is to varying degrees a creative process, it is inevitable that a certain number of strategies will become viewed as "outliers," those alternatives that the overwhelming majority of the strategic leadership views as not worthy of further consideration, even though at one time they appeared reasonable and worth considering. This occurs as a consensus builds in the strategic leadership team about the types of strategies necessary, preferred, and feasible.

Therefore, it is not unreasonable to make a final review of the strategies generated and screen out obvious outliers. When there is a significant difference of opinion and an easy decision to screen out an alternative is not readily forthcoming, the best course is to include the alternative in question for analysis, evaluation, and selecting in Step 9.

Chapter 4

STEP 9: EVALUATE AND SELECT A SET OF STRATEGIES FOR INCLUSION IN THE STRATEGIC PLAN

The rationale for detailed evaluation and selection processes stems from the need to ensure that strategic initiatives already in progress, along with newly proposed ones, are necessary, feasible, and desired.

During the processes of identifying and/or creating feasible strategies, it is neither effective to evaluate each option nor realistic to analyze and assess the interaction and impacts of several potential strategies on each other or within and between key result areas. This is easily demonstrated in brainstorming exercises where it is universally agreed that the processes that result in new ideas and approaches should not be analyzed or judged, for whatever reasons, until *after* the brainstorming session. Adopting this approach allows for the unhampered flow of ideas from the team so others may build on these ideas.

During the course of identifying feasible strategies, an alternative might be identified that all agree should be undertaken as soon as possible. In such cases, the processes of identification, evaluation, and selection occur almost simultaneously, and detailed evaluation and selection processes are not required. Although this does not commonly occur, it does demonstrate that these processes do not always proceed in the linear fashion in which they are being presented. For organizations engaging in a disciplined approach to strategic management for the first time, it is usually best to follow a sequential analytic approach and then modify it as experience, intuition and judgment suggest.

The evaluation and selection processes counterbalance the more creative processes of identifying and/or generating feasible strategies. What may seem very desirable and necessary while developing feasible strategy alternatives may not prove to be quite so desirable or necessary, if a particular strategy does not meet the tests of profitability, cost, feasibility, growth, and similar evaluation criteria, which are applied during the evaluation and selection processes. Thus, evaluation and selection play a key role in helping to ensure that the strategies provisionally selected in the previous step are those most likely to contribute to the achievement of the organization's vision, mission and goals.

Step 9 has the following tasks:

- Provide an overview of strategy evaluation and selection processes
- Identify and describe core evaluation and selection criteria
- Identify and describe contextual/situational evaluation and selection criteria
- Evaluate, select, and modify strategic initiatives currently being implemented
- Evaluate, classify, and select the strategies identified/generated in Step 8

Provide an overview of strategy evaluation and selection processes

The term *evaluation* as used in this task refers to the process of examining strategic alternatives to determine the extent to which a particular alternative meets specific criteria/requirements/specifications. The evaluation can be qualitative or quantitative, but as a general rule the process is qualitative, since what is required is estimating an initial "order of magnitude" for the purpose of determining inclusion in the strategic plan. In all cases an alignment of organizational values and senior leadership interest is required before a particular strategy is approved for inclusion in the strategic plan.

The criteria of interest are those pertaining to the impact a strategy will have on the organization and on achieving its desired future state. These criteria originate from two main sources: generally accepted criteria found effective in the practice of strategic management and those coming from the leadership of the organization itself. The latter criteria are especially important, since each organization has contextual and idiosyncratic features that need to be taken into account when evaluating and selecting strategies.

There are two significant types of evaluation that occur at this juncture: *intrinsic* and *comparative.*

Intrinsic evaluation pertains solely to the option itself, that is, the option meets the specified evaluation criteria to an assessed degree without any further consideration. It is similar to passing or not passing a quality control inspection within a manufacturing process.

Comparative evaluation is just that: comparing two or more alternative strategies meeting a given set of criteria to determine which is more "acceptable." Carried a step further, the comparison of strategic alternatives is used as the basis for selecting those alternatives that compete for final selection and inclusion in the strategic plan.

The selection process is driven by an examination of the results of the evaluation process. It considers strategies currently being implemented with those newly proposed. In most cases, selection relies heavily on the judgment of the team making the evaluations. However, no matter how explicit we are in setting and applying a set of criteria, there are always subjective factors introduced and used by individual team members in making their own evaluations and selections.

Consequently, it is not good practice to simply summarize individual ratings based on some scoring model. The use of these models needs to be accompanied by thorough discussions that include all members of the leadership team. This will allow team members to understand the reasons for the differences in the ratings and give them an opportunity to reconsider their selections with new information and insights. The result will be a consensus-based selection process that is much more robust and effective.

Ultimately each leadership team will develop a set of evaluation criteria that is consistent with their management system and style as well as the capabilities of their organization. Therefore, the following ideas are presented as checklists that each leadership team may find useful. We also highlight one guideline we have found especially useful in reducing the number of alternatives to a manageable subset: identify and use two types of evaluation and selection criteria as described below:

- *Core criteria* that must be used in processing all proposed strategic alternatives
- *Contextual/situational criteria* that are applied selectively, depending on their relevance to a given organization and their perceived utility to leadership in that organization

Identify and describe core evaluation and selection criteria

We recommend development and use of well-defined core evaluation and selection criteria *before* attempting to winnow down the set of strategy alternatives based on contextual and often idiosyncratic criteria. This will help to avoid the problems that inevitably surface as disagreements occur, that is, when discussions devolve into competing advocacies for a particular

Chapter 4

strategy based on an individual or group preference—one that all too often is not widely shared.

Often times the result of such an insular process is a set of unrelated strategies that do not meet the strategic needs of the organization, nor do they result in the most effective use of organizational capabilities or utilize the unique competencies of the board of directors, leadership team, and staff.

While there is no hard and fast rule on what distinguishes three core factors from contextual factors, many organizations, either explicitly or implicitly, have found the following core criteria (discussed briefly in Step 8) to be effective in making a first-cut evaluation and selection of strategic alternatives:

Criterion 1: Consistency with leadership perceptions

Ultimately, it will be almost impossible to initiate substantive modifications in organization strategy without the approval, cooperation, and commitment of top leadership—and increasingly all levels of leadership with responsibilities in the strategic management process. At a minimum it is necessary that leaders agree on the following:

- A shared perception of an organizational need for strategy
- A shared perception of the organization's willingness to fund, support, and implement a particular strategy
- A shared perception of the feasibility of the organization to undertake and complete the strategy successfully

Criterion 2: Expectation of goal achievement

In the process of identifying and generating alternatives it is very easy to find attractive opportunities and new uses of an organization's resources and capabilities. When doing, so it is also easy to lose focus of the strategic direction that has been set.

Therefore, each strategy alternative should be measured against the strategic direction, especially the goals, both current and newly established. This is not a yes-no process, since options will differ considerably on the extent to which they will facilitate achieving the strategic direction and still be considered desirable. In fact, it may be necessary to modify the strategic direction based on new information found in the process of developing new and feasible strategies.

Criterion 3: Linkage/synergy/impact across the organization's core functions

There are four key advantages of a strategy that creates linkage and impact across the organization:

- The contributions of each core functional area are linked in an integrated approach.
- This balancing, alignment, linkage, and synergy minimize the waste inherent in over- and underdeveloped functions.
- Management systems become more effective, since the scope and content of what is to be done in each core function are clearly defined, consistent across functions, and linked at each leadership level.
- Leadership and professional staff are more motivated and willing to contribute to a system that uses their skills and competencies more fully and allows them to continue growing and developing as professionals.

Identify and describe contextual/situational evaluation and selection criteria

In contrast, contextual and situational evaluation criteria vary widely in their perceived utility and application. Each organization eventually settles on a set of criteria that fits their style and comfort zone. However, as new opportunities emerge, threats multiply, and the environment becomes more uncertain, the need for more sophisticated evaluation and selection processes increases. Therefore, a continuing set of criteria is listed to facilitate the development of these processes.

Criterion 4: Identification of specific benefits/advantages to the organization

Consider both long- and short-term benefits and strategic and operational benefits. Identify impact areas, such as the following:

- Opportunities exploited
- Threats counteracted
- Strengths augmented
- Weaknesses addressed

Criterion 5: Identification of operationally defined and/or measurable alternatives

When it comes to implementing strategy, performance measurement is one of the most powerful and effective tools available. Strategy alternatives that include a measurable component are perceived positively for several reasons. Measurable objectives:

- communicate expected outcomes of strategic initiatives to all levels of the organization.
- provide a basis for planning, organizing, and executing assigned tasks.
- provide a basis for measuring, controlling, and evaluating performance.

- provide a basis for designing and developing training programs.
- can be used to deploy a strategy through multiple levels of leadership.
- are especially important in keeping strategies aligned as strategies are operational statements of desired outcomes.
- are based on the premise that clear-cut measures are among the most easily understood at all levels and act as immediate and powerful motivators.

Criterion 6: Linkage to current strategic initiatives being undertaken

Strategic management is a long-term and continuous process. Over time, there will be many strategies adopted in previous years that continue to be implemented. New options need to be assessed against the strategies already underway, since any of the following and similar interactions and relationships may exist:

- New strategies can build on and reinforce current initiatives being implemented.
- New strategies may have implementation tasks that require the use of the same resources and thus require parallel or sequential scheduling. In the latter case, especially where resources and/or capabilities are in great demand, a new strategic option may have to be deferred or put in a queue.
- Information acquired in a current strategic initiative may be very relevant to the success of a newly proposed option—even to the point of having to make major modifications in the proposed strategy.
- The timing of a new strategy may be contingent on a strategy currently being implemented.

Criterion 7: Risk(s) likely to be incurred

Increasingly, leadership teams are concerned with risk for several reasons, including the following:

- The increasing rate of change
- The unpredictability of trends and events in the organization's environment
- The increasing cost of implementing new strategies
- The difficulties that arise in attempting to estimate benefits that may not materialize
- The dysfunctional consequences of implementing new and untried approaches

However, at a minimum, an in-depth and frank discussion of risks needs to take place, especially to identify any foreseeable downside impacts on the organization. It is always useful to reduce risks where possible by using proven tactics such as the following:

- Test marketing on a small scale
- Pilot projects
- Close scrutiny by top leadership
- Frequent performance evaluation
- Incremental funding
- Using senior personnel to lead the assignment

Criterion 8: Ease of entry

This factor is a double-edged sword, since it benefits all competitors that are qualified to enter a given market or develop a product or service—or undertake any given strategy for that matter. A corollary consideration is the need to consider the window of opportunity, that is, the time when the benefits of a given activity outweigh the costs of entry. A combination of early entry, rapid response to opportunities, and superior execution enables ease of entry into a given advantageous situation.

Criterion 9: Ease of implementation

Ease of implementation may be underestimated, since the focus early on is often based on a preoccupation with the end results and not on the often complex processes of turning a strategic alternative into an ongoing process. While it is not always easy to determine in complete detail all that goes into a given set of implementation activities, it is usually possible to scope them out in sufficient detail to determine whether or not they can be implemented by the organization.

It is also important to bear in mind that ease of implementation is not a unique attribute. Many other organizations may find a given option is feasible for them to implement. This results in the competitive advantages of a particular strategy being less effective in delivering the product or service being considered.

Criterion 10: Duration of the implementation process

The longer a strategy requires for full implementation, the more likely it is to require a detailed work breakdown structure for the strategy, including realistic performance measures to guide process. While these are tasks that are covered in much more detail in Chapter 5, it is still necessary to determine that a given option can be organized with appropriate milestones to be accomplished in each operating period. This will allow the team to better estimate the feasibility and desirability of undertaking a given strategic alternative.

Criterion 11: Estimate of resources required

Better to overestimate than underestimate the resources required, since leadership attention may have moved on to new options. If this were to occur, there is a very real possibility that a strategy with many important benefits to the organization runs the risk of reduced funding and/or delayed implementation.

Criterion 12: Resources that need to be acquired

Every effort should be made to use available resources and competencies, but usually the more complex, large-scale, and strategically important strategies being considered also require the acquisition of new resources and/or the development/hiring of new competencies. This factor can easily be overlooked as assessments of this nature can be difficult to determine at the outset of a strategic initiative.

Also, the proponents of a strategy may be hesitant to present the full scope of the requirements of a proposed strategy, fearing a deferral, scaling down, or even rejection of the strategy. However, anything less than the full disclosure of all necessary resources that need to be acquired is likely to have even more negative consequences at a later date.

Criterion 13: Use of existing leadership competencies and capabilities

While most managers like to take on new challenges, these same managers may also be guilty of not accurately assessing their ability to carry out these new challenges. Before agreeing to put a particular strategy into the plan, it is essential to determine whether or not the current leaders are capable of carrying out all of the required management tasks. If not, and it is agreed that the strategy is necessary, then the gap must be addressed as the primary task at hand, and steps taken to correct this deficiency before launching.

Criterion 14: Order of magnitude estimate of financial resources required

Very few strategies can be accurately evaluated without a significant investment in information gathering and cost analysis. At this point, a detailed cost analysis is not likely to be necessary. However, it is usually sufficient to make an order of magnitude estimate of costs and resources required, since, if the strategy is accepted, a much more detailed cost analysis will be required in Step 10.

At this juncture, it is sufficient to make an estimate based on similar initiatives from the past, outside expertise, or estimated range of expenditures. In any case, the objective is to develop an adequate estimate with enough detail for management to make an informed decision, unless any of the following apply:

- A high level of expenditures is anticipated that requires more detail.
- The strategy results in a long-term project.
- The strategy is high-risk and complex.
- Difficulties in implementation are anticipated.

Criterion 15: Cash flow requirements

Multi-year strategies may have very different life cycle patterns, especially with respect to resource requirements. Significant upfront expenditures for physical plant, equipment, and personnel may be required, while other strategies will have gradually increasing yet significant expenditures. Leadership needs to know these cash flow patterns over at least the next few years in order to allocate available funds in accordance with the current and projected financial plan.

At this point, a detailed cash flow analysis is usually not required, but there still needs to be a credible, realistic pattern of expenses estimated for the expected duration of the implementation process. Later, precise financial analysis will be required, but since a given option might not even be in the strategic plan, making detailed analyses at this juncture is not recommended.

Criterion 16: Organization-specific criteria

Every organization has some degree of uniqueness, that is, the existence of specific features that leadership, either explicitly or implicitly and to varying degrees, takes into account in planning and managing the organization. It is also possible that a great number of organizations have other features such as unused competencies, location advantages, and client information that are not even recognized for the leverage they provide for formulating feasible strategies.

One of the most significant benefits of an explicitly designed strategic management system is that it leverages these factors to extract the maximum benefit possible from them. This is in sharp contrast to depending on an ad hoc, intuitive approach to formulating strategy.

As a consequence, all options should be evaluated in terms of these unique characteristics. These features provide a number of evaluation criteria that help crystallize the evaluation and selection of strategy—and in some situations even provide insights for the development of new strategies. For example, consider such organizational features as the following:

- Organization culture
- Potentially useful information on current clients already in the database

- Strategic partner competencies not currently being used by the organization

Criterion 17: Leadership-specific criteria

As in Criterion 16, over time, every organization develops a unique combination of leadership features specific to the organization. These features evolve based on the preferences, values, and experience of the leadership team in place and the management systems and processes they have developed. These all play a prominent role in determining which strategies will be selected. Therefore, it behooves the personnel involved in evaluating and selecting strategies to consider these features.

One effective approach is to use the core criteria to narrow the range of alternatives deserving more extensive analysis and review, followed by the selective evaluation of the remaining alternatives using the applicable contextual and situational criteria as required to examine a given strategy.

Evaluate, select, and modify strategic initiatives currently being implemented

Once strategic management has become an integral and effective part of the overall management process, there will be a continuous flow of new strategies. Each year new options are identified, and a subset is selected for implementation. However, along with the new options will come a carryover of current strategic initiatives in various stages of implementation. This carryover has a direct impact on the availability of staff and funds for new projects. It must be taken into account in evaluating similar options.

Existing strategies must be re-evaluated to determine if they are still consistent with the new strategic direction that has been set and with newly proposed strategic options. They should also be examined in terms of their performance level and overall progress rate. Several alternative dispositions of these strategies are possible, including: continuing as is, curtailing, expanding, accelerating, decelerating, downsizing, outsourcing, modifying, transferring to another business unit, deferring, and/or terminating.

The preceding evaluation criteria will be found useful in evaluating strategies that have already received leadership's approval and are now in the process of implementation. However, it will not be enough to make a rational and objective evaluation of progress, since some of the following conditions may prevail:

- Conditions that made these strategies appear so attractive when initially approved may have changed.
- Available resources may be severely limited.
- Progress may be seriously lagging expectations.
- Continuing to base decisions on sunk costs that may realistically never pay off, especially when combined with unrealistic optimism, may result in continuing to fund losing strategies.
- Lower levels of leadership may be assuring management that "all is going well and on schedule" when, in fact, it is not.

In any case, strategic alternatives approved in prior years must be rigorously evaluated in terms of their original objectives, performance measures, and the newly set strategic direction and proposed strategies. In a strategic planning process, evaluations need to be translated into the staffing and resources *required* for completion. It will then be possible to make a more accurate estimate of staffing, funds, and other resources *available* for the newly proposed alternatives.

In making these evaluations the same core criteria previously discussed can effectively be used here. Briefly, and in review, they include:

- Leadership perceptions with respect to the following:
    - The need to change current strategies
    - The willingness to change current strategies
    - The feasibility of changing current strategies
- Expectation of goal attainment
- Linkage/synergy/impact across core functions

The key considerations to take into account in evaluating strategies initiated in previous years are the changes that have occurred since their initiation. A prime example is that of a technology-based change requiring several years to complete. Changing conditions are present in all areas pointing to all types of changes, and being sensitive to obsolescence is the order of the day. What appeared to be a great opportunity last year can become a losing proposition. Rationally this is something most managers accept as a truism, but emotionally many of these same managers find it difficult to terminate a strategy that they championed only recently. Strategic leadership teams must be especially sensitive to these changes in order to identify the need to change early on and make it more likely that a "mid-course correction" is all that is required.

Evaluate, classify, and select strategies identified/generated in Step 8

From the beginning of the evaluation and selection process, there is a need to guard against a few obvious but often overlooked "subjective" tendencies that drive the formulation of new/revised alternatives:

- Selecting the proposals of higher-level and/or influential managers
- Making evaluation and selection a political process, that is, supporting each other's favorite but flawed strategy, initiative, or project
- Preferring short-term and/or more easily implemented options over more difficult, long-term, and risky strategies that will, it the long run, prove to be much more necessary and beneficial on a number of counts
- Preferring to use available capabilities and competencies instead of accepting the need to acquire new competencies, even new leadership and/or staffing
- Preferring technical options, albeit strategic in nature, instead of strategies requiring cultural, structural, and behavioral changes that are most often complex and challenging

Surprisingly, when these tendencies are recognized and a conscious effort made to not indulge in them, evaluation and selection reduce to a surprisingly rapid, efficient, and effective process, even in considering expensive, risky, and long-term options. This is possible when the subsurface tensions of competing interests are reduced, allowing a focused strategy to emerge.

When combined with an understanding of the components of a thorough OTSW evaluation, evaluating specific strategies becomes an opportunity to apply these implicit evaluation criteria. It is in those organizations that are not yet fully committed to the strategic management discipline that the evaluation process may be perceived as a tedious exercise.

Keep in mind the ultimate objective of these processes is to select that set of strategic alternatives, that, when added to the efforts already underway to achieve strategic goals, will significantly improve the processes of attaining them and at the same time best utilize existing capabilities, competencies, and resources of the organization.

Before even considering the use of the evaluation and selection processes that follow, it should be recognized that leadership in all organizations employs a decision-making system that it has found to varying degrees to be effective. Often this is not a team-based strategic management decision-making system. Therefore, the following process is included as an effective way to initiate a team-based process. It is not necessary to follow each stage in some lock-step fashion. The significant output should be a set of potentially actionable strategies that leadership is ready to consider in developing a strategic plan in Steps 10 and 11.

The key point here is that inevitably the strategic management team will generate more strategic alternatives than it can possibly use. At the same time, there is usually a manageable subset that should be selected and entered in the planning process. Even if many of these strategies cannot be implemented immediately, they can be included in a long-term plan that, in effect, serves as a repository of potentially actionable strategies to review, modify, and implement at a later date, if desired.

Using the evaluation criteria developed in this step either as a checklist of considerations or detailed analyses, the essential stages of the process are as follows:

- Evaluate strategies based on core evaluation and selection criteria
- Analyze and evaluate any of the remaining alternatives as necessary using relevant contextual criteria
- Repeat the evaluation and selection processes as required to complete a set of strategies for inclusion in the strategic plan (Step10)

- Compile a set of selected feasible strategies for inclusion in the strategic plan (Step 10)

Procedure 1: Evaluate strategies based on core evaluation and selection criteria as follows:

A three-phase evaluation approach is illustrated in Figures 4.4, 4.5 and 4.6, using each of the following criteria:

- Leadership perceptions and preferences
- Expectation of goal achievement
- Linkage/synergy/alignment between core functions

Task 1: Evaluation of leadership perceptions and preferences

Figure 4.4 includes an illustrative set of strategic alternatives in a comprehensive set of key result areas. In a given organization, the set of key result areas will vary. Include only the reduced set of strategic alternatives remaining after the first-cut screening in Step 7. The team may further reduce this set of alternatives being evaluated by consensus in the process of developing this initial list of strategic alternatives to be evaluated.

The purpose of this evaluation process is to consider only the alternatives initially deemed feasible but which need more detailed scrutiny in comparison with other alternatives. In this figure, the evaluation criteria are based on leadership perceptions and preferences as discussed above. The alternatives that are shaded are those that remain after this first-level evaluation process.

This evaluation approach will become clear in the example shown in Figure 4.4, as strategies are listed in rows against the management evaluation criteria in columns. In the last column labeled "Combined team rating," the lowest common

Strategy in the 21st Century

denominator from the three previous columns is used to make an overall rating of a particular strategy. Alternative approaches are possible.

Figure 4.4: Leadership Perceptions of the Likely Impact of Strategies

Strategic management team evaluates using a 1 to 5 rating scale (1 = low and 5 = high)

Feasible strategies by key result area	Perceived need to change	Perceived willingness to change	Perceived feasibility of changing	Combined team rating
External Dimensions				
Market/Product Mix				
Market penetration	5	5	4	4
Market development	4	4	3	3
Product development	4	5	4	4
Diversification	3	3	2	2
Suppliers				
Partner with suppliers	5	4	4	4
Consolidate suppliers	2	2	3	2
Vertically integrate	4	5	3	3

Chapter 4

Figure 4.4: Leadership Perceptions of the Likely Impact of Strategies (continued)

Feasible strategies by key result area	Perceived need to change	Perceived willingness to change	Perceived feasibility of changing	Combined team rating
Internal Dimensions				
People Alignment				
Invest in staff	4	5	3	3
Reorganize roles & responsibilities	5	4	4	4
Bring in new staff resources	3	3	5	3
Develop multi-cultural org.	3	4	2	2
Operations				
Product/Service Development				
Maximize internal resources	3	3	2	2
Outsource product development	3	3	3	3
Pursue blended approach	4	4	4	4

Figure 4.4: Leadership Perceptions of the Likely Impact of Strategies (continued)

Feasible strategies by key result area	Perceived need to change	Perceived willingness to change	Perceived feasibility of changing	Combined team rating
Customer Service				
Streamline internal processes	5	3	4	4
Outsource	2	2	3	2
Pursue blended approach	3	2	3	3
Marketing				
Product/Service				
Invest in R&D	5	4	4	4
Personalize existing products	3	3	3	3
Bundle services w/ products	4	4	2	3
Differentiate via quality	4	5	3	4
Improve customer service	3	4	3	3
Price				
Be the low-cost provider	3	3	4	3
Offer competitive pricing	5	3	4	4

Figure 4.4: Leadership Perceptions of the Likely Impact of Strategies (continued)

Feasible strategies by key result area	Perceived need to change	Perceived willingness to change	Perceived feasibility of changing	Combined team rating
Price (continued)				
Offer premium pricing	2	2	2	2
Place				
Build distribution network	4	5	4	4
Form a distribution alliance	3	3	2	2
Leverage the Web	4	4	3	3
Finance Growth				
Reallocate resources	4	5	3	4
Invest retained earnings	4	3	2	2
Reinvest operating margins	4	5	4	4
Sell assets to raise capital	2	2	2	2
Share risk and return	5	4	4	4
Incur debt	2	2	1	1
Seek government grants	1	2	1	1

Task 2: Evaluation of expectation of goal achievement

The strategies remaining need to be further narrowed down into a more manageable subset for inclusion in the strategic plan. One of the most effective ways to do this is to consider the strategies remaining from Task 1 and evaluate them with respect to the goals derived in Step 7 regarding setting strategic direction.

At the same time, this will also serve to limit the number of goals selected for implementation since *no more than two goals with the highest possibility of goal attainment should be selected.* The primary reason for limiting the number of goals will become apparent in Chapter 5 when goals and their corollary strategies are converted into a strategic operating plan. To illustrate, a single goal must be translated into a set of objectives that, in turn, are deployed at the cross-functional, core-functional, support-functional, and all leadership levels. As a consequence, the strategic operating plan resulting from *just one goal* can easily become a complex and challenging implementation process. In fact, we do not know of any organizations committing their management and organizations to strategic management for the first time that have successfully implemented more than two goals simultaneously.

This work can be done by using a matrix as shown in Figure 4.5, using the same five-point rating scale, or any preferred rating scale. The one or two goals with the highest ratings should be selected for planning purposes, unless the leadership team can reach a consensus about an alternative rationale for selecting more than two goals. To illustrate this process in Figure 4.5, Goals 1 and 4 of the National Food Services Association (see Table 4.16 on p. 173) were selected as the primary goals for inclusion in the strategic plan.

Figure 4.5: The Expectation of Goal Achievement

Strategic management team evaluates using a 1 to 5 rating scale (1 = low and 5 = high)

Strategies remaining from Figure 4.4 by key result area	Goal 1: Protect & Grow Core Business	Goal 2: Become Global Leader	Goal 3: Non-Traditional Membership	Goal 4: Position & Invest for Future
External Dimensions				
Market / Product Mix				
Market penetration	5	3	2	4
Market development	4	4	3	5
Product development	3	3	2	3
Suppliers				
Partner with suppliers	5	4	4	3
Vertically integrate	3	2	2	2
Internal Dimensions				
People Alignment				
Invest in staff	4	5	3	5
Reorganize roles & responsibilities	5	4	4	4

Strategy in the 21st Century

Figure 4.5: The Expectation of Goal Achievement (continued)

Strategies remaining from Figure 4.4 by key result area	Goal 1: Protect & Grow Core Business	Goal 2: Become Global Leader	Goal 3: Non-Traditional Membership	Goal 4: Position & Invest for Future
Operations				
Product development				
Outsource product development	3	3	2	4
Pursue a blended approach	5	2	2	4
Customer service				
Streamline internal processes	3	3	2	3
Pursue a blended approach	4	2	3	4
Marketing				
Product/Service				
Build R&D alliances	3	4	4	4
Bundle services w/ products	4	4	5	4
Differentiate via quality	2	2	1	3

Figure 4.5: The Expectation of Goal Achievement (continued)

Strategies remaining from Figure 4.4 by key result area	Goal 1: Protect & Grow Core Business	Goal 2: Become Global Leader	Goal 3: Non-Traditional Membership	Goal 4: Position & Invest for Future
Price				
Be the low cost provider	4	2	2	2
Offer competitive pricing	4	3	4	4
Place				
Build distribution network	4	5	4	4
Leverage the Web	4	4	4	3
Finance Growth				
Reallocate resources	4	5	3	4
Reinvest operating margins	4	3	3	4
Share risk and return	5	4	4	3

Task 3: Evaluation of linkage/synergy/alignment between core functions

One of the most overlooked features of evaluation and selection processes is the tendency to omit realistic assessment of the interactions newly proposed options would have on each other, on strategic initiatives currently being implemented, and on current operations. It can be likened to the prescription of multiple medications to one patient as a result of "individual" doctor diagnosed conditions; each doctor acts alone with no "group" consideration by a medical "team" of the potential negative interactions among the drugs and resultant impact on the patient.

There is no best "rule of thumb" or algorithm for doing this check of interactive effects of multiple strategies. It is more a matter of common sense and making the time to ask probing questions. Consider the following illustrative questions:

- Do the results of the newly proposed strategy in a given area lead to a more balanced strategy across the organization?
- Does this option add to the overall capability of the organization?
- Does it provide a platform with a broader scope and a more flexible and varied response capability?
- Does this option include all of the various functions that will be impacted at the strategic level?
- Should the emphasis on the option be modified or changed in any way to better interact with other strategies and operations that are already in place or currently being put in place?
- Is it actually a cross-functional strategy that will require a more encompassing organization structure and management process in order to be implemented successfully?
- Will this option prove to be cost effective in one functional area and not in another?

Ignoring these and similar questions results in the all too common turf wars among competing functional areas. For example, consider the plight of the U.S. automobile industry that could not seem to make a quality car until Japanese automakers showed the way. Before the Japanese took over a large segment of the automobile industry, quality and excellence in U.S. manufacturing traditionally took a backseat to marketing, design, and customer appeal.

Be mindful to include only those key evaluation criteria that are relevant in the given decision context. Usually four to six evaluation criteria will be more than adequate. Beyond that the influence of each factor does not facilitate the decision process. In selecting evaluation criteria, one of the most effective approaches is to use a balanced set of criteria. The advantage of this approach is that functional managers can see the relationship of their area of responsibility to all of the strategies in each of the key result areas. Using this approach has the following advantages:

- Leadership is directly involved in determining the relative importance of the evaluation criteria before the implementation process begins.
- A common set of evaluation criteria is considered by all members of the strategic management team on a systematic basis and not on the basis of each manager's favorite criteria.
- Team members have a basis for comparing and discussing their individual ratings and a framework for coming to a consensus when the ratings differ significantly.

With these considerations in mind, evaluate the results of strategies for Goal 1 selected in Procedure 1, Task 2, as shown in Figure 4.5. Repeat this process for the other selected goal, in this case, Goal 4. In Figure 4.6 the task is to eliminate those strategies that are not balanced, synergistic, linked, aligned, or impactful.

Strategy in the 21st Century

Figure 4.6: The Linkage/Synergy/Alignment Among Core Functions

Strategic management team evaluates using a 1 to 5 rating scale (1 = low and 5 = high)

Goal Statement: Protect and grow core business

Strategies remaining from Figure 4.5 by key results area	FINANCE Positive Financials & Acceptable Risks	MARKETING Meets Customer Needs	OPERATIONS/IT Operationally Feasible	HR Workforce Capability
External Dimensions				
Market / Product Mix				
Market penetration	5	5	4	4
Market development	4	4	3	3
Product development	3	4	2	3
Suppliers				
Partner with suppliers	5	4	4	4
Vertically integrate	4	5	3	3
Internal Dimensions				
People Alignment				
Invest in staff	4	5	3	3
Reorganize roles & responsibilities	5	4	4	4

NOTE: We have found it useful to facilitate the process by using these general criteria. These criteria may vary based on the type of organization.

Figure 4.6: The Linkage/Synergy/Alignment Among Core Functions (continued)

Strategies remaining from Figure 4.5 by key results area	FINANCE Positive Financials & Acceptable Risks	MARKETING Meets Customer Needs	OPERATIONS/IT Operationally Feasible	HR Workforce Capability
Operations				
Product development				
Pursue a blended approach	3	3	2	2
Customer service				
Streamline internal processes	3	3	4	4
Marketing				
Product				
Build R&D alliances	4	4	4	4
Bundle services w/ products	4	4	2	3
Price				
Offer competitive pricing	4	3	4	4
Place				
Build distribution network	4	5	4	4
Leverage the Web	4	3	2	3

Strategy in the 21st Century

Figure 4.6: The Linkage/Synergy/Alignment Among Core Functions (continued)

Strategies remaining from Figure 4.5 by key results area	FINANCE Positive Financials & Acceptable Risks	MARKETING Meets Customer Needs	OPERATIONS/IT Operationally Feasible	HR Workforce Capability
Finance Growth				
Reallocate resources	4	5	3	4
Reinvest operating margins	3	2	3	2
Share risk and return	5	4	4	3

Procedure 2: Analyze and evaluate the strategies remaining from Procedure 1 for contextually specific criteria.

Occasionally, some of the alternatives generated will require more analysis and evaluation using specific criteria, even before a provisional decision to include them in the strategic plan can be made by the team. This is especially true in cases of new and untried technology and entering new markets. It was not recommended that in-depth analyses be conducted before this time since they may have been eliminated; that is, it is simply a matter of conserving leadership time and energy.

In those situations where the decision requires lengthy analysis and evaluation, provision should be made to selectively utilize criteria described earlier in Step 9.

Procedure 3: Repeat the evaluation and selection processes as required to complete identification of a set of strategies for inclusion in the strategic plan (Step 10).

After completing the preceding processes, the strategic management team may feel that the results are still not satisfactory. After all, there is no guarantee that following a set of procedures will produce the desired results. Strategic management is rooted in strategic thinking, not process and procedures.

Employing the criteria, evaluation, and selection processes within an effective team-based approach to strategy can only offer a more efficient and effective way to develop and channel strategic management outputs. Ultimately, it all rests on the analytic and creative capabilities of the strategic leadership team.

Procedure 4: Compile a set of selected feasible strategies for inclusion in the strategic plan (Step 10).

After the foregoing evaluation, it is useful to compile a set of "core/primary" and "support/secondary" strategies that have been selected for inclusion in the strategic plan, along with any relevant comments that will help in integrating them into a comprehensive strategic plan. These options should be summarized in one figure, such as in Figure 4.7.

The comments column is provided to include any relevant comments about each of the selected options. These comments pertain to such factors as the following:

- Priority
- Time phasing
- Sequencing
- Long lead times

Strategy in the 21st Century

- Acquisition of resources and/or competencies
- Costs

In essence, note any significant component that needs to be taken into consideration during the planning and implementation processes. However, this summary sheet is not to be used as a substitute for a description of individual strategies as outlined in Step 8.

Figure 4.7: Selection of Strategies for Inclusion in the Strategic Plan

Goal Statement: Protect and grow business

Selected *Core (ital.)* & Support Strategies by Key Result Area	Comments Regarding Strategic Plan
Market / Product Mix	
Market penetration	• High priority
Market development	• Build capacity
Suppliers	
Partner with suppliers	• Help all understand that together we can do more. Ensure this piece is in place before launching market development strategy.
People Alignment	
Invest in staff	• Work with local business school and professional organizations to build overall management capacity
Reorganize roles & responsibilities	• Align behind new organization structure. Make this a #1 priority

Chapter 4

Figure 4.7: Selection of Strategies for Inclusion in the Strategic Plan (continued)

Selected *Core (ital.)* & Support Strategies by Key Result Area	Comments Regarding Strategic Plan
Operations	
Product development—Pursue blended approach *Customer service—Streamline internal processes*	• Use internal training department and targeted consultants • Work with ABC consultants to flow chart and improve process.
Marketing	
Product—Build a R&D alliance with other food related associations	• Ensure new product is rigorously tested before launch
Price—Offer competitive pricing	• Immediately do a fresh market assessment to refine pricing
Place—Build distribution network	• Retool the website to support distributors & alliance partners
Finance Growth	
Reallocate resources	• Reallocate resources targeted to new product development to building the distribution network
Share risk and return	• Partner up when we can on distribution

Defining the organization's strategic direction, the identification/creation of potential strategic alternatives in alignment with this direction, and subsequent evaluation and selection of feasible strategies have been the focus of this chapter on strategy formulation. However, the end result of these processes does not constitute a strategic plan. It remains to process the selected strategy alternatives using a planning approach to arrive at a long-term strategic plan and a short-term, that is, one- or two-year, strategic operating plan. These considerations and outputs are the focus of Chapter 5.

CHAPTER 5

Strategic Planning

The end result of the work in the previous chapter is a set of preferred strategies for inclusion in the strategic plan. Developing strategies is an exercise in strategic thinking. It includes setting the strategic direction, identifying and/or generating strategies, and evaluating and selecting a subset for inclusion in the strategic plan.

Strategic planning, the focus of this chapter, initiates a distinctly different set of strategic management activities: activities required to transform the organization's strategic goals and selected strategies into detailed action plans. The process for strategic planning occurs in two steps:

- Step 10: Develop a comprehensive strategic plan, including
  - A long-term set of strategies
  - A short-term set of strategies
- Step 11: Develop a strategic operating plan

It is important to note that implementation does not take place during the strategic planning phase. Instead, specific actions are planned paving the way for implementation of a "strategic operating plan" in Step 12.

STEP 10: DEVELOP A COMPREHENSIVE STRATEGIC PLAN

Developing a comprehensive strategic plan requires the ability to differentiate between different types of plans, strategic versus operational, and to apply the appropriate procedures to develop them. Most managers are sufficiently prepared to develop their own planning policies and procedures. Unfortunately, when it comes to planning, the tendency is to adopt a "one size fits all" approach to all planning assignments.

In the case of strategic planning an all too frequent result is to treat strategic planning the same as operational planning. Strategic plans sooner or later deploy into operational activities; however, if the links to strategy are lost, it is only a matter of time before strategic planning becomes a meaningless and disconnected top-management exercise yielding a set of fragmented and isolated operational activities lacking strategic focus.

Therefore, we begin with a few preliminary observations on planning per se before outlining the process of developing a comprehensive strategic plan. The objectives of this step are the following:

- Compare and contrast strategic thinking and strategic planning
- Consider strategic planning as a two-step process
- Recognize the features of effective long-term strategic plans
- Recognize the features of effective short-term strategic plans
- Identify and evaluate the various types of strategic activities currently underway
- Identify the appropriate planning format for each strategy included in the strategic plan
- Develop a comprehensive planning framework

- Make provision for a contingency plan
- Write a summary statement of a two-phase strategic plan
- Obtain management feedback, revisions, approval, and authorization to continue
- Produce an illustrative strategic plan

Compare and contrast strategic thinking and strategic planning

As noted, *strategy formulation* is primarily an exercise in strategic thinking. Strategic thinking, in turn, is both analytic and creative. It includes developing a thorough understanding of the organization's environment capabilities and resources and the setting of strategic direction based on the environment resources and capabilities filtered through the perceptions and preferences of leadership. Strategic thinking requires active questioning with respect to strategy:

- What did we do?
- What are we doing?
- What do we want to do?
- What can we do?
- What are we willing to do?
- What do we need to do?
- What should we do?
- What will happen if we do?

Questions such as these must remain reality-based, or they will begin to include include hypothetical premises. They may be intensive and/or extensive and, when taken together, form a strategy-focused thought process that results in the basis for strategic planning.

The primary deliverable coming out of this process is a set of strategies that, taken together, indicate the big picture direction and viable strategies to achieve them. However, as stated, these strategies do not constitute either a comprehensive long-term strategic plan or a short-term operating plan and certainly not a set of detailed deployable implementation instructions.

In contrast, *strategic planning* includes the set of activities that will develop these strategies and instructions for implementation. Strategic planners are concerned with a more constrained set of questions, such as the following:

- What is the set of potentially actionable strategies that are to be included in the plan?
- How do we prioritize these strategies?
- How do we time-phase these strategies?
- How do we scope and structure strategies for planning purposes?
- How do we select the strategies that are to be included in the next annual operating cycle as policies, initiatives/projects, or assignments?
- How do we write a strategic plan for leadership approval?

Consider strategic planning as a two-phase process

As a planning horizon extends farther into the future, the more a strategic plan will be subject to revision as conditions change and new opportunities arise. In contrast, the shorter the planning horizon, the more fixed plans become; that is, strategies to be implemented in the next operating cycle are selected and formally established in the strategic operating plan. This program then becomes fixed as funding begins, staff commitments are made, and the implementation process is initiated.

These two planning processes are part of an integrated planning process. However, for managerial, organizational, and operational purposes, they are best treated as a two-phased process meeting the needs of both long-run and short-run approaches.

With respect to the long-run, there needs to be a set of preferred and potentially actionable strategies that give management alternatives to act on, either proactively or reactively, as conditions and opportunities emerge. These strategies must already have been selected for their potential to realize the strategic vision and mission of the organization. Reviewing alternatives needs to be done in a forum that is free from the pressures and tensions of day-to-day implementation processes.

This planning process needs to be flexible with ample provision for change. This is best done by projecting and time-phasing strategies over a long-run time period—a period in which changes can more easily be made the farther into the future the plan reaches. In contrast, the strategic operating plan (as discussed in Step 11) needs to be a much more concretely fixed entity with as little change as possible.

In the process of identifying feasible strategies (see Step 8), it is usually the case that many more options are generated than can be implemented in any single operating period. Strategies that ultimately don't make the cut can be saved for future consideration. As such, they serve as an initial set of options to start the strategy formulation process in the next strategic planning exercise.

In contrast, in the short-term, the strategic planning process should include evaluating strategies that were initiated in the previous period *and are still being implemented in the current operating period and possibly future periods.* These are "in-process initiatives" that will have an impact on new strategies either because of the relation of their content or the limitation they place on the capabilities and resources available for implementing new and/or revised strategies.

Previously initiated strategies, along with the new strategies to be initiated, often require extensive and detailed implementation plans that are in sharp contrast to the more open-ended process of long-term strategic planning. In any case, long- and short-term planning cannot be effectively combined into a single process, even though both are essential components to planning the organization's future course of action.

Accordingly, Step 10 focuses on developing a two-phased strategic plan, while Step 11 further develops the short-term plan (hereafter referred to as the strategic operating plan) by designing specific implementation plans for each strategy. In Steps 12 and 13, the actual implementation processes themselves are outlined and discussed.

Features of effective long-term strategic plans

The end result of the long-term planning process is *a set of actionable strategies* (for each strategic goal) that may be implemented at some point over the life of the organization's planning horizon, that is, three to five or more years.

Long-term plans should be designed so that management can use them to accomplish the following objectives:

- Provide a basis for informed long-term strategic decision-making
- Provide a basis for planning by the strategic management team
- Provide linkage between long-term goals and strategies and the nearer-term objectives
- Provide a set of evaluation criteria for evaluating nearer-term planning performance beyond the immediate criteria of the nearer-term plan
- Provide a document that can be revised and updated on

a scheduled basis and intermittently, as required, by extenuating circumstances

To accomplish these objectives, long-term plans should incorporate certain features in their design. These features are summarized in Table 5.1.

> **Table 5.1: Features of a Long-Term Plan**
>
> - The primary focus is on successful deployment of an aligned and integrated organization strategy. This begins at the highest governance and management levels in the organization and includes the deployment of strategy throughout all levels of management and all functions.
> - It is coterminous with the longest planning period that is being used in the organization. Strategic planning reaches into the future as far as leadership is accustomed to laying out plans and making decisions. It needs to have the flexibility to make changes, modifications, and additions to strategy in an integrated, systematic way.
> - It provides an up-to-date information base for leadership discussions on strategic planning. It should be regarded as a "work in progress" wherein all strategies, except those included in the current annual operating plan, will be subject to change and reconfiguration.
> - Key result areas are fixed entities in the long-term strategic plan. It is essential to maintain the key result areas for each goal as identified in Step 8, since they provide a logical "goal-based" architecture and a rationale for implementing an integrated and related set of strategies. While some strategies will be deferred until later

> **Table 5.1: Features of a Long-Term Plan (continued)**
>
> operating cycles, the logic for balanced growth requires that attention be paid to all key result areas in each operating cycle. There may be a need to give more attention and resources to a specific key result area in order to take advantage of a window of opportunity or develop the organization's capabilities to the level compatible with its strategic expectations.
> - Strategies are provisionally prioritized. All strategies are not equally important so they should be prioritized by goal in terms of need, feasibility, cost, and benefits. This is not a refined process requiring a lot of analysis. Most leadership teams know how to prioritize a given list of options—the real challenge was attended to in Step 9 by developing and evaluating an initial set of alternatives for inclusion in the strategic plan.
> - Sequencing, relationships, and interactivity between strategies are identified. It is easy to overlook the impact that various strategies have on each other and the collective impact they can have on the organization. The way strategies build on each other is often overlooked as are precedence relationships that require sequencing.
> - Roles and responsibilities are identified. At this point, we are not referring to detailed implementation responsibilities but rather to overall responsibility for overseeing the strategic plan. This includes such responsibilities as the following:
>   - Overall authority and responsibility for executing each strategy; that is, a single individual should be assigned this responsibility for each strategy

Table 5.1: Features of a Long-Term Plan (continued)

- º Overall responsibility for coordinating the process of compiling, writing, obtaining approvals, rewriting (as required by top management), and distributing the plan
- º Overall responsibility for developing and maintaining a schedule to complete the strategic plan, including review, revision, and approvals required during the process

• Within the long-range plan provision is made for contingencies. No strategic plan is complete without providing for the need to change it by aborting some initiatives, starting or modifying others because of unforeseen events. Clearly, it is not necessary to make a Plan B or Plan C for every contingency. However, major concerns need to be identified to form a basis for developing alternative scenarios regarding a changing external environment, such as the economy, the competition, customers, suppliers, new technology, or fluctuating currencies. Internally, the primary concerns relate often to new product and process development that does not always go according to schedule. Another important internal consideration is the sudden departure of key managers or professional staff.

• Long-term strategic plans are not the same as operating plans. One of the main shortcomings of organizational planning is to combine strategic and operational planning; hence, it is useful to consider their differences. Many so-called strategic plans are actually operating plans based on, for example, five-year mar-

> **Table 5.1: Features of a Long-Term Plan (continued)**
>
> keting, operations, and financial projections of current operations. Operating plans differ from strategic plans in the following ways:
>
> - ○ They focus on programmed action plans, that is, the multitude of activities that are extensions of already implemented strategies that have become accepted on-going processes and programs.
> - ○ They are enacted through organization infrastructure and management systems that have already been established and accepted by organization personnel.
> - ○ They do not require the close involvement of the highest levels of management that strategic management requires, that is, formulating the initiatives, explaining the rationale for the new initiatives, motivating the organization to accept them, and closely following progress throughout the strategic management process.
> - ○ Operational planning may include projects and programs that are several times larger than some strategic initiatives. It is not a matter of size; it is a matter of needing to make a change or modification in the strategic direction that requires new and/or modified capabilities and competencies.
> - ○ An operating plan's primary focus is on the annual budget cycle, not the long-run strategic direction.
>
> - Long-term strategic plans require performance evaluation. A particular strategy may be executed efficiently and still come up far short of achieving leadership's desired objectives and expected results. Thus, provi-

> **Table 5.1: Features of a Long-Term Plan (continued)**
>
> sion for performance evaluation must be included in the strategic planning process. Strategies started in the previous operating cycle need to be evaluated before starting the new implementation program. These "legacy strategies" must also be evaluated periodically during the implementation process (Steps 11 and 12) and after implementation during ongoing operations management (Step 13).

The aforementioned features taken together are intended to convey an understanding of the essential structure and format of a long-term strategic plan. How they get combined in writing the strategic plan is left to the individual(s) charged with writing the plan, since this is a matter of organization planning policies and procedures combined with the writing style of those charged with producing it.

Features of effective short-term strategic plans (strategic operating plans)

Short-term strategic planning refers to the following processes that are described in this step:

- Selecting and time-phasing the strategies to be implemented in the next annual planning cycle, including:
  - Strategies initiated in previous planning cycles not yet completed
  - Strategies selected from the pool of strategies in the long-term plan that are set for implementation in the next annual operating cycle

- o Those strategies selected from this pool that will be implemented in a future operating cycle but require initiating some activities that have long lead times
- Writing the "short-term" portion of the comprehensive strategic plan that will be submitted to leadership for approval *before* preparing detailed implementation plans
- Preparing a detailed implementation plan for each strategy selected from the long-term plan (the activities required to do this are covered in Step 11)

Identify and evaluate the various types of strategic activities currently underway

Organizational leaders are continuously making decisions that can have an impact on strategy—ones that may not have been considered "strategic" at the time. This type of decision is common even in organizations that have advanced strategic management systems. Decisions may be made either implicitly or explicitly, intuitively or formally as part of a process that James Brian Quinn refers to as "incrementalism" (1980).

However, these decisions need to be evaluated periodically and always at the time that a strategic plan is written. Planning for new strategic initiatives should not start until progress and performance of legacy strategies started in previous periods are known. The two main reasons are:

- To ascertain the costs of continuing implementation and, therefore, the funding level available for strategic initiatives to be started in the next budgetary cycle
- To assess relationships with and the impact on new/revised alternatives proposed for inclusion in the strategic plan

Other points that need to be included in reviewing the current strategic plan include the following:

- A brief summary of progress on each major strategy and initiative
- Problems encountered that will impact the implementation process
- A recommended course of action regarding strategies and initiatives currently in progress

Format new and/or revised strategies

The term *format* is used to refer to how a strategy is organized, its scope, its objective(s), expectations from assigned personnel, and some indication of how it should be implemented. This is necessary to determine the prioritizing and time-phasing of the alternative strategies and to provide additional information that will help management determine which strategies to include in the strategic operating plan. In Step 11, the formats described below will be developed in much greater detail for each strategy being implemented.

The *format* for initiating a strategy is vitally important to the *content* of the strategy since it communicates to management the scope, content, and approach to be used. These considerations aid management in determining the allocation of funds and personnel, the level of effort required for implementation, and its duration. Unfortunately, the format of strategies is often neglected, and when it does receive attention only one favorite management approach is used—often inappropriately.

Currently project management is a favored management technique and indeed is a powerful tool for executing strategy. However, it runs the risk of being overused, so much so, that every new strategy is structured as a "project." Of course, more complex and cross-functional strategic initiatives require the structure and systems incorporated in project management, but many strategic initiatives are best managed using a less complex approach.

Management has other tools and concepts that are just as effective in planning and implementing strategic initiatives, that is, a committee assignment, a team assignment, an external contract, or an individual assignment. The key is to classify and then match the correct format with a given strategy, its purpose, and content. This is achieved by *starting with a succinctly stated strategic initiative*; that is, the strategic intent must be clearly evident so that the appropriate format can be selected. Making these classifications will aid in both planning and implementation by fitting strategies into an overall strategic plan and emphasizing exactly what leadership expects to achieve.

Develop a comprehensive planning framework

The purpose of a comprehensive planning framework is to provide leadership with a single graphic representation of all the strategic initiatives they have deemed potentially actionable. The framework should include provision for both past, current, and future planning periods.

It is not realistic to consider more than one year beyond the current planning period as part of the short-term plan, that is, the strategic operating plan (SOP), because of the changes that are very likely to occur beyond that time frame. Also, dividing the long-run into annual planning periods is not realistic. At most, some rough prioritizing and time sequencing may be feasible.

Accordingly, Figure 5.1 is an example of such an approach. The strategies that are included in the strategic operating phase, that is, "current" and "next" planning periods, provide the basis for the detailed implementation plan defined in Step 11.

Chapter 5

Figure 5.1: Relationship Between Strategic Planning and Strategic Operational Planning

Key Result Area	Core *(italic)* and Support Strategies	Format	Previous	Current	Next	Future
			\multicolumn{4}{c}{Planning periods (by year(s) and quarters) X = One Quarter}			
External						
Market / Product Mix	*Market Penetration*	Project	XXXX	XXXX	XXXX	
	Market Development	Committee			XX	XXXX
Suppliers	*Partner*	Project	X	XXXX	XXXX	XXXX
Internal						
People	Invest	Team	XXXX	XXXX	XXXX	XXXX
	Define roles and responsibilities	Project		XX	XX	
Product Development	Blended approach	Team		XXXX	XXXX	
Customer Service	*Streamline*	Project	XXXX	XX		
Marketing	*Distribution Network*	Project	XXXX		XX	XXXX
	R&D Alliance	Committee				XXXX

247

Figure 5.1: Relationship Between Strategic Planning and Strategic Operational Planning (continued)

Key Result Area	Core *(italic)* and Support Strategies	Format	Previous	Current	Next	Future
			\multicolumn{4}{c}{Planning periods (by year(s) and quarters) X = One Quarter}			
Finance	Reinvest earnings	Committee	XXXX	XXXX	XXXX	XXXX
	Share risk	Team			XXXX	XXXX

The key feature of Figure 5.1 is its extension to include all strategic initiatives currently in the process of implementation, as well as those in the strategic planning pipeline. Thus, it provides leadership with a comprehensive overview of the strategic plan throughout the organization, currently and in the future.

This "complete" overview (key result area, strategies, and format) of the strategic plan enables leadership to intervene more proactively in the planning process as a result of seeing past, current, and future planning initiatives. For example, it makes it easier to make adjustments in the planning and implementation processes, that is, to balance, realign, integrate, sequence, and prioritize the relationships between strategic initiatives in both the long-run and the short-run.

The strategies being implemented in the current year include those legacy strategies still in process from the previous year (or years). This is important, because legacy strategies impact the capacity, capabilities, and resources of the organization to implement new/revised strategies.

The strategic operating plan is shown as covering two years. It covers the actual implementations that will occur in the current year, as well as those requiring advanced preparation before the actual implementation of strategies in the following year.

Make provision for contingency plans

All strategic initiatives are not realized according to plan. In a very real sense, strategic planning is often experimental, since many deal with untried initiatives in new and uncertain circumstances. This points to the need for contingency planning before it becomes clear that a new or modified strategy is required. Unfortunately, the need for contingency planning often does not occur until implementation of the initiative has begun.

The purpose of introducing contingency planning here is to give direction to those implementing strategic initiatives regarding the need to be flexible to alternative scenarios and courses of action.

Consider contingencies with respect to size, scope, cost, and duration of strategic initiatives. For example, ask:

- Can this initiative be reduced in size?
- Can it be changed with respect to its scope?
- Can the total cost of the project be reduced?
- Can the planned duration of the implementation process be lengthened or put on hold?

Write a summary statement of a two-phase strategic plan

Writing a summary statement provides a rationale and explanation of the two-phase strategic plan. It outlines the assumptions and key points of the plan *for both* the long- and short-term in an integrated overview that incorporates the thinking of the strategic management team.

Table 5.2 summarizes suggestions on the format and content of this written plan.

Table 5.2: Suggested Format and Content of the Two-Phase Strategic Plan

- Introduction. Provide a solid introduction to the strategic plan up front. Corporate annual reports provide a good example of how leadership can make summary introductions that include salient features of the organization's progress, problems, prospects, and plan. The reader is provided an overall perspective of the state of the organization and its future direction. In writing an introduction to the strategic plan, leadership has a similar responsibility and can use a similar format with a few modifications. First, the strategic plan is primarily written for internal consumption by the organization and by key stakeholders. It should briefly cover key points regarding the existing plan with respect to progress, problems, and prospects already identified in the more detailed evaluation of the existing strategic plan.
- The written strategic plan serves both instructional and motivational purposes. In this "single summary" document the organization's leadership and staff can obtain an overall perspective on an integrated strategic plan reaching into the long-term and building on the organization's strengths. The document also serves to motivate and unite the broader team toward the achievement of shared goals.
- While this document serves as a plan of action, it would be more technically accurate to call it a "proposed" plan of action, a precursor to the detailed action plan that is the function of the strategic operating plan (see Step 11). The strategic plan is equivalent to an architect's design; the strategy implementation plan

> **Table 5.2: Suggested Format and Content of the Two-Phase Strategic Plan (continued)**
>
> is equivalent to a building contractor's blueprints; and the actual implementation process (Steps 12 and 13) can be viewed as the actual construction of the building.
>
> - Provide an outline of the new/revised strategic direction. In Step 7 it was recommended that all components of the strategic direction be included in summary form and approved by the board or leadership team. These statements, as approved, should be included in the strategic plan to set the stage for all that is to follow and make clear the rationale for revising or setting a new strategic direction. When members of the organization are given information that helps them to understand the new direction (needs connected to benefits), they are more likely to buy in and be motivated to implement the required changes.
> - Description of the organization's strategic plan, including at least the following:
>   - A summary statement of the organization's strategy. This statement should be developed to be in step with the planning horizon customarily used in the organization, that is, three to five years—give or take. It should include the description of high-impact strategic initiatives in broad and general terms. These descriptions set the stage for developing well-defined strategic initiatives that are to be introduced during the next annual budget cycle.
>   - Significant strategic outcomes. There must be some salient, easily identified outcomes that further rein-

> **Table 5.2: Suggested Format and Content of the Two-Phase Strategic Plan (continued)**
>
> force the need for and desirability of the new strategies. These need to be highlighted.
>
> - Deployment of the organization strategy. The objective of describing strategy deployment is to convey a sense of how the strategy cascades into the functional areas on a long-range basis. It does this without going into the detailed organization and management of each key result area and related strategic initiatives—that is the function of the strategic operating plan. In the strategic plan the longer-term options are still subject to continued consideration with some being significantly modified as near-term events and trends unfold.
> - Identification of strategic initiatives that are to be implemented in the next annual operating plan. These initiatives will become components of the strategic operating plan considered in Step 11. This is the pivotal link between strategic planning and implementation, that is, to make the transition explicit in terms of the strategic initiatives that are to be executed.
> - Scope and nature of the implementation program. Every significant activity requires an estimate of the nature and scope of the actions to be taken in order to develop a feasible implementation program. Therefore attention to the following factors is advised:
>   - The risks, uncertainties, and potential obstacles that might delay or otherwise impede the implementation process

> **Table 5.2: Suggested Format and Content of the Two-Phase Strategic Plan (continued)**
>
> - ○ The amount of training and education that is required; learning curve estimates for new activities are not always accurate
> - ○ Resources that need to be acquired; delays and shortages are commonplace
> - ○ Resistance, even opposition, that is likely to occur
> - ○ The time it takes to reach expected returns on the investments made
> - ○ New (to the organization) implementation processes that are not easy to estimate
>
> - These and related factors need to be taken into account in order to establish a feasible and cost-effective implementation program. The difficulty is that these estimates have to be made at the outset when the necessary information is often not available. Nevertheless, an effort is required to make as careful a set of estimates as possible to help offset the all too common tendency to attempt to do too much ineffectively and/or inefficiently. Taking these factors into account helps avoid overcommitment and underachievement.

Obtain management feedback, revisions, approval, and authorization to continue

The level of top management commitment to and involvement in the strategic management process does not obviate the need for a formal approval process. Once the strategic management team has finalized a two-phased plan, it needs the approval

Strategy in the 21st Century

of the board, leadership, and/or executives assigned strategic management responsibilities.

At this point, the approval process has the following objectives:

- To ensure that *all* members of leadership that are included in the strategic planning process have reviewed the plan and have made suggestions for additions, modifications, and/or deletions
- To ensure that the members of leadership that are responsible for approving plans, authorizing expenditures, and acquiring resources have reviewed and approved the plan
- To provide for revision of the plan until all suggestions have been considered and either accepted, modified, or rejected

This approval process does not entail a detailed budget review, nor should it be viewed as a request for funds and other resources. It is a time to ensure that the plan has leadership approval to proceed to the next stage of planning, that is, detailed implementation planning that will include budgeting, scheduling, and requests for the acquisition of resources and staffing.

Produce an illustrative strategic plan

Table 5.3 provides a fictitious strategic plan for the National Food Service Association (see Table 4.16 on pp. 172–173).

Chapter 5

> **Table 5.3: Sample Strategic Plan for the National Food Service Association**
>
> - **Analysis of current plan.** The existing National Food Service Association plan has been highly effective in terms of providing high quality education and training offerings. Unfortunately these standard offerings have not generated sufficient financial returns to support the ongoing operational needs of the association.
> - **Rationale for new strategic plan.** Moving forward we believe additional value can be added to member organizations by offering new products and services that will enable critically needed stability and expansion of the workforce. Additionally, strategies outlined below will result in significantly greater financial returns to support the broader set of strategic needs of the industry. By expanding our distribution network both domestically and internationally, the association will be well-positioned to meet the needs of U.S. members while providing a leadership role at the global level.
> - **Shared Vision.** In 2012 National Food Service Association enables an educated and trained workforce with management bench strength for the future.
>
>   The NFSA has grown to become the industry leader in education solutions for equipment safety, responsible service delivery, and workforce development, generating $80M annually. We leverage an extensive network of industry relationships to outdistance all competitors and have extended our reach to multiple international locations. The NFSA makes a real difference by delivering meaningful products and services meeting the highest quality standards. Adherence to

Table 5.3: Sample Strategic Plan for the National Food Service Association (continued)

core values has resulted in outstanding employee satisfaction, customer satisfaction, and profitability.
- **Mission.** Protect and grow the food service industry through workforce development certification, education, and training.
- **Values.** We exist to serve the food service industry and, in doing so, hold to and are guided by the following values:
    - Our team—Committed to each other, passionate about our mission, celebrating our successes, and balanced between work and life
    - The way we work—Professionalism and mutual respect for each other
    - Ethics—Honesty, integrity, and a strong belief in doing what's right leads us to intelligently and constructively disagree
    - Customer satisfaction—Listening, understanding, and striving to meet the customers' needs
    - Financial viability—We make and keep our commitments toward growth and self-sustainability
- **Policies.**
    - We will pursue international opportunities in support of our domestic customers.
    - We will finance growth through reinvesting operating margins and sharing risk.
- **Goals.**
    - Protect and grow the core business.
    - Position and invest for the future.

Chapter 5

Table 5.3: Sample Strategic Plan for the National Food Service Association (continued)

- **Core and Support Strategies (for Goal 1)**

Key Result Area	Core *(italic)* and Support Strategies	Format	Previous	Current	Next	Future
			\multicolumn{4}{c}{Planning periods (by year(s) and quarters) X = One Quarter}			
External						
Market / Product Mix	*Market Penetration*	Project	XXXX	XXXX	XXXX	
	Market Development	Committee			XX	XXXX
Suppliers	*Partner*	Project	X	XXXX	XXXX	XXXX
Internal						
People	Invest	Team	XXXX	XXXX	XXXX	XXXX
	Define roles and responsibilities	Project		XX	XX	
Product Development	Blended approach	Team		XXXX	XXXX	
Customer Service	*Streamline*	Project	XXXX	XX		
Marketing	*Distribution Network*	Project	XXXX		XX	XXXX
	R&D Alliance	Committee				XXXX
Finance	Reinvest earnings	Committee	XXXX	XXXX	XXXX	XXXX
	Share risk	Team			XXXX	XXXX

- **Deployment and expected outcomes.** Deployment of these strategies will occur incrementally over the next

> **Table 5.3: Sample Strategic Plan for the National Food Service Association (continued)**
>
> three years. Expected outcomes include a 30 percent increase in staff retention at the local member level and a 25 percent increase in net revenue.
> - **Contingency plans.** A critical assumption driving this plan is that the US economy does not slip into a lengthy recession. It is likely that efforts and costs will also be curtailed regarding development of our planned research and development network. If a prolonged recession were to occur, additional efforts will be made to expand our online training offerings. Online offerings will enable member organizations to continue training their workforce without occurring additional travel costs and loss of productivity.
> - **Budget Estimates.** Incremental new investments are required to execute the full range of strategies proposed range between $2MM and $3MM.

STEP 11: DEVELOP A STRATEGIC OPERATING PLAN (SOP)

In many situations it can be difficult to translate the strategic plan into an effective strategic "operating" plan. Often times a gap develops between the intended strategic direction and strategies as they come down from the top of the organization *and* the level of employee understanding of how their daily activities contribute to achieving the vision. This gap appears almost by necessity because a strategic plan is, by its nature, a series of long-term goals and strategies, while most managers are trained to gauge their progress by assessing achievement in meeting operations level "here and now" demands and deliverables.

Translating the big picture to everyday operational activities has been the desired end result of strategic planning from its earliest manifestation on the corporate scene. To front-line workers, the corporate strategy can seem highly irrelevant to their daily existence. Their sense of disconnection and powerlessness to affect the outcome can be overwhelming. They often feel, "Why should this matter to me? Success at the top never reaches us down here." *To avoid this problem, careful attention must be placed on development of a practical strategic operating plan.*

The strategic operating plan is the physical manifestation of strategy formulation converging with implementation. It is a set of marching orders detailing exactly *what* will have to be done to transform selected and approved strategies into operating activities with measurable results during the annual budgeting and operating cycle.

The strategic operating plan's development/work steps are:

- Identify implementation planning guidelines
- Define accountability linkages between the strategic plan and the strategic operating plan
- Identify strategic objectives in core functions
- Develop a strategy deployment map for each goal
- Identify management roles and responsibilities necessary to implement the strategic operating plan
- Develop implementation plans for strategic objectives
- Develop implementation plans for strategic objectives requiring nonproject formats
- Reconcile strategic operating plan requirements with available implementation capabilities and resources
- Write a summary implementation plan

Strategy in the 21st Century

- Obtain management approval/authorization of the strategic operating plan
- Distribute and communicate the strategic operating plan

Identify implementation planning guidelines

Much time and effort has been invested by the organization and its leadership team up to this point in the strategic management process. Before going any further, it is important to recognize that much of the potential return on the work already done can be lost in translation, as the process moves from the strategic planning phase and into the implementation phase. Stories abound about professionally facilitated planning processes resulting in slick four-color, beautifully wordsmithed calls to arms that never get implemented. Too often plans are approved then molder in limbo waiting for the day when "best intentions" meet "when things slow down" —usually when the next strategic planning process begins. Such an experience does great damage to the organization's collective psyche, ratcheting up the level of employee cynicism about the value of strategic planning.

Another frequent pain-point occurs when those charged with implementing the strategy do not understand how their day-to-day works supports the overall strategy. Again, confusion occurs, and the strategic management capacity of the organization is undermined.

To avoid pitfalls leaders and managers will face here, it is worthwhile to remind ourselves of some "golden oldie" universal truths to implementation management. These basic management principles have stood the test of time and are good to revisit anytime strategy implementation takes center stage.

Table 5.4 summarizes some of the most important and effective implementation guidelines.

Table 5.4: Effective Implementation Guidelines

- **Guideline 1: Strategic Operational Planning**
    - Focus on no more than two major organization goals to begin the implementation planning process. Detailed implementation planning will be based on more than two goals in most cases and will expand the requirements and demands on management and staff beyond initial considerations.
    - Evaluate strategies initiated in previous planning periods before continuing them into the current planning period.
    - Select projects to implement that deploy across all core functions, contribute to the development of those functions, and contribute significantly to goal attainment.
    - If this is the first major strategic planning effort in the organization, carefully select the tactics and key strategic projects that have the greatest observable benefit to the organization.
- **Guideline 2: Organization**
    - Provide an appropriate format and structure for each strategy. Remember, every strategy is not a project.
    - Deploy that structure in the core functions of the organizations.
    - Make explicit any external relationships required for a given strategy.
- **Guideline 3: Operations**
    - Develop implementation procedures and tactics required to implement a given strategy.

Table 5.4: Effective Implementation Guidelines (continued)

- Clarify relationships between ongoing operations and strategic implementation activities.

- **Guideline 4: Management Systems**
Provide efficient management systems for the implementation plan, including:
    - Performance monitoring, measurement, evaluation, and control.
    - Engagement of subject matter expertise as required.
    - Scheduling, milestones, assignment of personnel.
    - Acquisition and allocation of resources.
    - Budgetary controls, approvals, authorizations, and top management oversight.

- **Guideline 5: Staffing**
Select the people who have the ability to do the job and:
    - Confirm that they clearly understand what you expect and let them know you sincerely believe in their ability to carry out the task.
    - Negotiate a deadline and secure commitment that they will follow through.
    - Provide latitude for them to use their own imagination and initiative.
    - Let each know in the beginning you will follow up and then do it.
    - Don't do the job for them.
    - Recognize and reward them commensurably with the results they produce.

Table 5.4: Effective Implementation Guidelines (continued)

- Include implementation and change management responsibilities in job descriptions and performance evaluations.
- Assign nonmanagement personnel to implementation tasks to broaden the implementation effort and develop interest in the plan and its success.
- Ensure that the required personnel are made available for new/revised strategies being implemented, as necessary through recruitment, promotion, transfer, training, job restructuring, and/or assignment/reassignment of duties.

- **Guideline 6: Management**
  - Explain the importance of the strategic plan and sustain interest in its implementation.
  - Assign and align roles and responsibilities at all management levels that are required to implement a given strategy.
  - Obtain leadership approval of the implementation plan and its budget.
  - Communicate the implementation plan to members of the organization and relevant stakeholders.

- **Guideline 7: Resources**
  - Provide for the acquisition and allocation of required resources.
  - Ensure the efficient and effective utilization of resources.

> **Table 5.4: Effective Implementation Guidelines (continued)**
>
> ○ Provide for the development and upgrading of current resources as a consequence of introducing new strategies and resultant operations.
>
> - **Guideline 8: Report and Documentation**
>
>   ○ Record the significant events, problems encountered and solved, barriers overcome, and suggestions for future implementation processes.
>   ○ Record this experience in a way to facilitate the development of effective implementation processes.

Define accountability linkages between the longer-term strategic plan and a strategic operating plan

Defining the functional linkages between the longer-term strategic plan and the nearer-term strategic operating plan is the fundamental requirement to move from the state of planning into the state of implementation. Once these relationships are clearly communicated, it enables operational alignments to develop into final form and eventually occur.

The majority of strategies are implemented by people working in one or more core organizational functions or teams, that is, finance, marketing, sales, operations, information technology, and human resources. Managers of these core functions have a critical role to play in leading their own internal, and often cross-functional teams, during the execution phase of the strategic management process. Figure 5.2 defines these core functional linkages for our continuing case study.

Figure 5.2: Strategic Plan with Functional Linkages for One Goal

Goal - Protect and grow the core business

Key Result Area	Core *(italic)* and Support Strategies	Functional Linkage – Format	Previous	Current	Next	Future
			Planning periods (by year(s) and quarters) X = One Quarter			
External						
Market / Product Mix	*Market Penetration*	Marketing & Sales – Projects	XXXX	XXXX	XXXX	
	Market Development	Marketing – Committee			XX	XXXX
Suppliers	Partner	Finance & Operations as a policy – Team	X	XXXX	XXXX	XXXX
Internal						
People	Invest	Human Resources – Team	XXXX	XXXX	XXXX	XXXX
	Define roles and responsibilities	Operations – Project		XX	XX	
Product Development	Blended approach	Operations – Team			XXXX	XXXX
Customer Service	*Streamline*	Operations – Project	XXXX	XX		
Marketing	*Distribution Network*	Marketing – Project	XXXX		XX	XXXX

Strategy in the 21st Century

Figure 5.2: Strategic Plan with Functional Linkages for One Goal (continued)
Goal - Protect and grow the core business

Key Result Area	Core and Support Strategies	Functional Linkage – Format	Previous	Current	Next	Future
			\multicolumn{4}{c}{Planning periods (by year(s) and quarters) X = One Quarter}			
Internal (continued)						
	R&D Alliance	Marketing – Committee				
Finance	Reinvest earnings	Finance as a policy – Team	XXXX	XXXX	XXXX	
	Share risk	Finance as a policy – Team				XXXX

Norton and Kaplan (1992, 1996) were among the first to recognize the need to define carefully the relationship/dynamics between strategy and operations. They helped us understand the importance of executing the overall organizational strategy through a balanced operational approach. Norton and Kaplan's "Balanced Scorecard" methodology (See Figure 5.3) specifies four strategic perspectives leadership teams must consider when building the bridge between the strategic plan and the strategic operating plan. They include the financial, customer, internal business, and learning and growth perspectives.

In each perspective, the leadership team must define one or more strategic objectives, performance indicators, targets, and initiatives (projects) to construct a Balanced Scorecard.

A fundamental premise of the Balanced Scorecard (BSC) is that the four perspectives are linked in a synergistic or "cause

Chapter 5

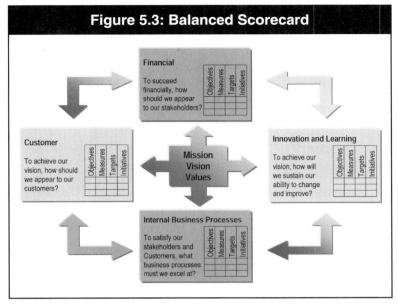

Reprinted by permission of Harvard Business School Press. From *The Balanced Scorecard: Translating Strategy into Action* by Robert S. Kaplan, David S. Norton/Hollis Heimbouch, Carol Franco. Boston, MA 1996, pp 8-9. Copyright © 1996 by the Harvard Business School Publishing Corporation; all rights reserved.

and effect" manner. Financial objectives are desired outcomes that have all too often led to a myopic and short-term focus almost exclusively on financial performance. They need to be supplemented by the three other perspectives, which are performance drivers that lead to financial results.

The customer focus drives examination of the business processes that need to be developed to meet customer needs. This, in turn, drives a need to improve current processes and many times drives identification of new required processes. These processes then drive management and staff to learn and grow with a new emphasis on innovation.

It is not necessary to accept the four perspectives as the only way to link the strategic plan and the strategic operating plan. For example, a case can be made for information technology as a separate integrating perspective. In nonprofit and govern-

Strategy in the 21st Century

mental organizations the "mission perspective" is often considered separately.

Table 5.5 compares the Balanced Scorecard model to a functional model for building a bridge between the two plans. Note the essential equivalent nature and logic of the two approaches.

Table 5.5: Comparison of Balanced Scorecard Model to a Traditional Functional Approach

Balanced Scorecard Approach	Traditional Functional Approach
Financial Perspective	Finance Function
	Sales Function
Customer Perspective	Marketing Function
Internal Business Perspective	Operations Function
	Information Technology Function
Learning & Growth Perspective	Human Resource Function

Whether an organization employs the four basic perspectives of the Balanced Scorecard, modifies the perspectives, or uses a traditional functional approach is not the key issue. The critical point is to link and align organization level goals and strategies with a "balanced" set of operational objectives rather than maintaining a singular focus on financial outcomes.

Throughout the remainder of Step 11 we will examine a functional approach to building the strategic operating plan. In subsequent steps, as relevant, the Balanced Scorecard methodology will be included.

Chapter 5

Identify strategic objectives in core functions

Essentially leadership teams must answer five basic questions for each strategic goal in order to begin the process of linking and translating the organizational strategy into operational objectives, metrics, projects, and assignments.

Table 5.6 summarizes the key questions to ask and answer to link and to translate strategy into operational objectives.

> **Table 5.6: Questions to Ask and Answer in Translating Strategy into Operational Objectives**
>
> - *Finance Function.* What are the desired financial outcomes we must achieve to satisfy our stockholders and other key stakeholders?
> - *Marketing Function.* What customer needs, desires, and expectations must we meet in order to meet our financial expectations?
> - *Operations Function.* Where must we improve internal operations to satisfy our customers and meet our financial expectations?
> - *Information Technology Function.* Where must we improve our use of information technology to strengthen operations, satisfy customers, and meet our financial expectations?
> - *Human Resource Function.* Where must we learn and grow as people and as a team to operate efficiently, satisfy customers, and meet our financial expectations?

The answers to these base questions become the primary drivers of the strategic operating plan. The leadership team should carefully consider each question and document the results. After each question has been answered for each goal, answers should be restated as clear and concise strategic objectives.

When writing strategic objectives, careful attention must be placed on stating them correctly. *Strategic Objectives should always be stated as outcomes and not as activities.* Only when objectives are stated as outcomes do they provide a stable foundation for execution of the strategic operating plan. While objectives evolve over time, they should resist being easily changed. An operating plan needs to be stable and understood by all. At this point in building a strategic operating plan emphasis should not be placed on creating measurable and quantifiable objectives. This occurs later in the process.

Table 5.7 presents a balanced set of objectives for one strategic goal covering each of five core functions outlined above.

Table 5.7: Sample Set of Balanced Objectives

Goal : Protect and grow the core business

Finance Objectives:

- Exceed top line revenues
- Exceed bottom line revenues over expenses
- Reduce total expenses
- Improve customer loyalty year after year

Marketing Objectives:

- Deliver up-to-date, relevant, and effective standard offerings that meet customer expectations
- Provide integrated customer information and performance analysis
- Enhance instructor quality

> **Table 5.7: Sample Set of Balanced Objectives (continued)**
>
> *Operations Objectives:*
>
> - Establish and maintain a customer-centric prospect to order, fulfillment, and customer service process
> - Manage effectively and improve the product management and decision making processes
> - Improve overall effectiveness and efficiency of the sales and customer relationship management processes
> - Develop relevant, effective, and accurate content based on sound science, best industry practice, and law
> - Enhance intellectual property protection, customer privacy, and exam security
>
> *Information Technology Objective:*
>
> - Provide innovative, flexible, and stable IT services
>
> *Human Resource Objective:*
>
> - Cultivate and retain a highly competent and motivated staff

Develop a strategy deployment map for each goal

A strategy deployment map is a graphic representation of the cause and effect relationships among strategic objectives linked to one particular goal. Developing a deployment map at this point provides the strategic management team an effective and simple means of checking for imbalances and/or ineffective

Strategy in the 21st Century

linkages among the strategic objectives. It also provides management with a summary view of the integrations taking shape within the implementation plan.

A strategy deployment map highlights cause and effect relationships among key business objectives. It is a highly effective tool in facilitating internal communications regarding the strategic operating plan and serves as a significant first step toward aligning the work force behind the plan.

A deployment map as depicted in Figure 5.4 portrays the process of translating one particular goal into a balanced set of objectives across each strategic function with cause and effect relationships identified between objectives.

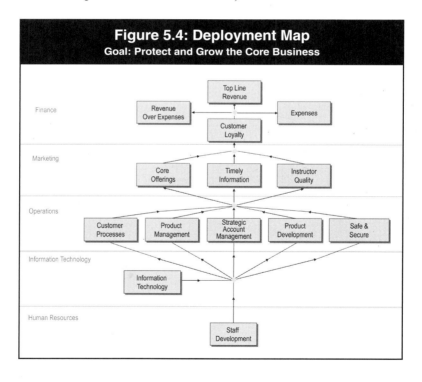

Chapter 5

Identify management roles and responsibilities necessary to implement the SOP

It is vitally important for the senior leadership team to be transparent regarding what specific leader has *authority and responsibility* for each component of the strategy and the strategic operating plan. Unless roles and responsibilities are clearly defined, implementation will falter and expected outcomes will not be achieved.

- At the *strategy level* a single individual should be identified to hold overall authority and responsibility for executing each strategy. This individual will likely be a member of the leadership team and will be responsible for management oversight of a given strategy but not necessarily for the tactics or projects employed within a strategy.
- At the *objective level* a single individual should be identified to hold overall authority and responsibility for the attainment of a particular strategic objective. This individual will likely be a member of the senior leadership team.
- At the *project level* a single individual should be identified to hold overall authority and responsibility for executing a given strategic project. This individual will not necessarily be a member of the leadership team but will be someone who has the commitment level and resources to appropriately execute a particular project.

In Chapter 6 these roles and responsibilities will be described in detail. At this point, the objective is to include the specific assignments of individuals in the implementation of the strategic operating plan.

Develop implementation plans for strategic objectives

The actual implementation of a strategic operating plan works best when all levels of the leadership team work together to further *translate* high-level goal statements by defining key performance indicators for each strategic objective. A key performance indicator (KPI) is a measure for which the organization has data that help quantify the achievement of a desired strategic objective. Key performance indicators give an "indication" as to whether a particular objective is being achieved *and* help to answer the question: "How would we know if we achieve the expected result?"

Workers in any organization must be able to translate the high-sounding phrases of the strategic plan into everyday talk. Once the entire team equates the goals, strategies, and objectives of the plan with measurable key performance indicators containing specific targets, the abstract notion of strategy is replaced with a clear understanding of deliverables and the challenge they provide.

Effective use of key performance indicators to evaluate the soundness of the strategic direction is a necessity for well-run organizations in today's tumultuous global economy. It is necessary to maintain a reliable stream of performance information to assess the effectiveness of the current strategic operating plan and to drive development of the next generation of relevant objectives to pursue. Chris Argyris (1993) has described this process as *double-loop learning*—learning that changes people's assumptions and, therefore, their responses.

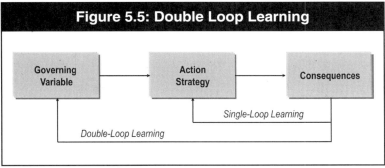

From *Knowledge for Action: A guide to overcoming barriers to organization change* by Chris Argyris. Reprinted by permission of John Wiley & Sons, Inc., Global Rights Department.

Ultimately, a balanced set of key performance indicators provides feedback regarding the validity of the hypotheses that underlie the strategic outlook. Responses predicted at the beginning of the strategy formulation process are continually checked for validity each time a performance measurement is conducted. When new learning occurs, necessary changes are made at the strategic and operational levels of the organization.

An effective strategic operating plan requires development of performance indicators, targets for each indicator, and alignment of strategic initiatives/projects to accomplish the targeted performance level and therefore achieve the objective. Below is a set of four tasks to guide this process.

1. Identify key performance indicators for each objective and build an effective performance measure for each indicator.

Every leadership team would love to discover the "silver bullet" of performance measurement, that is, a single miracle indicator that, closely monitored, would signal to the organization they are on track to faster growth and unparalleled success. Unfortunately this scenario is the stuff of fantasy. No indicator alone can predict future results for an entire organization.

Today's business environment demands a balanced approach to performance measurement, one that employs a blend of indicators focused on where the organization is measured in comparison to where it wants to be. Performance indicators should be established for dual tracking of internal performance, such as operations and training, and external performance focused in the areas of customer satisfaction, sales, and market share.

Organizations that use a balanced approach to performance measurement are moving to influence their external and internal environments. Those that do not will spend more time reacting to unforeseen "events" in their operating environment—moving from firefight to firefight.

An effective technique for developing acceptable indicators is to engage the broader involvement of team members in the development process. Questions to answer when evaluating a potential indicator are as follows:

- Is the indicator *valid*?
  - Does it truly measure what it should, which is accomplishment of the objective?
- Is the indictor *valuable*?
  - Will it help the leadership team better understand what is truly happening?
  - Will it enable the leadership to steer through the ups and downs of the business cycle that every organization experiences?
- Is the indicator *easy* to track?
  - Do the data already exist, or would it require a gargantuan or expensive effort to track the information?
- Does the indicator hold the team to an appropriate level of *accountability*?

- Does the indicator *communicate* a positive message to the team? (for example, staff retention sends a positive message to the work force versus staff turnover, which sends a negative message)?
- Is it *a leading or lagging* indicator?
  - Does it help predict in advance a desired organizational outcome by providing some leading indication or does it lag behind, simply reporting on outcomes after the fact?

Ideally, a strategic management system is best served when it includes a balanced set of leading and lagging indicators. Leading indicators will likely be discovered in the human resource, information technology, and operations functions as milestones are reached in tactical efforts and process improvements are initiated. Lagging indicators will likely be discovered in the marketing, sales, and finance functions once results are measured and numbers become available.

Figure 5.6 illustrates a practical and effective exercise a planning team can complete to help identify performance indicators by doing the following:

- Step 1: Brainstorm a targeted set of potential indicators for each strategic objective included in the strategic operating plan.
- Step 2: Rank each indicator from 1 (Low) to 5 (High) for A–F.
- Step 3: Assign a priority based on the team's consensus.
- Step 4: Select those vital few indicators that best fit the situation.

Figure 5.6: Performance Measurement Exercise
**Sample Human Resource Management Objective:
Cultivate and retain a highly competent and motivated staff**

Potential Indicators	A Valid	B Value	C Ease	D Accountable	E Communicate	F Lead/Lag	Final Rank
On time delivery	4	4	2	4	4	5	3
Overtime	3	4	5	4	3	4	4
Employee Satisfaction	5	5	3	5	5	5	1
Margins	3	5	5	5	5	2	6
Employee Retention	4	4	4	5	5	4	2
Sales Lead to Close Ratio	3	4	4	3	4	5	5

2. Construct a performance measure for each indicator.

Working with the leadership team, final selection of key performance indicators should be made and at least one complete performance measure constructed for each indicator. Information required to construct a performance measure includes the following:

- Formula for calculating the indicator.
- Source of variable level information. *A variable is a quantity that may take on any of a set of values, for example, total number of customers served in one year.*
- Baseline information on every variable included in the formula. *A baseline is the organization's actual performance for the most recent reporting period.*
- External benchmark information(if available). *A bench-*

mark is an external comparison point, for example, an industry-wide statistic.
- Reporting frequency.
- Data collection and reporting responsibility.
- Acceptable targets or target ranges for each indicator. *A target is the specific performance level the organization seeks for a particular indicator.*

Figure 5.7 provides a sample performance measure.

Figure 5.7: Sample Performance Measure

Function:	Human Resource Management
Objective:	Cultivate and retain a highly competent and motivated staff
KPI:	Employee retention rate
Baseline:	70% of employees remain 5 years or more
Benchmark:	60% = industry standard
Target:	**85% retention rate by 12/31/__**
Formula:	(B/A) * 100
Responsibility:	VP Human Resource Management

Variable	Data Source	Baseline	Target	Actual
Variable A = # Employees	HRM Report	100	102	98
Variable B = # Employed >= 5 yrs	HRM Report	70	86	71

Table 5.8 presents a sample goal, partial set of objectives, key performance indicators, and targets.

3. Define tactical guidelines.

Within the scope of strategic management, the term *tactics* refers to the means by which a strategy is carried out to achieve

Table 5.8: Sample Set of KPIs with Targets

Goal : Protect and grow the core business

Finance Objective:

- Exceed top line revenues over expenses
  - KPI = Profit per customer
  - **Target = 32%**

Marketing Objective:

- Deliver up-to-date, relevant, and effective standard offerings that meet customer expectations
  - KPI = Percent repeat business
  - **Target = 40%**

Operations Objective:

- Establish and maintain a customer-centric prospect to order, fulfillment, and customer service process
  - KPI = Average cycle time from order to delivery
  - **Target = 72 hours**

Information Technology Objective:

- Provide innovative, flexible, and stable IT services
  - KPI = Employee satisfaction rating with IT services
  - **Target = 90%**

Human Resource Objective:

- Cultivate and retain a highly competent and motivated staff
  - KPI = Percent staff retention
  - **Target = 85%**

a particular goal. In the military, *tactics* refers to maneuvering forces in combat. This process requires adjustments that must be made immediately in response to changing conditions and unexpected events. As a result, tactical decisions and adjustments in war are left in the hands of battlefield commanders at the scene of combat.

The concept of *tactics* applies equally well to organizations that have deployed a strategy into the organization's core functions, and the desired objectives must be coordinated in and amongst core functions. In short, tactics refer to *how* to use the means available to carry out a strategy. However, top management is usually more concerned with strategic outcomes, that is, *what* needs to be accomplished. As a consequence, tactical guidelines are easily overlooked.

This does not mean tactics need to be fully detailed in the implementation plan; this is simply not practical. It does mean that tactical considerations must be accounted for while making plans to implement strategic objectives. Doing this helps to ensure achievement of the expected results.

The following considerations regarding tactics are useful in this regard:

- If implementing a strategic objective is going to need significant tactical decision making, ensure that either the management team has the required experience or that more experienced management is made available to monitor and coach the implementation team as required.
- While senior management should not be expected to intervene in the day-to-day implementation process, it may provide useful "tactical guidelines," that is, advice, tips, and suggestions on how to go about a particular assignment based on their expertise and/or experience.

- Managers and/or staff from other areas may need to be made available to assist because of their ability to operate in new and difficult situations.
- The more that lower levels of management are included in all stages of the strategy management process, the less there is a need for tactical guidelines. This occurs as lower level managers acquire expertise and experience in strategic management tools and techniques.

4. Identify the tactics for each strategic objective and include them in strategic projects to be executed.

For each objective the responsible objective level manager must work with his or her team to refine the tactics to be used to achieve a particular objective, especially the vital strategic projects to be launched in the upcoming periods. Below is the continuing case study including sample strategic projects for each objective.

Table 5.9 demonstrates how high-level strategies are integrated into the SOP.

> **Table 5.9: Sample Strategic Operating Plan with Projects**
>
> **Goal : Protect and grow the core business**
>
> *Finance Objective:*
>
> - Exceed top line revenues over expenses
>   - KPI = Profit per customer
>   - Target = 32%
>   - **Project 1: Launch "Go deeper, Go faster" program**
>   - **Project 2: Build a distribution network**
>
> *Marketing Objective:*
>
> - Deliver up-to-date, relevant, and effective standard offerings that meet customer expectations
>   - KPI = Percent repeat business
>   - Target = 40%
>   - **Project 1: Design and execute a formal product management process**
>
> *Operations Objective:*
>
> - Establish and maintain a customer-centric prospect to order, fulfillment, and customer service process
>   - KPI = Average cycle time from order to delivery
>   - Target = 72 hours
>   - **Project 1: Define roles and responsibilities across functions**
>   - **Project 2: Steamline the customer service process**

> **Table 5.9: Sample Strategic Operating Plan with Projects (continued)**
>
> *Information Technology Objective:*
>
> - Provide innovative, flexible, and stable IT services
>   - KPI = Employee satisfaction rating
>   - Target = 90%
>   - **Project 1: Outsource internal technical support and training**
>   - **Project 2: Build a robust internal IT team focused on new product development**
>
> *Human Resource Objective:*
>
> - Cultivate and retain a highly competent and motivated staff
>   - KPI = Percent staff retention
>   - Target = 85%
>   - **Project 1: Launch a formal internal mentoring program**

Develop implementation plans for strategic objectives in nonproject formats

While new strategies are most often developed using the tools and concepts of project management, as indicated in the preceding section, there are many strategies that are best initiated in other organizational formats. Table 5.10 summarizes useful strategic implementation formats.

These formats facilitate the planning process by helping determine the most appropriate approach to be used so strategies are not automatically organized as projects. Many strategies

Table 5.10: Useful Strategic Implementation Formats

- ***Projects.*** In general, project management is most effective and efficient when outcomes include a degree of risk and uncertainty; the assignment is complex, multifunctional, multidisciplined, and long-run; and where outcomes are new, even unique. As such, this constitutes unprogrammed activities and new challenges for the personnel involved.

  Therefore, project management should only be used for those strategic initiatives where it can be justified. Too many organizations have attempted to use project management for increasingly smaller in scale assignments. This is ineffective and inefficient in most cases, since much simpler organization and management techniques are available for the purposes of strategic management.

- ***Committee assignments.*** In spite of the many criticisms of committees, they serve an important purpose in organizations, since they can maintain long-term surveillance over a wide variety of trends, concerns, and policies that need continuous monitoring, evaluation, interpretation, and feedback and provide important advice to leadership. In strategic management there are many activities of this nature, especially those that require long-term, incremental change.

  The work of a committee is not the type of work easily translated into key performance indicators to be measured and tracked on a dashboard. A committee is a more subtle and important asset to the strategic

Table 5.10: Useful Strategic Implementation Formats (continued)

thinking processes that experienced planners are doing continuously.

Strategy seldom comes in an epiphany; quite the opposite is true—strategies are much more likely to emerge incrementally from current practice. The value of systematic strategic management is to recognize these strategies in their emergent state and to foster the development of those that are the most promising. For example, an organization that is considering entering international markets might assign a committee to investigate the necessary policies, problems, and prospects of moving the organization in this direction. This may not be a move that can be accomplished in a given budget year. Nevertheless, if the organization is considering a move in this direction, a committee assignment could be the right strategic format for this initiative. In the future this low-cost investment in a committee study could lead to a major strategic project.

Special support should be given to these committees, as they provide a primary input into the organization's strategic information system.

- *Team assignments.* Team assignments refer to activities that management has decided to initiate on an exploratory and limited basis before approving a full-scale project. This intermediate step should be used in those situations where the outcomes and/or means of achieving them are in the early stages of development, but at the same time the benefits and competitive advantages

> **Table 5.10: Useful Strategic Implementation Formats (continued)**
>
> accruing to early adopters will more than offset the risks. These are action-oriented activities, as opposed to the deliberative and advisory nature of committee assignments.
> - ***External contracts.*** Securing external assistance from an experienced consultant may be the best course of action for undertaking assignments that are outside the expertise and experience available within the organization. Even when an organization has developed an advanced strategic management system and the competencies required to use it, organizations still find it useful to get outside advice and counsel.
> - ***Individual assignments.*** At times, a strategy requires additional study, analysis, research, or simply more information before leadership will approve it and commit to its implementation. These assignments are usually low-cost and can be assigned to an individual within the organization without interfering with on-going activities.

are not ready for immediate implementation in the next operating cycle—a primary requirement of strategies organized in a project format. They require further analysis, study, deliberation, or consensus building in order to launch a full-blown project. These preparatory activities have a high priority; that is, except for the additional information required, they are strategies that management would like to launch as soon as possible.

Examples follow on the appropriate use of these alternate organizational formats:

- ***Committee assignments.*** With respect to strategic management, and especially strategic thinking, the key strengths of a committee are as follows:
    - To engage in long-term deliberations on key issues and points of disagreement among members of the strategic management team
    - To monitor and evaluate new strategies that management needs and offer recommendations to management
    - To make in-depth analysis and evaluations requiring shared opinions from several core functions
    - To analyze selected costs and benefits that management wants to include in future strategic operating plans but for which sufficient information is not yet currently available

    For example, consider the following situations:
    - An organization is considering expanding its international operations and needs to identify their best options (from their perspective).
    - An organization is considering a new product that has a narrow entry window in the very near future.
    - An organization wants to invest in green technology and reduce its carbon footprint.
    - An organization is considering the impact of plant closures and early retirement plans.
    - An organization is considering outsourcing and offshoring and needs additional information and policies on how to proceed.

Since committee organization, procedures, and reporting systems are well-developed in most organizations, these committee assignments are best made using the organization's established procedures and practices—subject to the following caveats:

- Clearly define the expected outcomes.
- Appoint or have the committee appoint/elect a chairperson.
- Specify committee membership.
- Dissolve the committee as soon as management is satisfied with the outcome(s).
- Require meeting agendas and meeting notes.
- Require reports on a scheduled basis.

- *Team assignments.* A team-based approach is useful for assignments preceding the organization of a strategic project because teams can:
    - Be easily created and terminated
    - Be highly focused on specific outcomes
    - Be *either analytic or action-oriented*
    - Be highly creative and, depending on the desired outcomes, innovative
    - Develop a high level of synergy in developing and evaluating a concept or test approach

  For example, consider the following situations:
    - An organization wants to launch a test market study for a new product or service before launching a full-scale operation.
    - An organization wants a focus group to explore some aspect of a new strategy before committing to a full-scale project.

- An organization wants to test a new approach to customer service with a few established customers before ramping up to a new strategic approach in a given product line.
- An organization wants to interview several subject matter experts in diverse areas of subject matter expertise.
- An organization wants to explore the impact of a strategy in several core functions of the organization that will be impacted by a new cross-functional strategy that management wants to implement in the near future. Currently, there is not enough experience with the strategy, and management wants as much additional information as possible, including opinions in each core function impacted.

- ***External contracts.*** Often organizations plan to embark on a particular course of action but lack a key piece of information or set of opinions before committing to a significant effort that requires a project organization format. Outside resources should be limited to the following types of situations.

  - The necessary experience and expertise does not exist inside the organization at the current time, and it is premature to think of adding in the next operating cycle.
  - Outside resource use is classified as a potential long-term planning alternative rather than referenced in the strategic operating plan. The expertise included in the concept should include the judgment, opinion, and counsel of the experts identified in the contract. Ordinarily, it is advisable to use only senior personnel, in cases requiring these personal inputs.
  - Outside expertise and opinion should be limited to specific strategic information for which the organi-

zation has internal counterpart expertise at a level of comprehension sufficient to evaluate the use of the information and/or advice being sought.

Consider the following examples:

- An organization wants to enter the Chinese market and needs information and advice on which of their products is most appropriate to incorporate in a market entry project.
- An organization needs technical information and advice about several new IT systems—other than what they can learn from vendor personnel.
- An organization is considering its first acquisition of a smaller organization operating in a new (to the organization) market.

   Note: These external contracts do not apply to operating projects with significant costs attached to them, for example, a million dollar upgrade in the IT system. This type of project may well have strategic impact and implications for new strategic alternatives. However, this occurs as a byproduct and not necessarily in the domain of the strategic management team.

- *Individual assignments.* Some assignments are most effectively and efficiently done by individuals who have the required combination of experience, expertise, and knowledge of the organization and its strengths and weaknesses, such as in the following situations:
  - The assignment is very focused and any opinions included by the individual are clearly identified and usually optional in nature, since the individual's report should be submitted to the strategic management team for review and evaluation.

- The individual can make the analysis more efficiently and economically than a team or committee.
- The assignment can be limited to one core function, management discipline, or knowledge area.
- The individual can complete the assignment with minimal supervision.
- Inputs required from other individuals can be limited to information gathered from interviewees and included in study outcomes.
- Individuals making these analyses/studies can be allotted the time and resources to complete these assignments in a timely manner despite their being in demand for other assignments.

Examples include the following:

- Gathering information on specified locations for opening offices in new markets
- Gathering information on competitors regarding products and markets
- Conducting primary research using interviews, questionnaires, opinion surveys, and focus groups on topics eventually requiring projects but for which vital information is still in question
- Conducting secondary research using relevant resources

Note: "Individual assignments" does not mean that only one individual can or should be used on the assignment. The scope and nature of the information being gathered may require several individuals but not as a committee or team. They are simply employees assigned to one individual to accelerate the study.

In summary, it is essential to remember that the primary advantage of these different organizational formats is to facilitate the strategic management process by attending to the myriad of details that require attention *before* initiating a full-scale project. They also serve to keep track of these details and provide a means of addressing them in an organized manner. Lastly, using these alternative organizational formats will contribute greatly to the process of making strategic thinking a continuous process—one organized to reinforce and facilitate strategic planning.

Reconcile requirements of the strategic operating plan with available implementation capabilities and resources

In the course of developing implementation plans for *each* strategy, it is customary to confirm that required personnel and other resources are available. *This is not enough to ensure implementation.* No matter how large or small, every organization has limited resources, and these resources must be allocated carefully. Nothing is gained when resources are allocated "on paper" but, in reality, spread too thin to be effective.

Therefore, it is imperative to determine the *aggregate* implementation requirements to ensure that the appropriate resources will be available. This is an interim step, since it still remains for top management to approve the implementation plan, as discussed below. At that time, top management needs to know that the strategic operating plan, as presented, is feasible and required resources, if approved, will be made available. With this understanding in place they should be able to start.

Determining available resources is an important set of calculations. The implementation requirements for a given strategy naturally compete with the resource expectations for other strategies and with present demands made by ongoing activities in the organization. In fact, these ongoing activities often cause even more competition for the use of some resources.

Once the strategic management team has a realistic comparative estimate of committed versus available resources, then adjustments based on priorities, scheduling, scope, scale, and content modifications can be made. If these estimations are being made for the first time, there will inevitably be miscalculations. In such cases, it is advisable to err on the side of *overestimating* required resources (present demands) and *underestimating* available resources (future needs).

Write a summary implementation budget

In Step 10, we recommended that the strategic management team submit a two-phased strategic plan to management for provisional approval—provisional since only an order of magnitude estimate of the funding required is expected at that stage in planning.

What remains is to submit a detailed request for funding and the approval for the resources, especially staffing, that should be outlined in sufficient detail to permit management to authorize expenditures and the use of resources.

In summary, what is required in this report are the following:

- Any changes made in the strategic operating plan since the two-phase plan was submitted
- A summary of the funds and other required resources, especially staffing
- Summary descriptions, including funding and resource requirements, for each of the implementation plans for each strategic objective in the strategic operating plan

Chapter 5

Obtain management approval and authorization for the summary implementation plan for the strategic operating plan

Once the strategic operating plan is built, the income and expenses associated with the plan must be budgeted and approved by the board, owners, or relevant stakeholders.

As with the strategic plan, each organization will have its own approval process for management decision making. Since the operating plan contains a precise description of the strategic actionable initiatives and projects to be undertaken, it requires top leadership approval, as well as any intermediate levels or approval required by the organization. This approval process needs to be formalized and followed to complete the strategic operating plan process.

In many organizations the team charged with leading the strategic planning process is often separate and potentially removed from the group designated to guide the budgeting and resource allocation process. The budget implementation process is typically focused on a fiscal year of operation while the goals, objectives, and initiatives require years of sustained effort to achieve. Hence, budgets are commonly made up of financial measures that bear little connection to the longer-range focus of the strategic operating plan.

The integrated nature of the strategic operating plan demands that the leadership team work with performance criteria for all four perspectives, not just the financial measures. This naturally forces the comptroller and management team to develop a comprehensive strategic focus in order to analyze, understand, and decide between present and future resource demands and effectively deploy them across the entire strategic operating plan.

By defining the **key drivers** of revenue and profit growth, the strategic operating plan development process permits leaders to become more comfortable committing to aggressive strategic goals. The process also makes it quite obvious which current programs are successfully working toward the agreed-upon financial outcomes and which should be jettisoned. Plan revisions will occur based on budgetary and resource constraints and revisions in authorized funding levels and priorities for their use. Consequently, it may be necessary to make any or all of the following changes in the strategic operating plan:

- Reallocate funds to other strategic objectives *within* a given core function
- Reallocate funds among the strategic objectives in *other* core functions
- Expand the resources available for implementing new organization-level strategies
- Modify the scope of the strategy and/or the strategic objective itself
- Adjust the rate of progress and duration of the new/revised strategies based on management, staff, and other resources available
- Reschedule strategic initiatives and projects as necessary because of funds availability

Distribute and communicate the strategic operating plan

Once the strategic operating plan and supporting budget are approved, careful attention must be placed on developing and then approving a *staff level communications plan*. One of the key challenges for implementing a strategic operating plan is to communicate the intent of the plan with employees and key stakeholders.

Chapter 5

What is to be communicated requires careful preparation because when the messages are disseminated widely, they cannot easily be withdrawn. Effective communications should never be confused with spin. When presenting the case for the plan and detailing any required changes, it is important to give the bad news along with the good, for example, work force restructuring. The entire strategic management process will be undermined by loss of trust if employees lose confidence in the accuracy and honesty of what they are told by senior leadership.

Senior leaders need to deliver messages personally in face-to-face meetings whenever possible. When written information is provided, it should be presented in a manner that reaches all who are impacted, and that means taking into account the specific needs of different groups of employees.

A frequent characteristic of both strategic and operational planning has been an intense burst of initial communication within the organization—then nothing! An important requirement for effective strategic and operational planning is clear and continuous communication—from the top to the bottom of the organization and back up, creating a feedback loop with the organization's most important resource: people.

Active participation of your team in strategy development serves as a powerful internalization process, as employees start to buy into the plan because of their direct involvement in establishing its very content. Ensuring that clear and comprehensive communications is shared and maintained serves to reinforce the team's commitment and energize the members as you move toward implementation.

Comments on the use of project management tools and concepts

The implementation approach emphasized in this book is the creation of a balanced set of objectives and projects with major impacts on strategic direction. Therefore, project management skills and competencies are a required competency for the effective and efficient introduction and management of strategic objectives.

An extensive set of project management tools and concepts has been developed by the Project Management Institute. They are outlined and discussed in their *Guide to the Project Management Body of Knowledge*. Since the 1950s, project management has evolved into a complete management system that has been applied in virtually every industry in a myriad of applications.

Organizations lacking this competency are urged to have key management personnel become certified by the Project Management Institute (http://www.pmi.org). The extent to which a given organization becomes proficient in these tools and concepts depends on the level of development of the organization and the scope, complexity, and multifunctional nature of the strategic and/or operational projects being implemented.

• . • •

The strategic operating plan's implementation process is often undervalued and neglected compared to the planning, managing, and controlling dedicated to ongoing operations. As organizations move into a continuous change mode of operating, implementation skills and change management become valued attributes of all managers and the basis for promotion and career development.

In short, there is a developing body of knowledge that management must acquire that, heretofore, has been neglected. This is the focus of Chapter 6.

CHAPTER 6

Strategy Implementation

Once a strategic operating plan has been developed, it is ready for implementation. Work turns to integrating the strategic operating plan with the ongoing processes of the organization. All developmental steps to this point have been *thought* processes, that is, environmental and contextual analysis and evaluation, creation of alternative strategies and their evaluation and selection, and development of a strategic plan and a corollary actionable strategic operating plan, *but no concentrated action program has yet been initiated.*

The focus now becomes *how* to actually implement the strategic operating plan as a plan of action. Unfortunately, strategic management "implementation" processes are not well covered in the literature as strategy "development" processes are. This gap is perhaps due to the differences in the sources of literature on strategic management, such as the following:

- Strategy development, which focuses on *what* is to be done, is the natural domain of academics, researchers, and high-level consultants whose primary purpose is to help senior management understand and define the "big picture."
- Strategy implementation is the domain of the managers, staff, operational consultants, advisors, and experts en-

meshed in "day-to-day" operations where processes for integration and implementation of strategic plans happen.
- Plan developers tend to focus on generalizations, model building, and theories, while those charged with execution focus on specific techniques and practices to carry out the strategies coming forth from the plan.
- Execution and achievement at the initiative level is easily translated into generic processes and model building. At most, lessons learned manifest as tips, bromides, and partial case descriptions and are usually restricted to success stories. In short, information and insights on results in the implementation area remain fragmented and anecdotal.
- When strategy practitioners do have an interest in generalizing their experience it is proprietary—limited to future use within the organization or with their next client.

Drawing from our real world practice and understanding of the literature, we recognize that implementation proceeds along several dimensions simultaneously. For example, even modest changes in strategy can lead to managerial, operational, cultural, and technical changes at differing rates and levels of resistance requiring different levels of response and adjustment in attitudes and behavior.

For example, strategies that emphasize changes at the technical level pose fewer implementation challenges than do managerial and organizational changes. These, in turn, pose less demanding problems than do cultural changes—the most complex dimension of change and the least amenable to direct intervention.

To leverage existing knowledge and information about implementation, we find it useful to divide the implementation process into two phases. The first phase (Step 12) deals with integrating and aligning the strategic operating plan into current management operating processes and systems.

During the first phase, the primary objective is to prepare management, staff, and the work force, as various subunits of the organization, to understand, manage, and operate accepted strategies and their tactical deployments within each required subunit.

The second phase, or Step 13, pertains to delegating responsibility to line management for strategic processes that will be integrated with ongoing processes that they currently manage at the level of day to day operations. Even though the new strategies may not be fully understood and accepted and the boundary between implementation and ongoing management is not always clearly defined, it is crystal clear that there is an inflexion point where the primary responsibility shifts to the ongoing management of the organization. Identifying this shift in responsibility for implementation is one of the main reasons for dealing with implementation in two distinct, albeit, not easily differentiated steps.

STEP 12: IMPLEMENT THE STRATEGIC OPERATING PLAN

Implementing a newly developed or refined strategy differs from simply implementing operational changes. Changes in the components of strategic direction, that is, vision, mission, values, policies, and goals of the organization, reverberate through the existing organization structure and its operations. In contrast, planned-for changes originating at an operations level are usually carried out *within* the framework of a current strategic direction and strategic operating plan.

How this added dimension is handled is the key to the successful implementation of strategy. Organizations routinely implement large-scale changes in operations yet become highly challenged when it comes to executing even the smallest strategic initiative requiring a fundamental change in organization culture or shared values.

Strategic and operational changes are intimately intertwined, but it is focusing on strategy as the priority consideration that drives change throughout the organization and distinguishes it as being strategic. Consequently, in this step we focus on how to develop strategic management processes and their prerequisite ancillary support systems to implement strategic *change,* as opposed to the more limited process of programmed and/or operational change.

To do so, we face a basic dilemma, that is, how do we generalize about strategy implementation processes if these are so dependent on a unique organizational context and situation? The approach we use is to identify the basic implementation processes; identify the contextual and situational determinants; and adapt, modify, and apply the principles and practices from relevant sources.

Accordingly, the objectives of this step are as follows:

- Understand the rationale for an explicit *strategy implementation process*
- Identify the key managerial roles, responsibilities, and capabilities required to implement a strategic operating plan
- Identify key contextual/situational variables that impact implementation processes
- Assess the impact of these managerial features and contextual/situational variables on the implementation of a strategic operating plan

Chapter 6

Understand the rationale for an organized and disciplined strategy implementation process

When execution is viewed as the fundamental requirement of effective implementation, we should heed the words of Larry Bossidy and Ram Charan in their book entitled *Execution: The Discipline of Getting Things Done*. Bossidy and Charan point out on page 6, "*Execution is not only the biggest issue facing business today; it is something nobody has explained satisfactorily.*" If they are correct, and we believe they are, this implies that all the work in previous chapters is to set the stage for the biggest challenge of all: translating the strategic operating plan into action—without the benefit of a proven body of knowledge.

This in no way minimizes what has been done to arrive at an appropriate strategic operating plan. Bossidy and Charan simply state what most executives feel at one time or another:

"*Strategies most often fail because they aren't executed well. Things that are supposed to happen don't happen. Either the organizations aren't capable of making them happen, or the leaders of the business misjudge the challenges their companies face in the business environment, or both*" (ibid, 15).

Why is this so often the case? Most simply, top executives do not view execution from the proper perspective. Table 6.1 summarizes what Bossidy and Charan (ibid, 21), believe are three key premises top executives constantly ignore.

It is instructive to also consider change management as conceptualized by Jeanenne LaMarsh in *Changing the Way We Change: Gaining Control of Major Operational Change* (1995).* LaMarsh begins with setting the vision—a desired future state. However, this vision cannot be fully defined at the outset, that is, "the future is never an 'end'—instead it is a guideline, a flexible framework that sets the outside boundaries for change. It

---

* LaMarsh, Jeannene, *Changing the Way We Change: Gaining Control of Major Operational Change* © 1995, pgs. 18, 57–61, 91. Reprinted with permission of Pearson Education, Inc. Upper Saddle, NJ 07458

Table 6.1: Key Premises Executives Ignore Related to Execution (Bossidy and Charan)

1. **Execution is a discipline and integral to strategy.**
   Effective strategy formulation and strategy planning are based on the organization's capability to execute. Execution, in turn, includes the ability to implement strategic and operational change. It complements the emerging discipline of change management. In essence, execution, implementation, and change management are variations of the process of getting things done and are most effective when considered as disciplines.

2. **Execution is the major job of the business leader.**
   This premise is best expressed by Bossidy and Charan: *"An organization can execute only if the leader's heart and soul are immersed in the company… The leader is the only person in a position to achieve that understanding. And only the leader can make execution happen, through his or her deep personal involvement in the substance and even the details of execution"* (ibid, 24). In order to get things done, he or she must be in charge of three core dimensions: people, strategy, and operations.

3. **Execution must be a core element of an organization's culture.**
   The discipline of execution must be accepted and practiced by every member of the organization. It rests on a deeply held belief embedded in the organization's culture. Bossidy and Charan liken the discipline of execution to the Six Sigma processes of continual improvement, in which the focus is on deviations from the control limits, followed by swift action to correct the causes of the deviations from acceptable performance.

From *Execution* by Larry Bossidy and Ram Charan, copyright © 2002 by Larry Bossidy and Ram Charan. Used by permission of Crown Business, a division of Random House, Inc.

is ill defined, adjusting, and impermanent" (LaMarsh, 4). She likens the vision to an umbrella; that is, it defines the broad framework of the future company. "The umbrella is made up of individual spokes and connecting fabric: the elements that define *process, structure, people, and culture* in the future" (ibid. 18-19). These same elements, or *spokes of change*, can also be used to describe the present state of the organization.

With the beginning and end states described, LaMarsh elaborates on moving from the present toward a desired future. In her words, *"the company travels from present to the future through a period of time that is no longer the old way, but not yet the new way. The 'delta' is where change occurs. It is where people stop operating in the old way, learn new ways, make mistakes, mourn the loss of the old, and test the new way. The delta is a state of limbo"* (ibid. 57).

Table 6.2 summarizes salient features of the delta and highlights the challenges of change while emphasizing the need for an organized and disciplined approach to implementation.

Table 6.2: Features of the Delta and the Challenges of Change (LaMarsh)

- *The delta is not the old way.* People do not know what to expect in the delta—even with education and training and constant reassurance by management. This is because the managers responsible for implementation are themselves not certain of all the ramifications.
- *The delta is not safe.* Even the most senior managers are not exempt from the prospect of major changes in their duties and responsibilities, transfers, demotions, even dismissals. Strategic change does not necessarily mean changes that are positive and optimistic. People know this, and many are predisposed to expect the worst.

Table 6.2: Features of the Delta and the Challenges of Change (LaMarsh) (continued)

- *The delta is expensive.* This is where the funds are spent, resources acquired, education and training occurs. Old systems and processes may run parallel to new systems and processes until there is a reliable and stable new process.
- *The delta is sad.* Over time the old ways became familiar—and they worked, albeit perhaps not as effectively and efficiently as the new ones. Relations became familiar and comfortable.
- *The delta is exciting.* On the positive side, most managers and employees know of changes that could and should be made. Over time when nothing is done to correct the situation, interest in changing along any dimension gradually diminishes. On the other hand, when management announces strategies that will ripple throughout the organization, people are energized. Changes move an organization into unknown territory, but they also bring the prospect of a new and better strategic position to exploit new and emerging opportunities.
- *The delta is stressful.* The organization needs to continue operating while undergoing changes in many dimensions of the organization. Time, resources, availability of the right people at the right time, unforeseen problems and unexpected events, and many more factors elevate the pressure and stress of both managers and employees.

LaMarsh, Jeannene, *Changing the Way We Change: Gaining Control of Major Operational Change* © 1995, pgs. 18, 57–61, 91. Reprinted with permission of Pearson Education, Inc. Upper Saddle, NJ 07458

Chapter 6

In essence, Bossidy and Charan have articulated a managerial approach while LaMarsh employs an organizational perspective. They complement each other well and, taken together, provide a compelling case for recognizing implementation as a priority responsibility of leadership to develop an organized and disciplined approach to implementation.

We have combined Bossidy and Charan's three core dimensions of execution, that is, *people, strategy, and operations,* with LaMarsh's umbrella "spokes" of change management, that is, *process, structure, people, and culture*, to develop an organized and disciplined approach to implementation. We also integrate the dimension of *external forces*, often overlooked in making operational changes but essential in making strategic changes.

Figure 6.1 depicts the types of factors that impact implementation processes.

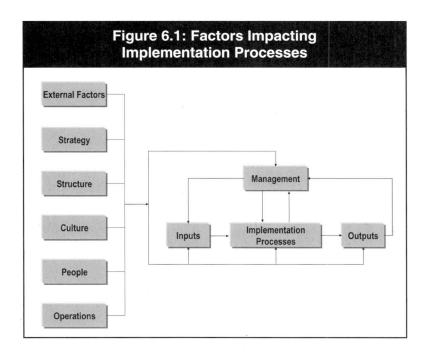

Identify the key managerial roles, responsibilities, and capabilities required to implement a strategic operating plan

In this chapter we limit our discussion to strategic management processes related to execution, implementation, and change management. To be effective, it is important to identify the roles and responsibilities required to implement a strategic operating plan and then adapt them to fit contextual and situational variables that shape organization realities.

Since organizations vary widely in their ability to make strategic changes, the use of this framework will depend on the level of expertise and experience organizations have had in this arena. Organizations with extensive expertise and experience can view this framework as a checklist to ensure an appropriate approach to implementation. Those organizations without much formal experience with strategic management can use the framework to build an effective approach to implementing strategic change, development, and management.

Regardless of the level of development of strategic management processes in an organization, management is responsible for ensuring that the organization's capacity, resources, and capabilities meet the implementation requirement of the strategic operating plan—and that they will be available as required.

Management Implementation Roles

In designing the strategic operating plan, assignments were made for what is to be implemented. Corollary to this is the need to consider how it is to be implemented. The "how" will differ from one organization to the next by the way their implementation processes are organized and managed and each organization's unique set of realities.

In most organizations, the existing management team, as organized in the existing hierarchy and reporting structure, is responsible for designing, implementing, and ultimately managing the strategic operating plan as part of ongoing operations. However, as the process of implementing change becomes more continuous and grows in scope and complexity (both strategically and operationally), a set of change management roles begin to emerge that require recognition, training, and development.

Though these roles are not formally included on the organization chart, they are ones that must be filled to prepare an organization for conducting the implementation process. They include the following:

- **Sponsors**—the executives and managers with the authority to make changes in the current strategic direction, the organization structure, and/or the processes required to implement and manage the change process. The level and scope of the changes that fall within the domain of each manager should be contained in a set of organization policies and procedures, as well as the manager's position/job description.
- **Champions**—the individuals throughout the organization that identify strongly with the need for given changes. They are self-appointed and need the unwavering support of management to be recognized by other managers and staff members. In the case of strategic changes, these individuals are more likely to be located at higher levels in the organization. However, as organizations become "flatter" and communication channels open up to more and more employees, champions for change begin to emerge throughout the organization. The challenge is to harness the energy and enthusiasm of these champions in cultivat-

ing support for the strategic operating plan in their sphere of influence in the organization.
- **Change agents**—the individuals responsible for any part of the implementation process. As LaMarsh points out, *"anyone and everyone who takes responsibility for figuring out how to make changes happen and how to support the targets (of change) are the change agents"*(LaMarsh, 91).* They can also be sponsors and champions of change, as well as targets of change themselves, but primarily they understand change, know how to manage change, and deal with the people involved in the changes they undertake.

With respect to dealing with people in an environment of change, LaMarsh provides a comprehensive description of how change agents can be effective:

- *Listen and listen and listen and listen.*
- *Translate the messages to targets and sponsors in language that is meaningful to them.*
- *Build team strength at the project level, in the senior management group, and among target groups.*
- *Develop coaching and counseling techniques.*
- *Build organization and structure into the delta wherever and whenever possible.*
- *Use some process, such as fishbone diagramming, to keep the changes in the delta identified, monitored, and tracked.*
- *Use that process to keep the organization focused on changes in the delta while maintaining regular company business.*
- *Know when to solve problems and how to do it effectively.*

---

* LaMarsh, Jeannene, *Changing the Way We Change: Gaining Control of Major Operational Change* © 1995, pgs. 18, 57–61, 91. Reprinted with permission of Pearson Education, Inc. Upper Saddle, NJ 07458

Chapter 6

- ○ *Know when to delegate and how to manage the delegated (ibid.93).*

    Clearly, change agents do the heavy lifting when implementing new or revised strategic operating plans.

- **Targets of change**—the people within the organization directly impacted by implementation of the strategic operating plan and the changes it brings about. Those who will be affected must be identified to assess how they will be affected, what changes they can expect, and why. Since people vary dramatically in how they react to change, their potential for resistance needs to be understood and dealt with constructively.

    This can be a make or break experience for those instituting change (change agents) and those directly affected by it (targets of change). Confronting resistance, fears, and opposition to proposed changes are key challenges facing change agents. Constructively helping their fellow staff members to expect, accept, and develop tolerance to the changes coming their way is the good work of the change agent.

Taking on roles like these come naturally to some managers and staff personnel. It is important to be aware of these individuals and to call upon them during the implementation process. It is equally important for leaders to give them their full support. Ensuring these roles are filled with adequately trained personnel is a priority before any implementation process begins.

Management Implementation Responsibilities

Implementation, like many management processes, has a defined set of responsibilities. However, as noted above, with a few notable exceptions, implementation has not been fully developed as a management discipline. For example, processes such as communication, delegation, leadership, team work, and many others are well-defined, taught, and integrated into the mainstream development of modern professional managers, but nowhere does implementation, or for that matter execution or change management, receive equivalent attention.

In short, implementation is not adequately defined in the literature for use in implementing strategic operating plans. Therefore, the following set of 12 management responsibilities is intended to develop a basis for assessing an organization's implementation readiness, that is, the basic responsibilities, which must be adequately covered to ensure a successful implementation. For each implementation responsibility described below a set of questions is included to aid in defining the responsibility in a given organization.

1. Sustain commitment, involvement, and leadership of the implementation process.

During the first year of implementing a strategic operating plan, there is a concentrated effort on the part of management and staff to implement a new strategic initiative, that is, to make the plan operational and integrated within the existing organization and management structure.

In time, as management interest and attention shift to other concerns, attention to the need to sustain interest and enthusiasm for the new strategy becomes increasingly important. Many members of management and staff have questions about the value of the changes, especially as they relate to their careers and opportunities in the organization.

When top managers do not understand the root causes of these questions and reactions, they are very likely to use inappropriate methods to deal with them, for example, by falling back on a command and control system that only increases the problems of implementation. What is required is a sustained commitment to, and involvement in, the implementation process that is based on a full understanding of its nuanced complexity. This is a responsibility that must be accepted by all members of the implementation team.

Top executives and managers are often first to walk away from this responsibility thinking this is now the responsibility of lower-level managers by rationalizing, "this is not my job." Nothing could be further from the truth. Without the commitment and involvement of top management throughout the implementation process, suboptimal results—even failure—are likely.

The implementation management team should examine its willingness and ability to accept this responsibility. To do so it is useful to analyze and dialogue, asking questions such as the following:

- Is management willing to lead the implementation team throughout the process?
- Does management have confidence that it can and will carry out this leadership function?
- Are the rest of management and the other members of the organization willing to accept leadership roles throughout the process?
- Are there significant weaknesses in the leadership team that need to be shored up before beginning implementation?
- Are there others in management or the organization at large that should be asked to play a major role during implementation in view of the crucial role of leading the implementation process?
- Is there any key result area that does not have implementation leadership capability in place? If so, how can it be strengthened?

2. Identify the scope and dimensions of the implementation requirements of the strategic operating plan.

Every strategic operating plan should have an identifiable scope and measurable dimensions. Therefore, it is somewhat paradoxical that the total implementation of a strategic operating plan is seldom measured—except in terms of the budget and resources required. These measurements do not get at the process of implementation itself. For example, what presents a major challenge to one organization may be a "walk in the park" to another organization. Why? The capacity, capabilities, and the resources of the organization to implement vary widely across an organization. This stems from a basic tendency to underestimate the implementation process.

This was perfectly understandable, even acceptable, in more stable and less challenging environments. In today's environment of constant and increasing change—both internal and external—this is no longer acceptable, and it is a critical responsibility of top management and the implementation management team to face, measure, and overcome today's challenges.

The task of summarizing budgets, required resources, and management and staff requirements is relatively straightforward. Estimating the *noneconomic and nonquantitative challenges* of implementation is much more difficult. To aid in this process it is useful to ask the following and similar questions:

- Are there elements of the strategic operating plan that have a precedent in the organization that can be drawn on for applicable experience and implementation models?
- If not, does the implementation need to draw on outside expertise to undertake the given implementation?
- Are there implementation challenges resulting from changing the strategic direction of the organization, and is the implementation team prepared to meet them?

- Is the rate of the implementation process required by the strategic operating plan compatible with the organization's capacity to accept and integrate required changes?

3. Assess the existing implementation capabilities of management.

Before the team can begin the process of implementing the strategic operating plan, there should be a realistic assessment of the implementation capabilities of the current management team. This assessment is often done implicitly during the process of formulating and planning strategy.

Even when it comes to developing the strategic operating plan, however, it is very likely that the implementation capabilities of the organization are not considered in sufficient detail. This is not an unrealistic assumption, as noted at the outset of this step: "*Strategies most often fail because they aren't executed well*" (Bossidy and Charan, 15). One of the primary reasons for this lack of attention to the implementation process, as already noted, is that top management all too often considers this a responsibility of lower levels of management, not realizing that they have a major leadership responsibility for implementing the strategic operating plan.

Secondly, implementation requires a combination of skill in dealing with both "people" and "technical" processes. However, since few managers have excellent skills in both areas, there is a need to assess the combined pool of implementation skills available. Leadership teams require necessary implementation capabilities in both areas as listed in the following questions:

- Are the implementation capabilities (people and processes) at the required level of development to implement the strategic operating plan?
- Are the following implementation capabilities at the required level of development?

- Technical knowledge and skills?
- Communication skills?
- Interpersonal relationships?
- Change management?
- Organization design and development?

4. Match the implementation capabilities to the strategic operating plan requirements.

The quantitative aspect of matching implementation capabilities, that is, funding, staffing, and other required resources, with implementation requirements was introduced in Step 10. In Step 10 the objective was to present management with a feasible plan to obtain approval, funding, and authorization to begin implementation. In the current step, there are two additional phases in the process of matching implementation capabilities and requirements:

- Phase I. Before initiation of any implementation activities

  This is essentially an initial fine-tuning process to match implementation capabilities and requirements. It begins with top management and deploys down and out to all teams and individuals assigned to implement the strategic operating plan. The objective is to ensure that all personnel with implementation responsibilities have the capability, capacity, and resources to carry out assigned implementation responsibilities. This is an assessment that is often glossed over on the assumption that "of course we can implement this plan. I know we can." If our experience teaches us anything, this is not only a false assumption but also a dangerous one to make.

- Phase II. During the implementation process

  The second phase is to maintain a continuous and in-depth dialogue between all manager and staff members with assigned implementation responsibilities. Implementation capacities and requirements are in a constant state of flux in what LaMarsh refers to as the *delta,* that is, that unknown chasm between the safe harbor of familiar responsibilities and a new desired future state—the vision. During the time in the delta, the organization needs continual monitoring and adjustment between the implementation capabilities and the requirements of the strategic operating plan. Addressing the following and similar questions will be of assistance in making this assessment:

- Will personnel with the required skills be available?
- Will required equipment and resources be available?
- Are there significant shortages in the availability of the required capabilities in any of the key result areas?
- Will these shortages cause significant delays in the implementation of the strategic operating plan?
- How can these shortages be addressed?

5. Develop a comprehensive implementation approach.

In assessing the match between capabilities and requirements, the need for a comprehensive implementation approach will emerge. A comprehensive approach refers to the inclusion of the scope, timing, scheduling, and other features that determine the shape and phases of the implementation process.

Table 6.3 summarizes several alternative implementation approaches.

Top management must be involved in the selection of the implementation approach(es), and all members of the implementation team should give input into the final selection of an implementation approach. Many of these approaches have limited use except in certain circumstances, but regardless of the implementation approach selected, it is a decision that will have a major impact on the organization and its ongoing operations.

Table 6.3: Alternative Implementation Approaches

- *Incremental.* Small operational steps until implementation is thoroughly understood, accepted, and integrated in ongoing operations. Widely used and effective. It provides ample opportunity to learn, correct mistakes and improve.
- *Turnaround.* Only used in crisis situations when no alternative is possible. Requires outside expertise to cut through the mind-set of the current management team.
- *Pilot/test program.* A small-scale project that serves as a "proof of concept" regarding development of a new process or service or entry into a market.
- *Crossover.* Applicable when a new process will replace a current process, and the new and current process are run in parallel before "crossing over" to the new process. Used when the new process is not yet reliable and/or problem free.
- *Parallel programs with alternative implementation approaches.* Used in multisite organizations when uncertainty exists regarding the effectiveness and/or efficiency of alternative implementation approaches.
- *Turnkey project.* Used when a client has little or no experience in the organization or operation of the facility. The contracting organization in effect carries out all implementation responsibilities and leaves the client with a ready to operate "turnkey project."

Each approach noted in Table 6.3 has different advantages and disadvantages, that is, different ways in which they impact the organization and varying probabilities of success. The entire management team has a vital interest in choosing the implementation approach that best fits the organization. Consider the following (and similar questions) to select the approach that best fits with your organization's needs:

- What is our current implementation approach?
- Can we use any of the comprehensive implementation approaches listed above?
- What are the critical factors in our organization to take into account when selecting our implementation approach?
    - Urgency
    - Interference with ongoing operations
    - Preservation of data from the current process
    - Impact on the work place climate with respect to causing uncertainty, tension, loss of production, morale, etc.
    - Financial risk/exposure
    - Impact on customer relations
    - Management turnover
    - Compatibility with current organization and its culture
    - Payback/cash flow
    - Adherence to schedule
    - Development of the strategic management capability
    - Duration of implementation
    - Implementation a stretch for us
    - Board policy

6. Articulate and communicate the strategic operating plan.

Executive management is prone to forget that what has become familiar to them in the process of formulating and planning strategy is largely unknown to most of the organization.

Secondly, executive management sometimes assumes that strategic implementation processes do not require its committed, continued, and detailed involvement. The net result of these two tendencies is to initiate implementation without a full and complete explanation of the strategies and the impact they will have on the organization and its entire work force.

When executive management does not accept responsibility for articulating and communicating these new and/or revised strategies and the rationale for making them, there is no reason to assume those out of the information loop will accept the required changes in strategy, organization, jobs, expectations about the future, and other dimensions of change. All team members need and deserve an explanation of the scope and nature of the changes being made and how they will impact them. Consider these and similar assessment questions:

- Are there one or more members of executive management team that can do an excellent job of articulating and communicating the strategic operating plan at an organization-wide level?
- Are there members of the implementation team that are prepared to articulate and communicate the strategic operating plan at division and department levels? Will they accept this responsibility?
- Has the implementation team, including members of top management, agreed on the key points to articulate and communicate to all members of the organization?

7. Motivate management and staff personnel to implement the strategic operating plan.

It is not enough to articulate and communicate the strategic operating plan. This alone will not be sufficient to motivate management, staff, or the work force in general to get behind the plan and facilitate its implementation. Along with change comes uncertainty, rumors, doubts, and stress—all adding to resistance to change. Not only must changes be made clear and be understood, but they also must be accepted.

As part of acceptance, each employee impacted by the strategic operating plan needs to understand what is at stake in the plan for him or her individually. In some cases, this is not an easy task, since the impact of strategic changes will impact employees differently, some by being promoted, others transferred or required to learn new skills. Others may be demoted or possibly let go, and it is not reasonable to enlist this group in the implementation of the strategic operating plan. The following questions address this topic:

- Is our team ready and willing to assume a leadership role in motivating the other members of management, their direct reports, and the personnel assigned to them for the implementation of the strategic operating plan?
- Do we need to provide any training, coaching, or mentoring in order for some members of the team to carry out this responsibility?
- Have we identified the most often asked questions that relate to motivation?
- Have we answered these questions?
- Have we made provision to share new questions that we have been confronted with individually?
- Do we accept responsibility to ensure that personnel who have asked questions and/or expressed doubts and reservations about various aspects of the strategic operating plan are provided with immediate and straightforward responses?

8. Schedule implementation processes and projects.

Depending on the aggregate scope, level, and rate of change that implementing the strategic operating plan requires, it may be necessary to have a formal means of scheduling the implementation process. Many initiatives may require use of the same scarce resources. For example, it may be necessary to have the equivalent of a clearinghouse (that is, Project Management Office) with one individual in charge who is authorized to coordinate and schedule the use of the required scarce resources that are outside the control of a particular manager or team leader.

In simple strategic operating plans containing few cross-functional initiatives, coordinating the use of staff and resources may be done informally, since managers across functions are able to make these arrangements at team meetings. It is only as the change management process becomes more complex that formal arrangements for coordinating resources are found to be necessary. Consider the following questions to aid the implementation team in understanding and accepting this responsibility:

- Can we, acting as a team, schedule the use of personnel and resources that are required on several strategic initiatives at the same time and by means of informal communication processes within the implementation team?
- Or are more formal scheduling arrangements required, such as creating a Project Management Office under the direction of one person?

9. Coordinate and direct the implementation process.

This is the heart and core of the implementation process. From this point forward, all personnel with responsibilities for implementation are actively engaged in all the foregoing responsibilities. Their primary objective will be to use their individual and collective managerial skills to integrate the strategic operating plan as seamlessly as possible into the day-to-day functioning of the organization.

Chapter 6

It is no longer possible to easily separate out and concentrate on a single phase of the implementation process for very long, when new events, unexpected difficulties, personnel changes, unavailable but required resources, and a host of other intervening variables come into play. This is not much different from ongoing operations in the existing system.

This is precisely the problem! It is all too easy to get drawn into the current system with which everyone is familiar and to lose track of the implementation process. Since many managers and employees are often not heavily invested in the new strategy, it is of no great concern to them whether the strategic operating plan is implemented or not. This is the situation in organizations that are not strategy-focused and not managed by an experienced and committed strategy implementation team.

Complex but routine operational changes that do not impact the strategic direction and the implementation of new goals are often mistaken for strategic changes. The importance of effectively managing this type of implementation challenge, while not strategic, should never be underestimated.

At the same time, strategic changes differ significantly from operational changes. Strategic changes cascade through all of the components of the strategic direction. These changes in strategic direction, in turn, require changes in the culture of the organization and the behavior, attitude, and performance of all the members of the organization, albeit in different ways, and therein is the challenge. In stark contrast, operational changes are usually made as expansions and improvements to/in the existing strategic direction and operating system.

Most managers need to learn to deal with these complex, interrelated, and not easily changed dimensions of the organization, its structure, or operations. For example, there is a hierarchy in the level and complexity of the change process.

Technical and operational changes are usually much easier to implement than are changes to organization structure, interpersonal relationships, and work place climate. These variables, in turn, are easier to change than the components of the strategic direction, organization culture, and the impact on organization members.

How to deal with these various dimensions of strategic change is not an easily acquired skill, but it is much easier if the scope and complexity of the strategic implementation process are understood from the start. To aid members of the implementation teams, consider the following questions:

- Are we prepared to coordinate and direct the implementation process *in all required dimensions* of the balanced scorecard?
- In addition, do we have the skills to coordinate and direct the implementation of a change in strategic direction? At the organization level? At the functional level?
- Are there shortcomings and/or gaps in any of these dimensions?
- How are we going to address these shortcomings and/or gaps?

10. Measure and control implementation performance.

The twin steps of rigorously and systematically *measuring* and *controlling* all processes in an organization do not exclude the implementation process. Often the need for measurement and control during implementation is explained away by observing that it will only be for a limited time, or that the situation is too fluid and uncertain to evaluate performance. Nothing could be further from the truth.

Planning execution without an effective measurement and control system in place will ensure that implementation is neither efficient nor effective. It is not the mere setting of schedules and performance measures that ensures implementation. It is the mandate that management operates effectively and efficiently at all times to the best of its ability. This is not possible without accurate and realistic performance measures at all levels of management.

Consider the following questions to ensure an understanding and acceptance of this implementation responsibility:

- Do we understand the need for a measurement and control system for the implementation process?
- Do we have one in place at the organization level? At the functional level? At the strategic objective and initiative level?
- If not, who and how will we develop one where required?
- Has a reporting system been established at each implementation level?
- Do all members of the team understand the use of these measurements and controls?

Figure 6.2 presents a comprehensive measurement and control process.

Figure 6.2: Sample Annual Performance Measurement Calendar

Month	Project Reporting	Metrics Reporting	Objective Reporting	Plan and Budget Development	Sr. Staff SFO* Review Meeting	Board Meetings
January 20__				• Kick-off 20__ "confirmed" Projects • Confirm 20__ Budget Forecast	1/9/20__ • Review Q4 and overall 20__ results • Prepare SFO information for Bd.	1/21 – 1/23/20__ • 20__ Budget Approval
February 20__	2/1 – 2/4/20__	2/5 – 2/7/20__				
March 20__	3/1 – 3/4/20__	3/5 – 3/7/20__				
April 20__	4/1 – 4/4/20__	4/5 – 4/7/20__	4/8 – 4/10/20__	• Forecast new Projects • Review Budget	4/24/20__ • Review Q1 results • Prepare SFO info. for Board	
May 20__	5/1 – 5/4/20__	5/5 – 5/7/20__				5/16 – 5/18/20__ • KPI Dashboard Review
June 20__	6/1 – 6/4/20__	6/5 – 6/7/20__		• Review and update Env Scan		

* SFO—strategy focused organization

Chapter 6

Figure 6.2: Sample Annual Performance Measurement Calendar (continued)

Month	Project Reporting	Metrics Reporting	Objective Reporting	Plan and Budget Development	Sr. Staff SFO* Review Meeting	Board Meetings
July 20__	7/1 – 7/4/20__	7/5 – 7/7/20__	7/8 – 7/10/20__	• Forecast new Projects • Review Budget • Update of OTSW		
August 20__	8/1 – 8/4/20__	8/5 – 8/7/20__		• Update of OTSW • Refine KPIs & Evaluate Targets	8/28/20__ • Review Q2 results • Prepare SFO info. for Board	
September 20__	9/1 – 9/4/20__	9/5 – 9/7/20__		• Define 20__ Projects • Begin Project Priority setting		9/20 – 9/24/20__ • Approve 20__ targets • Review Q1-Q2 Results
October 20__	10/1 – 10/4/20__	10/5 – 10/7/20__	10/8 – 0/10/20__	• Review 20__ Projects • Confirm 20__ Priorities • Draft Budget		
November 20__	11/1 – 11/4/20__	11/5 – 11/7/20__		• Refine Budget	11/25/20__ • Review Q3 results • Prepare SFO level info. for Bd.	

Strategy in the 21st Century

Figure 6.2: Sample Annual Performance Measurement Calendar (continued)

Month	Project Reporting	Metrics Reporting	Objective Reporting	Plan and Budget Development	Sr. Staff SFO* Review Meeting	Board Meetings
December 20__	12/1 – 12/4/20__	12/5 – 12/7/20__		• Prepare Budget	Establish 20__ Forecast and Initiatives	TBD (Executive Committee Only) • Review 20__ Projected Results • Budget vetted

11. Adapt, change, modify, and revise the implementation process.

Implementation management, in and of itself, is a process undergoing constant change as new and unexpected challenges are encountered. It is why there is no a priori set of principles and practices that can be prescribed and applied with a cookie-cutter approach. Not only is the current situation undergoing change, but the future situation remains unknown and subject to change. Managing an organization under these conditions requires sensitivity to the need to adapt, change, or modify the processes being implemented and to make requisite adjustments in the strategic operating plan.

If implementation were well understood in the hands of skilled managers, then the implementation process and responsibilities would be clear and dealt with effectively. However, since implementation is one of the most underdeveloped of management skills, it is important to establish a systematic and flexible implementation approach. This is especially true with respect to the ability to adapt, change, or modify the strategic operating plan. It is one thing to use a narrowly-focused ap-

Chapter 6

proach to a stable implementation task and quite another when the organization's environment, key players, and work force are all undergoing change simultaneously.

Accordingly, considering the following types of questions will aid in assessing the ability to carry out implementation:

- Have we identified those points within the implementation process that are likely to pose problems?
- Have we anticipated the types of problems likely to occur at these points? And what adjustments to the schedule for implementation or within the strategic operating plan are required?
- Are we prepared to monitor all performance reports during the implementation process; to look for scheduling delays, cost overruns, unforeseen circumstances; and to respond with appropriate remedial actions including modifications to the strategic operating plan? And ultimately answer, who will do this?

12. Evaluate the impact of the strategic operating plan on the progress and performance of the organization.

The last thing an organization needs is an empty victory, that is, an implementation process that is up and running but valued little by management, the professional staff, and the workers. The essence of a successful strategy is tangible movement and realization of a shared vision based on a set of core values along with a commitment to achieve that vision by carrying out the mission of the organization.

Consequently, management has a responsibility to remain vigilant about how implementation is impacting the morale, attitudes, and performance of the organization—and to take measures to address any dysfunctional consequences of the implementation process.

This can only be done effectively if a performance measurement and control system has been set up to monitor the implementation process. Its primary purpose is to determine the performance and progress *during* implementation. Using a performance measurement and control system makes it possible to review and assess the effectiveness of the new strategic operating plan as an integral part of the entire organization. The evaluation of integrated operations must begin during implementation and then be continued as part of the ongoing management process (see Step 13).

However, during the course of the current operating year there will be plenty of indications as to whether the strategic operating plan is making a positive contribution to the organization and its performance. These indications, trends, and events need to be monitored closely and distinguished from the temporary disruptions that occur as a result of the implementation process. To aid in understanding and preparing for this responsibility, consider the following questions:

- Have we formulated a set of evaluation criteria that will help us monitor and evaluate the impact of the strategic operating plan's various initiatives on the strategic management of the organization?
- For example, have we formulated evaluation criteria paying attention to:
  - Increased level of awareness of the importance of a strategy-focused organization?
  - Increased ability to manage in a strategy focused manner?
  - Sustained acceptance and increased motivation to work to achieve the strategic direction of the organization?
  - Measurable progress in achieving the goals and objectives that were used to generate strategic initiatives or at

least avoid dysfunctional consequences?
  o Improved results in each of the key result areas?

- Has the entire implementation team used these or similar criteria to determine the impact of the strategic operating plan on the organization?
- Have we detected any adverse impacts on the organization, its strategic direction, management, work force, or operations that are likely to last beyond the current year?
- Has the implementation team met at least quarterly to make an in-depth evaluation of the impact of the strategic operating plan on the organization?
- Have we included evaluation of the strategic operating plan in, at least, quarterly written reports to management?

In conclusion, the preceding set of 12 management implementation responsibilities become effective to the extent that contextual and situation-specific conditions are taken into account and used to modify the implementation approach. In the next section a number of these conditions are outlined and their impact described.

Identify key contextual/situational conditions that impact implementation processes

While many operational processes and procedures are becoming commoditized and standardized, this has not yet occurred to any significant extent in the disciplines of strategic management. This is due to the creative and evaluative dimensions of strategic management that are not easily replicated and to contextual and situational conditions that are unique to each organization. Each management team needs to identify and

Strategy in the 21st Century

describe those conditions that are significant in its organization.

Some of the more salient key contextual conditions are listed in Table 6.4.

Within each category, there are several illustrative features that need to be taken into account in determining how to fine-tune and adapt implementation responsibilities within a particular organization. These contextual and situational conditions need to be considered at each level of implementation management, that is, organizational, core function, subunit, and project.

Table 6.4: Key Contextual/Situational Conditions

Human resource process features

- Employee skill level and distribution
- Disparity in level of development of functional areas
- Previous implementation experience of the work force
- The scope and complexity of required new competencies
- The staff education level and learning capabilities
- Relevant personnel performance evaluation
- The current reward and compensation systems and practices

Operational process features

- Degree of integration between strategic management and the operating function

Table 6.4: Key Contextual/Situational Conditions (continued)

- Level of operations processes and systems development
- Level of technology development
- Extent of organized innovation processes
- Operations management implementation capabilities
- Operational implementation tools and concepts
- Strategy deployment linkage
- Experience in using the tools and concepts of change management

Organizational features

- Stage and level of organization development
- Vertical versus horizontal relationships
- Differences in the level of functional area development
- Level of process development
- Work place atmosphere
- Communication systems
- Information processing capability
- Reporting and documentation capability

Cultural features

- Entrepreneurial versus bureaucratic values and policies
- Cultural diversity versus cultural homogeneity
- Management cultural characteristics
- Professional staff cultural characteristics

Table 6.4: Key Contextual/Situational Conditions (continued)

- Administrative staff cultural characteristics
- Cross-cultural communications barriers

Features of external relationships

- Owners
    - Distribution of ownership
    - Public versus private ownership versus nonprofit
    - Scope and type of intervention in the organization

- Board members
    - Role in setting strategic direction of the organization
    - Scope and type of intervention in the organization
    - Ratio of internal managers on the board

- Customers
    - Impact of key customers on strategic decisions
    - Customer requirements impacting key result areas

- Suppliers
    - Impact of key suppliers on strategic decisions
    - Role in implementing the strategic operating plan
    - Supplier capabilities impacting key results areas

> **Table 6.4: Key Contextual/Situational Conditions (continued)**
>
> - Joint ventures, strategic partners, strategic alliances
>   - Impact of relationships on implementation of the strategic operating plan
>   - Active versus reactive relationships
> - Advisors, consultants, contractors
>   - Role in implementing the strategic operating plan
>   - Responsibilities of advisors, consultants, contractors
> - Volunteers
>   - Full time
>   - Part time

Assess the significant contextual and situational conditions that impact the implementation of the strategic operating plan

The assessment outlined below is usually done intuitively and instinctively by the management team after long experience in a given organization. So long as the implementation process remains straightforward and focused primarily on operational change, this type of implementation approach will be adequate. However, as strategic operating plans become more complex and larger in scope, it is useful to pool insights and experience, in order to build a shared approach to implementation that will meet the needs of larger and more sophisticated strategic changes.

Strategy in the 21st Century

Figure 6.3 provides a sample template to evaluate key contextual and situational features. It should be noted that the exact features to be evaluated are not the same for every organization. This tool should be adapted to the specific needs of a particular organization.

Figure 6.3: Assessment of Significant Contextual and Situational Conditions on the Implementation Process

* Rank as follows: **Low** (monitor closely); **Medium** (significant improvement required); **High** (do not proceed without major improvement/adjustment, including modifying the strategic operating plan)

Factors modifying the strategic operating plan implementation process	Importance of strategic operating plan implementation impact*	Comments, suggestions, and recommendations requiring attention during strategic operating plan implementation
Internal Features		
Implementation roles		
Implementation responsibilities		
Managerial process features		
Human resource features		
Operational features		
Organizational features		
Cultural features		

Figure 6.3: Assessment of Significant Contextual and Situational Conditions on the Implementation Process (continued)

* Rank as follows: **Low** (monitor closely); **Medium** (significant improvement required); **High** (do not proceed without major improvement/adjustment, including modifying the strategic operating plan)

Factors modifying the strategic operating plan implementation process	Importance of strategic operating plan implementation impact*	Comments, suggestions, and recommendations requiring attention during strategic operating plan implementation
External features		
Owners		
Customers		
Suppliers		
Strategic relationships		
Strategy advisors, etc.		

STEP 13: STRATEGIC MANAGEMENT AS AN ONGOING PROCESS

At the beginning of this chapter, the case was made for employing a two-phased implementation process. Initially, there is a formal implementation process that focuses on the strategic operating plan and how to implement and then integrate the plan within ongoing operations. However, at the end of that phase, the implementation process is still not complete.

This remains true even in organizations that have begun to accept change as part of their daily routine. This is due to the rate at which changes and innovations can be introduced and assimilated by the organization and its members. As pointed out in Step 12, technical changes are usually more easily introduced than operational changes to processes, systems, and procedures. And secondly, operational changes are more easily assimilated than changes to organization structure and infrastructure.

Lastly, changes in interpersonal relationships, reporting relationships, and organization culture require even more time to introduce and become accepted as routine. Accepting and committing to the new or revised strategic direction as part of the organization's culture can be the most difficult implementation challenge of all—especially when it is taking the organization into uncharted waters. Changing attitudes and beliefs is very difficult to accomplish, while superficial compliance is easily attained because people want to keep their jobs. However, if one of the central tenets of the strategic direction is to pursue a shared vision that respects and derives from the core values of the organization, then changing attitudes and behaviors becomes a formidable task—one that is usually not completed in the initial implementation of the strategic operating plan.

Some changes can take years before they are truly accepted. In fact, some people will never accept the new/revised processes, the new organization structure, systems, policies, management style, or performance measurement system—or whatever dimension of the change that *they* find unacceptable. This stems from the very nature of strategic change; that is, it is *not* primarily operational. If it were, the change process would be much more routine and programmed. Strategic change, on the other hand, requires that significant attention also be paid to the impact the new/revised strategies have on the organization's strategic direction, organization, and culture.

Chapter 6

Clearly, we cannot set up an implementation process for each strategy that continues indefinitely into the future. The sooner a strategy is operational and line management takes over the process, the sooner the organization will become truly strategy-focused. This stems from considerations such as the following:

- Implementing new/revised strategic initiatives is fast becoming a necessary competency for survival, growth, and profitability.
- The complexity and rate of change, both external and internal, is increasing at an increasing rate.

As a consequence, the need to respond effectively and efficiently to these changes must be developed and continuously improved, that is, to do whatever the organization must do to acquire a highly efficient strategic management response capability. This capability needs to be developed in depth at all levels of leadership and management.

An effective way to develop leaders and managers with this response capability is to require their maximum feasible participation in all phases of the strategic management implementation process. It is in this process that management comes to grips with the challenges of winning over and motivating the work force to accept and commit to the strategic operating plan.

This approach also has the advantage of requiring that the implementation team set very aggressive implementation objectives and turn over the implementation process to ongoing management as soon as possible.

Accordingly, the objectives of this step include:

- Compare and contrast initial implementation processes and ongoing implementation processes
- Integrate implementation team roles and responsibilities into line management job descriptions

- Identify, understand, accept, and prepare to carry out the *new implementation responsibilities* of the line organization
- Manage remaining implementation tasks
- Assess the impact of the strategic operating plan on the organization
- Develop a framework for evaluating and continuously improving the current strategic management capability

Compare and contrast initial implementation processes and ongoing line implementation processes

The differences in requirements between the two implementation phases must be examined in greater detail before proceeding to the ongoing management of the implementation process. This is due to the tendency of many managers to assume the implementation process is over at the end of the initial implementation phase by simply leaving line management to operate the new/revised strategic operating plan.

However, operating in this manner creates a yearly accumulation of incompletely and ineffectively implemented strategies. The solution is to turn over the completion of the implementation tasks to line management. This allows the implementation team appointed for the next strategic operating plan to focus its attention on the new strategic initiatives in the next annual operating cycle. However, this is only possible if line management realizes that there are several implementation tasks that they must accept as their responsibility. This is not an abrupt change marked by a hand-off of all responsibilities to an entirely new team. In most organizations, the same personnel are involved in both phases of the implementation process.

What is usually missing is distinguishing between the two phases of implementation: the initial, or formal phase, focused

Chapter 6

on integrating new strategic initiatives and getting them operationalized, and its much longer counterpart focused on sustained execution under the direction of line management. Therefore, the first task is to understand the often very different perspectives, attitudes, behaviors, and skills that must be brought to the implementation process.

These differences are highlighted below to emphasize the need to adjust to these differences to ensure that strategic change and prerequisite improvements occur.

Table 6.5 summarizes the various dimensions of implementation and their variances in complexity, completion times, and acceptance by members of the organization.

> **Table 6.5: Dimensions and Challenges of Implementation**
>
> - The **Technical Dimension** focuses on the well-defined processes involving new products, services, technologies, equipment, information technology, and/or industry specific processing equipment and systems. In these often larger projects, these processes are most effectively implemented by using a project management approach. Many times these are multiyear projects and as such are probably best left in the hands of the project manager, rather than turning them over to a line manager.
>
>   During the initial implementation cycle, both management and staff are focused on solving the technical challenges that the new technology presents. Questions arise during this period pertaining to the other dimensions of implementation (see below), and the project

> **Table 6.5: Dimensions and Challenges of Implementation (continued)**
>
> manager must be prepared to deal with them. However, it is the line manager that accepts responsibility for the new changes as part of ongoing operations after the project ends, and she or he must be prepared to deal with questions and issues arising in the other dimensions of change.
> - The **Operational Dimension** is not as easily identified as is the technical dimension of implementation. Members begin to think about the implications of the new technology and their impact on the operations in which they are embedded. Questions are asked about the future of the operation and more broadly about the organization itself.
>
>   An implementation may be very successful in the eyes of management, but the work force has a more personalized agenda: one that connects their job, their future in the organization, and ultimately the future of the organization itself. In a sense they may be on the horns of a dilemma when viewing positively the change for the organization to survive, while potentially harboring negative concern that their own future may be in jeopardy. Issues of this sort become an important implementation challenge for line management. It may not have been a concern of the initial implementation team, but once execution gets underway, any issues that do exist may intensify, becoming major problems for line management.
>
>   Dealing with these and similar challenges will be discussed below; the objective at this point is to clear-

> **Table 6.5: Dimensions and Challenges of Implementation (continued)**
>
> ly recognize the different dynamics in each phase of implementation, including potential long-run consequences and how line management can/should address them.
>
> - The **Organizational Dimension** of the implementation process can easily cause implementation problems. For example, consolidating operations, downsizing, entering new markets, and going overseas all result in significant organizational change.
>
>   At the organization level, the change might have been "officially" completed in a matter of months, but there still remains a multitude of implementation tasks that ripple throughout the organization. New reporting structures are required, and new opportunities require new approaches. New jobs are created, others changed, others eliminated.
>
>   The initial implementation team may have identified these ripple effects, but the team has neither the authority nor responsibility to make the necessary adjustments in the organization structure or to deal with the long-run effects on the impacted organization members. These organizational impacts may easily require attention for years before they have become thoroughly integrated and accepted as part of mainstream operations.
>
> - The **Cultural Dimension** of change is the most daunting and presents the most difficult set of implementation challenges for the following reasons:

Table 6.5: Dimensions and Challenges of Implementation (continued)

- They are based on the organization's set of shared values that will resist being easily changed.
- Conflicts may arise between the need for organizational change and the individual's need for stability, security, and predictability.
- An organization's culture has unique characteristics that are not easily analyzed and changed.
- Culture emerges and evolves but at different rates and along different value vectors.
- Organizational cultures can have vastly different tolerance levels for and receptivity to change.
- Cultural change, above all else, is a long-term, incremental process.

These, and related characteristics of organization culture, will test line management's implementation skills, since these changes are addressed and unfold over the long haul in parallel with plan execution.

Table 6.6 summarizes implementation task characteristics that are major challenges to the line manager.

Table 6.6: Implementation Task Characteristics

- **Multitasking**. All implementation tasks require that the implementer have some skill in multitasking. However, during the initial implementation processes, the focus

> **Table 6.6: Implementation Task Characteristics (continued)**
>
> is narrowed to a few key tasks. In contrast, the rippling effects of the strategic operating plan, as it begins to impact the more complex dimensions of the change process, are left for line management to address.
>
> - **Task duration**. By definition the initial implementation tasks last for one year, except in those cases of a narrowly-defined technical implementation, such as new information technology that is primarily a set of well-defined technical and operating tasks that do not impact the strategic direction of the organization.
>
>   In contrast, longer-duration strategic initiatives transferred to line management may require several years for complete integration into ongoing operations. For example, arrangements to outsource low-cost labor parts to China may be completed in less than a year. Integrating and coordinating the new Chinese partner with a domestic distribution facility may be an ongoing implementation challenge that can take years.
>
> - **Task ambiguity**. When a strategic operating plan is developed, great attention is given to stating the objectives and the tactics, or projects, for achieving them in clear, concise, and measurable terms. The purpose of this approach is to have an effective and efficient implementation process based on clear and unambiguous objectives and tactics. However, once an initiative is introduced to the organization at large, there is a strong likelihood that a range of interpretations will emerge about why the changes are being made and about their value. At a minimum, there are likely to

> **Table 6.6: Implementation Task Characteristics (continued)**
>
> be unanswered questions by employees about management's motives, intended outcomes, and the impact on individuals and the organization. All these interpretations need to be addressed, and this becomes a line management responsibility.

Table 6.7 summarizes the types of short-run and long-run barriers the team will likely encounter. The latter are especially important to line managers.

> **Table 6.7: Implementation Barriers**
>
> - **Level of top management support.** During the initial implementation phase, top level management gives the new strategic operating plan careful attention and scrutiny. However, once this phase is over, their attention is often redirected to more pressing but not necessarily more important matters.
>
>   Once the tasks of implementation become ongoing and a line management level responsibility, they are viewed as "normal" operations. This may well be the case with respect to simpler and more operational projects, but when it comes to anything that can have a significant long-term impact on the organization's strategic direction and capabilities, top management needs to continue to give these factors their close attention.
>
>   Long-run implementation tasks fit this category of concerns because of the cumulative impact that in-

Table 6.7: Implementation Barriers (continued)

complete and fragmentary implementations can have. Unfortunately, this set of events occurs all too often—even when these tasks are understood, there is still a strong tendency to focus on the short-term, more operational and tractable types of strategic initiatives. This remains a major reason for management affinity with project management, that is, completing a project provides an illusory sense of closure.

- **Resistance to change.** In the initial implementation phase, resistance is usually focused on the problems caused by the introduction of changes in technology and operations, the rationale for making the changes, and the impact of the changes on each individual and work unit. These and similar problems can usually be dealt with effectively by the initial implementation team—assuming that they are made aware of them and are trained to cope with them.

  These technical and operational problems will continue to cause some resistance if not dealt with decisively at the outset. However, these are not usually the problems that will challenge line management after the initial implementation phase ends. The unsolved problems and unresolved issues that persist are of greater concern: those dealing with the organization as a whole, its future, and the changes that impact the organization's culture. Members of the organization at all levels of management and the work force are quick to raise questions about why changes are being made.

> ### Table 6.7: Implementation Barriers (continued)
>
> Questions proliferate and permeate the work place whenever changes are instituted. This is human nature, and care must be taken to answer them forth rightly.
>
> - Why this change?
> - Why now?
> - Why me?
> - Why our unit?
> - What will happen to us?
> - What about my promotion?
> - What will this mean in the long run?
> - Who really is going to benefit from all of these changes?
> - How is this better than our old way of doing things?
> - Is this really necessary?
> - Can someone explain the reasons for doing all this?
> - Is this only the beginning?
> - Are you trying to tell us something by doing all of this?
> - Why weren't we included before you decided to do this?
>
> In essence, the difficult (longer-lasting) implementation problems carry over and, by default, become the responsibility of line management.
>
> - **Unforeseen trends and events.** In the course of the initial implementation phase during the first year, unforeseen trends and events are always a possibility, but they are not a primary concern of the implementor.

> **Table 6.7: Implementation Barriers (continued)**
>
> In contrast, in the long run, unforeseen trends and events increasingly become factors for line management, who must continually monitor trends and events, not only with respect to the new strategic operating plan but also to the cumulative impact of previous plans.
>
> - **Availability of resources.** In most organizations, resources are made available through the budgeting process. In the initial implementation phase, there is usually a formal budget allocation for the strategic operating plan. However, once implementation is handed off to line management, it is usually not a budgeted or measured process.
>
>   Line management is simply expected to absorb the implementation responsibilities as part of their normal duties and responsibilities. If these responsibilities are not measured, reported, evaluated, and rewarded, they receive a very low priority in the eyes of most managers.

Table 6.8 summarizes primary implementation skills and abilities required for line management to be effective. Line management needs a different set of implementation skills and abilities than those required in the initial implementation phase.

> **Table 6.8: Line Management Implementation Skills and Abilities**
>
> - **Innovative thinking and problem resolution.** Line management may be required to develop its own set of innovative, or custom fitted, solutions as the implementation process continues. This is especially true when an outside vendor is responsible for the initial phase of the implementation process and then leaves. As the new strategic initiative becomes increasingly more integrated within ongoing operations, new problems, opportunities, and unforeseen developments will always occur; and those charged with responding to them need to be ready to do just that.
> - **Content versus process focus.** During the initial implementation phase, the focus is, of necessity, on the content of the strategic initiative being introduced. Of course, the managers in charge of the initial implementation must deal with the many concerns of both individuals and groups experiencing changes in their work, but the focus remains primarily on the substance of the change itself.
>
>   After the initial implementation, line management is much more likely to have a higher incidence of problems and issues arising from both individuals and groups than did the implementors during the initial implementation cycle. This occurs as all the moving parts or dimensions of change become the focus of attention.
>
>   Managers, staff, and work force will have had more time to adjust to the changes and to reflect on the impact of implementation on themselves, fellow workers,

> **Table 6.8: Line Management Implementation Skills and Abilities (continued)**
>
> and the organization. This requires that line managers have the ability to deal with the many process issues and problems that arise. They must have the empathy and skills to deal with both individuals and groups that voice problems and concerns.
> - **Motivational skills.** All managers must possess satisfactory motivational skills in the day-to-day process of managing their operations. More difficult motivational challenges are to be found in dealing with the long-term impacts of new strategies. This will require more attention, continuous in nature, on the part of managers to address individual concerns and situations. Managers will need to be more attuned and skillful as motivators of their team's strategically-focused efforts.

Integrate implementation team roles and responsibilities into line management job descriptions

To maximize the probability that implementation occurs as designed, it is important to incorporate explicit expectations into job descriptions for each implementation role.

Table 6.9 outlines the transfer and integration of these responsibilities into appropriate job descriptions.

Table 6.9: Implementation Roles and Responsibilities

- **Transfer and integrate the following implementation roles:**
  - Sponsors and champions. The roles of sponsor and champion continue beyond the initial implementation phase. After the first wave of enthusiasm dies down and new initiatives occupy top management, it is easy to forget that sponsoring new initiatives is not a short-term task. This is also true of functional managers that sponsor change in their areas. These roles need to be accepted and continued for the duration of the implementation process.
  - Change agents. Line managers that have not been subject to major and sustained changes must learn the skills and approach of change agents. Initiating change is only the beginning; sooner or later, change management tasks become integrated and specified change agents will have moved on to the next strategic operating plan, leaving line management to assume responsibilities with the implementation process.
  - Targets of change. New individuals, work units, and departments are impacted as the effects of a new initiative spread beyond the point of introduction.

- **Transfer and integrate the following implementation responsibilities:**
  (See Step 12 for a more detailed explanation of these responsibilities)
  - Sustain commitment, involvement, and leadership of the process.

Table 6.9: Implementation Roles and Responsibilities (continued)

- Ensure the adequacy of the implementation capabilities of management.
- Articulate and communicate the strategic vision.
- Lead and motivate line management in ongoing implementation.
- Monitor and control the ongoing implementation processes.
- Adapt, change, and modify the strategic operating plan as necessary.

Identify, understand, accept, and prepare to carry out the new implementation responsibilities of the line organization

The following responsibilities are all derived from the initial implementation phase (Step 12) and should be continued. It is key that the following be understood, accepted, and acted upon by line managers:

- Integrate and direct the remaining implementation tasks.
- Motivate organization personnel to accept the strategic operating plan.
- Identify and deal with continuing and significant areas/activities with high levels of continuing resistance.
- Maintain strategic management performance levels.
- Audit and report on strategic management performance.

Manage remaining implementation tasks

Once the full scope of the implementation responsibilities are identified and accepted, management can most effectively deal with them by organizing a set of programmed activities to implement them. The reason for a formally programmed approach is to sustain implementation of strategies over time. Once a program is defined it becomes a matter of simply applying a straightforward management process along the following lines:

- Identify the remaining implementation tasks:
  - Tasks to be completed by implementation team personnel.
  - Tasks assigned to line management.
- Prioritize continuing implementation tasks.
- Identify required implementation approaches.
- Implement using these approaches.
- Monitor, measure, and control results.
- Take actions as indicated.
- Assess performance and progress periodically.
- Submit and maintain reports.

Assess the impact of the strategic operating plan on the organization

The strategic operating plan articulates the best set of strategic actions that management is able to devise, *given* the current and projected assessment of the opportunities perceived to be available. However, this in no way guarantees that the execution of the strategic operating plan will have the desired impact on the organization or its strategic direction. To repeat Eisenhower's World War II admonition: *Plans are nothing, Planning is everything.* That is to say, plans, however well executed, do not *ipso facto* achieve the results desired in the larger context of the strategy.

Plans often fail to achieve the desired results and instead produce unintended consequences that need to be evaluated and subsequently dealt with. Close scrutiny is required to assess a plan's impact on the organization and its strategic direction. This work should be treated as an ongoing task of line management. A periodic assessment should be completed at least quarterly, which can be incorporated as a part of the overall performance measurement and evaluation process. Criteria should be identified in the following categories to ensure that the strategic operating plan is achieving intended outcomes. The specific criteria will be determined by the situational factors in play, by contextual factors present, and by management's cited concerns. The criteria include:

- Achievement of the strategic operating plan objectives
- Effectiveness of strategic operating plan implementation management
- Impact on the strategic management capability
- Impact on the strategic direction of the organization
- Impact on the organization structure
- Impact on core functions
- Effectiveness of individual strategies

Develop a framework for evaluating and continuously improving the current strategic management capability

Figure 6.4 shows a framework to evaluate the current strategic management capability on a periodic basis and develop the results to be discussed with the strategic management team.

Strategy in the 21st Century

Figure 6.4: Framework for Evaluating and Improving Strategic Management

Rating scale: 1=Non-existent, 2=Needs major improvement, 3=Needs minor improvement, 4=Satisfactory, 5=Excellent

Evaluation Criteria	Skills & Comp	Process Develop	Support Systems	Current Level	Develop Priority
Strategy Assessment					
Step 1 Make initial assessment					
Step 2 Organize the strategic management team					
Step 3 Conduct external analyses					
Step 4 Conduct internal analyses					
Step 5 Develop a strategic information system					
Step 6 Evaluate analyses					
Strategy Formulation					
Step 7 Set the strategic direction					

Figure 6.4: Framework for Evaluating and Improving Strategic Management (continued)

Rating scale: 1=Non-existent, 2=Needs major improvement, 3=Needs minor improvement, 4=Satisfactory, 5=Excellent

Evaluation Criteria	Skills & Comp	Process Develop	Support Systems	Current Level	Develop Priority
Strategy Formulation (continued)					
Step 8 Formulate strategic options					
Step 9 Evaluate and select options					
Strategic Planning					
Step 10 Develop strategic plan					
Step 11 Develop strategic operating plan					
Strategy Implementation					
Step 12 Execute implementation					
Step 13 Provide ongoing implementation support					

Epilogue

This strategic management process, when implemented and managed in its entirety, enables leadership teams to bring harmony of purpose between day-to-day operations and the strategic focus of the organization.

As stated in the Introduction and Chapter 1, we believe a disciplined team will outperform the "all-knowing leader" most every time. It is important to keep this in mind as you integrate the strategic management discipline into your organization. Today's operating environment is far too complex for one person or small group to understand. It demands the inclusion, brainpower, and perspectives of many when seeking alignment behind a chosen strategy.

One of the most salient features of our approach to strategic management is that it is team-based and includes all levels of leadership and management. Our approach differs markedly from the all-too prevalent mindset that strategy is an exclusive role for "others." For 30 years we have worked to overcome this tendency by emphasizing a continuous, seamless, and inclusive, team-based approach to strategy. This philosophy guides our work each step of the way.

Beyond our team-based approach we continue to build on what we know and have learned in our three-plus-year journey writing this book. Five topics will be focal points of our own professional development in the period ahead:

1. Linking strategic management and "good governance"
2. Linking strategic management and "innovation"
3. Building a practical and effective strategic information system (SIS)
4. Developing tools and techniques to facilitate execution
5. Integrating the discipline of strategic management with online learning technologies and "easy to use" strategic management software

Linking strategic management and "good governance"

We wrote this book believing in the strategic importance of building a "leadership partnership" between an organization's board of directors and its executive management team. We strongly advocate the absolute necessity of doing this.

At the time of our book's publishing, we are reminded that individuals, families, and organizations are suffering under the weight of a deep global recession. Political and economic leaders report, at the time of this book's publishing, that the recession is ending and that our economic situation will slowly improve. For organizations and individuals still fortunate enough to survive and maintain their livelihood, this is welcome news. However, for those who have seen their organizations slump with jobs eliminated, health care insurance canceled, and savings exhausted, it is now a matter of hanging on, hoping their lot in life improves.

Reflecting on this painful period, one marked by "revelations" of recklessness, greed and "system" failure, organizational leaders must answer difficult questions and make fundamental changes if there is to be any hope of breaking the cycle of systemic bad behavior. What lessons must we learn? What changes must we make? Who is responsible for making these changes? Where do we begin to find the answers?

Epilogue

To our way of thinking the answers come by looking to and understanding what is meant by "good governance."

Boards of directors of public or private organizations must apply their intellect in such a way as to maintain the integrity, resource base, and effectiveness of their own organization to positively impact their shareholders/stakeholders and, at the very least, do no harm to society and its citizens.

This requires that a board member with fiduciary responsibility lock into the mindset of "I am a leader." And, in doing so, be thoughtful, probing and engaged in the big picture and not just a passive steward of the day-to-day. It means boards must insist on transparent reporting of defined outcomes and exercise the discipline of good governance actively and consistently.

Good governance embraces several key principles including the following:

- Genuine commitment to the organization's vision, mission, *values*, policies, goals, and strategy
- An appropriate representation of key stakeholders on the governing board
- Clearly defined roles and responsibilities that are understood and clear lines of accountability between the board and the CEO
- Positive working relationships between board, management, staff, and collaborative partners
- A process for diligently monitoring and reporting achievement of clearly defined strategic objectives
- A balance between risk taking, stability, and flexible response to environmental changes
- An abiding respect for values-driven organizational norms and behavior

There is a correlation between governance and quality of life for all. When we work to strengthen and employ good governance at the highest levels, the people and institutions we serve flourish. When we stray from this fundamental truth and allow the "masters of the universe" to point the way forward, we are all diminished.

Our work moving forward will explore this "delicate balance" between the roles of the board of directors and the CEO, with a special emphasis on the linkages within strategy management.

We are particularly interested in this point as it relates to service organizations, such as associations, nonprofits, and governmental organizations. We have done much pioneering work in the independent and public sectors over the past 30 years and this will continue to be a primary focus of our work in the years ahead.

Linking strategic management and "innovation"

As the last century drew to a close, it became obvious that strategic management had to move beyond incremental improvements and reliance on a well-known repertoire of responses in each functional area, such as the "4 Ps" of marketing. The increasing rate, scope, and impact of change, coupled with aggressive and very competent competitors operating on a global scale, made such traditional methods of strategic management less and less effective.

In essence, it became increasingly obvious that strategic management had to become more creative and innovative if an organization was to develop and maintain leadership. Kim and Mauborgne, in their *Blue Ocean Strategy* (2005), have visualized the challenge as one of *creating* the uncontested market

Epilogue

space of the blue ocean and leaving the red ocean of competition in the existing market space.

In doing so, Kim and Mauborgne have recast the process of strategic management as a comprehensive challenge in creativity and innovation. A new process that requires creating and defining the desired market space itself, that is, the blue ocean, as the very first step in the strategic management process.

Once you engage in the process, it becomes a question of how to migrate to a newly defined blue ocean from the current red ocean of existing competitive markets. Again, this requires creative and innovative thinking, accompanied by major adjustments in the structure of the organization and the acquisition of new capabilities and competencies.

In essence, there are two key processes of strategic management that we have defined as being primarily creative and innovative steps. These are as follows:

- Setting the strategic direction (Step 7). In the blue ocean metaphor this is equivalent to creating the uncontested market place.
- Identifying and/or creating alternative strategies to orient and move the organization in this strategic direction and ultimately achieve its goals (Step 8). In terms of the blue ocean it is the challenge of determining how to migrate to this new future state.

Increasingly, these processes will be integrated elements in our approach to strategic management in competitive organizations. However, since we are also working with organizations and agencies that are not focused directly on competitive markets, that is, nonprofit organizations, associations, and government agencies, we also find the need to pursue other appropriate innovative approaches, including scenario planning.

Strategy in the 21st Century

By visualizing what alternative future conditions or events are probable, we can develop responses in order to benefit.

This need is driven by the myriad of existing and new challenges these organizations and agencies face. For example, we do not have proven and tested approaches to the challenges of "the greening of the United States," global relief, the energy crisis, waste and pollution, healthcare, and education. Addressing these problems strategically will require creative and innovative approaches yet to be identified. We look forward to engaging these challenges.

Building a practical and effective strategic information system

Earlier in the epilogue we stated strategic management enables leadership teams to bring harmony of purpose between day-to-day operations and the strategic focus of the organization. While this statement is certainly true, it oft times is true for a fleeting period only. Disruptive change can occur at any time and any place. A case in point is the housing and capital market meltdown of 2008. Any strategy derived from strategic information gathered prior to September 2008 was rendered largely obsolete.

To substantiate this point, think about how your team might answer the questions listed below now versus the fall of 2008:

- What political trends are driving changes in your organization?
- What economic trends are driving changes in your organization?
- What social and cultural trends are driving changes in your organization?
- What trends in technology and science are driving changes in your organization?

- What environmental trends are driving changes in your organization?
- What is the overall state of your industry and your organization's position relative to competitors and those who influence the industry?
- Which market trends will impact the markets/customers you serve and the needs that you fill?
- What is the profile of your customer, and what customer needs do you fill?
- What is the profile of your competitors, and what is your competitive advantage?
- What is the nature of your supply chain, and where are the bottlenecks that need to be addressed?

Going forward we are keenly interested in exploring *practical solutions* for organizations to update their Strategic Information System (SIS) on a continuous basis rather than waiting until the next environmental assessment cycle begins. One area we are particularly interested in examining is the notion of "listening posts," that is, monitoring centers throughout an organization where specific individuals with core expertise in a given area are responsible for analyzing a single dimension of the external environment on a real time basis. As we envision this process now, a single individual would be assigned one or more of the questions noted above and be held accountable to the leadership team for updating the SIS and reporting out on a quarterly basis regarding emerging trends and potentially disruptive changes on the horizon.

This same logic can be equally applied to the internal dimension of the organization. What if one individual within the organization were charged with maintaining an up-to-date repository of strategic information for one or more of the questions listed below? Would it make a difference in overall performance? Would the organization be able to adapt to change more quickly? We are interested in exploring these questions:

- What internal capabilities do you have within your own organization that gives you a competitive advantage?
- What internal issues yet to be dealt with, decided, or settled require the organization's attention?
- How would you characterize or describe the general work atmosphere/culture between the board and management, within management, and between management and staff?
- What issues within your organization impact your ability to develop and deliver new products and/or services to customers?
- What issues within your organization impact your ability to grow your customer base?
- What issues within your organization impact the quality and timeliness of product and service delivery?
- What issues within your organization impact your delivery of customer service?
- How would you characterize or describe the organization's current location and ability to access required resources?
- How would you characterize your organization's strategic management competencies and overall strategic management system?

Developing tools and techniques to facilitate execution

Like so many academic disciplines it is much easier to understand the theory of strategic management than to harness its power. There are practical *barriers* at work in every organization that make it much easier to "talk the talk" than to "walk the walk" of becoming a strategy-focused organization.

Epilogue

Each one of these barriers is summarized below:

- Accessing a repository of up-to-date strategic information is absolutely vital if an organization is to remain strategically focused. In the real world *data and information are scattered* across file cabinets, research reports, websites, and most importantly in the heads of the organizational leaders and their operational staff.
- There is *rarely enough time* to give strategic management the attention it requires. People are already busy trying to complete their immediate job responsibilities and keep up with their own personal life. This results in delays or poor implementation of the process itself.
- Even if the time is available, the people needed to effectively contribute to an organization's strategy are often times scattered around the planet with *distance being a major barrier* to meaningful strategic collaboration.
- The challenge of bringing the necessary people together, in one room, for the time necessary to think through a strategy and build a system is a barrier. This inevitably means incurring additional *travel and coordination costs* that may or may not be in the current operating budget.
- Adding to the cost consideration is a perception of *diminished staff productivity*, at least in the short run.
- And finally, there is the ever present constraint of the "human condition" itself. While some team members naturally embrace structure, process, and timely actions, a large proportion of most teams *lacks insufficient discipline* to build and maintain a well functioning strategic management system.

After more than 30 years of confronting these barriers on a daily basis, we have come to understand and appreciate that none of them ever goes away. Nevertheless, the negative influences they inflict can be minimized to a large extent. We believe the key to mitigating their effects is in skillful employment of the web.

We have built and refined a practical, web-based strategic management software tool named MAPPware® to address these barriers (www.mappware.com). The writing of this book has helped us understand where our product development needs to focus to minimize these constraints. Further refinement of this tool and the development of new online strategic management tools will be a major focus of our work.

Integrating the discipline of strategic management with online learning technologies and "easy to use" strategic management software

Our own journey has led us to a point where we now have a deep understanding and appreciation for the field of strategic management. The articulation of this book bears witness to our travails and growth in understanding.

Additionally, our team has designed and developed an eight-session (award winning) Certificate in Strategic Management Program (CSM) that incorporates all of the material in this book (www.csmlearning.com). CSM is offered online and comes bundled with MAPPware to facilitate the efficient deployment of the principles and techniques advocated throughout the book.

Our vision is to become the "back office" to others who seek to apply the discipline of strategic management. This demands that we continue to refine and improve our portfolio of strategic management products and services. A central element of our product development efforts is to produce a formal instructor "certification" program, one that will certify qualified strategic management professionals to teach the Certificate in Strategic Management Program and reach audiences in different sectors and spheres of activity.

In a broader sense, education, training, and development of strategic thinking is indispensable to the continued development of the strategic management discipline. Over the next decade we hope to impact many different education and training delivery systems with our work, that is, graduate, undergraduate, certificate, certification, on-the-job mentoring, coaching, and facilitating. This is a unique feature of our strategic management focus and comprises a set of competencies that we plan to develop further. At our core we are educators, and we continue to build our own competencies and move to the next level.

In the end it comes down to making a lasting difference. We believe a program that integrates our insights into strategic management and a team-based philosophy and makes practical use of the web and online learning technologies is the way forward.

Respectively and respectfully,

RANDALL ROLLINSON AND EARL YOUNG
rrollinson@lblstrategies.com
773-758-6921

APPENDIX 1

Distilled Wisdom

The Art of War, by Sun Tzu
(Translated by Lionel Giles)

Around 2300 years ago, Sun Tzu is credited for having written *The Art of War*, a compilation of essays that remains, to this day, profound wisdom on the conduct of war. In summary, there are several important themes developed by Sun Tzu that we can effectively apply to strategy challenges in business and organizational life today.

ENVIRONMENTAL SCAN

1. **Strategic Planning and Rational Analysis**
   - Planning based on rational analysis of the best quality information available.

2. **Importance of Information and Related Processing Capability**
   - Secure the best information available. Protect the sources and processing capabilities from compromise.

3. **Importance of Knowledge, Wisdom, and Understanding**
   - A theme that is embedded in virtually every other theme, especially in regard to knowing self and opposition.

4. **Study of the Past and Analyze Current Conditions to Create an "Edge"**
   - Leads to knowledge, which, if properly focused, can lead to success.
   - Strive to become the superior force in more than mere numbers. This is achieved through focused knowledge and experience, which, in turn, is gained by studying and observing situations, conditions, people, and events; remembering what was observed; comparing the observations to one another as well as to contemporary circumstances; and disciplining application of the results of the observations in the pursuit of strategic objectives.
   - Know yourself, your opposition, and the environment within which interaction will occur.

Appendix 1

STRATEGY

5. **Staying Focused on Strategic Objectives**
   - Keep attention of all resources and related action focused on achieving strategic objectives as promptly as possible. Avoid becoming distracted by the nuances and intricacies of implementing complex strategies and tactics.

6. **Suitability of Strategies and Tactics to Situation**
   - Match the suitability of strategies and tactics to the market's phase, section, pattern, and volatility.

7. **Inherent Advantages and Disadvantages**
   - Understand and guard against the inherent disadvantage in every advantageous situation. Likewise, remain alert and capitalize on advantages that arise in distressed situations.

8. **Opportunistic Flexibility in Adapting Strategies and Tactics to Situation**
   - Capitalize on emerging opportunities created by changing market conditions. Employ a well thought out trading plan and remain flexible in adapting tactics to ever-changing market conditions within the context of each predetermined strategy.

SELF

9. **Ethical Conduct**
   - Be moral and ethical; let it guide your thinking, decision making, and actions.

10. **Reliance on Your Own Preparation**
    - Rely on your own preparations. Do not hope for success based on the opposition not preparing.

11. **Competent Management**
    - Develop a balanced management skill set to enable prudent resource utilization.

12. **Disciplined Emotions**
    - Minimize emotional influences (hope, fear, greed).

ORGANIZATION/MANAGEMENT

13. **Disciplined Organization and Financial Management**
    - Discipline, efficient and effective organization, and utilization of all resources (people, plans, tools, capital) in the capacity to which they are best suited, in all situations, is critical to success.
    - Ensure appropriate financing and provisioning of all activities (prior to and during).

14. **Clear Communication**
    - Ensure clear communication in all aspects of the development, testing, and implementation of strategies and tactics.

15. **Deception and "Shaping"**
    - Practice deception in plans, strategy, and tactics (and its corollary) when facing adversaries.

Appendix 1

WARNINGS

16. Avoidance of Being Deceived and "Shaped"
- Take precautionary steps to avoid being deceived by the opposition.

17. Rewarding, Replenishing, and Investing in Support Structure
- Be sure to allocate appropriate parts of the profits of successful strategies to all resources employed in the portfolio management and risk management activity.

18. Patience, Positioning, and Timing
- Develop patience and discipline in positioning and timing the use of all resources in adapting to ever-changing circumstances.

19. Avoidance of Catastrophic Loss
- Avoid catastrophic mistakes by promptly adapting strategies and tactics to current circumstances, thereby keeping the consequences of mistakes small and manageable.

20. Preservation and Protection of Resources
- At all times seek to keep all resources in profitable and advantageous positions. Likewise, quickly liquidate unprofitable positions and minimize exposure to situations with inordinate risk to uncertain market movements.

APPENDIX 2

An Annotated Bibliography of Publications About Teams

Underlying all successful strategy-focused management systems is the management prerequisite to have a clear and comprehensive grasp of the principles and practices of teams in regard to their organization, operation, and function as a key feature of strategic management process design.

However, the literature is too vast and varied to summarize easily—even in a book devoted to the topic. At the same time, it is still useful to have a compilation of some of the leading books on teams that are especially relevant to strategic management.

Therefore, the following brief annotated bibliography of publications about teams and teamwork is included as a useful guide to a representative selection of works on the application of the principles and practices of teams—in effect, a gateway to understanding and using this well-developed and eminently practical literature.

The following references are listed alphabetically. The chief criterion used in summarizing the contents of these sources has been their usefulness to those involved in strategic management and not their contributions to the literature, their methodology, or the basis of the information.

In short, it is left to the readers to determine the relevance of each reference to themselves, their management team, and, more generally, their organization. The selection of these references indicates the authors' assessment of their importance and relevance to strategic management.

Note: Some authors use the term *small groups* but with respect to their team structures and functions.

Annotated References

1. Hackman, J. Richard, ed. *Groups That Work (and Those that Don't). Creating Conditions for Effective Teamwork)*. San Francisco: Jossey-Bass, 1990.

    Focus. Identification of factors and conditions that foster excellent team performance, high quality outcomes, and the enrichment of each team member's experience; an analysis of why some groups (teams) fail and others succeed; and suggestions on how to improve team performance.

    Approach. This is an in-depth analysis of 27 small work groups in seven diverse categories showing how teams were organized and how they operated to get things done. Summary conclusions and evaluations regarding each category are made by experts in the field.

    Relevance to strategic management. There are three case studies of top management groups with respect to setting organizational directions. Summary comments focus on relationships between teams and their CEOs, the impact of team member qualifications, delegation of power, executive decision making, and relationships with managers and staff members *not* selected as team members.

    Recommended readership. Executives and senior managers that do *not* have an effective track record of organizing and working with teams reporting directly to them and "first time" appointees to top management teams.

2. Hughes, Marcia, and James Bradford Terrell. *The Emotionally Intelligent Team: Understanding and Developing the Behaviors of Success*. San Francisco: Jossey-Bass, A Wiley Imprint, 2007.

    Focus. A discussion of the value of emotional and social intelligence of teams. Identification and analysis of seven skills revealing a team's emotional and social intelligence, including team identity, motivation, emotional awareness, communication, stress tolerance, conflict resolutions, and positive mood.

    Approach. Theory, information, and guidance are offered to business managers based on the principles and effective practices of emotional and social intelligence. The authors have incorporated this information and guidance in a test instrument for measuring team member performance in each of the seven competencies.

    Relevance to strategic management. All team members must understand and have skill in using emotional intelligence for the team to function efficiently and effectively. This premise is not usually recognized explicitly, nor is it monitored by management, team leaders, or team members. Developing and assisting management in the organization and implementation of strategy requires a very high degree of emotional and social intelligence.

    Recommended readership. All executives, managers at all levels, and team leaders and members engaged in developing and/or implementing strategic decisions. Often this dimension of team behavior is completely overlooked making this a recommended reading for all strategic management teams, regardless of their level of strategy-focused management performance.

3. Katzenbach, Jon R. *Teams at the Top: Unleashing the Potential of Both Teams and Individual Leaders.* Boston: Harvard Business School Press, 1998.

   Focus. Recognizing and resolving the inherent conflicts between the discipline and demands of executive leadership and those inherent in being members of a top management team. A key point is knowing when and how to use the two disciplines.

   Approach. Anecdotal material based on the author's consulting experience (Director of McKinsey and Company at time of writing) and well-known companies, such as Enron, Ben & Jerry's, Champion, Citicorp, and Mobil.

   Relevance to strategic management. This book is directly applicable to developing new and/or improved strategies to cope with new challenges, unexpected events, and rapidly changing events using teams and, when required, transitioning to individual executive responsibilities.

   Recommended readership. This book is recommended for the entire management hierarchy of an organization—especially those experiencing difficulty in using teams at the top.

4. Katzenbach, Jon R. and Douglas K. Smith. *The Wisdom of Teams: Creating the High Performance Organization.* New York: Harper Business: A Division of Harper Collins Publishers, 1993.

   Focus. A comprehensive overview of team organizing, managing, and operating principles and practice at each level of development. Emphasis is on performance and structural factors in an evolutionary path to high performance teams.

Approach. Analyses, evaluations, and insights on team performance based on 46 cases familiar to the authors. One appendix includes commonly asked questions about teams, commonly assumed "answers," and answers based on the book. A second appendix lists the teams researched for the book.

Relevance to strategic management. Lessons learned with respect to the following topics: team performance, achieving high performance teams, team leaders, overcoming team obstacles, team performance at the top, and top management's role in leading high performance team.

Recommended readership. Executives and senior managers that want to further develop their understanding of how to use teams effectively in developing and managing team-based strategic management systems.

5. Katzenbach, Jon R. *The Discipline of Teams: A Mindbook-Workbook for Delivering Small Group Performance.* New York: John Wiley and Sons, Inc., 2001.

Focus. Discipline as the common denominator of teams. There are three sources of discipline: the leaders, peers, individuals. Each are used to characterize types of small groups. Primary emphasis is on the application of team disciplines.

Approach. The term *mindset* refers to an analysis and discussion of key topics identified in chapter headings. The *workbook* consists of a separate section at the end of each chapter containing a series of questions and exercises to provide an opportunity to apply the principles set forth in each chapter.

Relevance to strategic management. Understanding that the most important characteristic of teams is *discipline*—not bonding, togetherness, empowerment, or any similar characteristic—and knowing how to apply this discipline. One chapter is devoted to virtual teams, their opportunities and obstacles, which is especially useful for multi-site team membership.

Recommended readership. Management teams that want to acquire skill in applying the disciplines of team management, organization, and operation. The exercises provide a guide for in-house training and development.

6. Mackin, Deborah. *The Team Building Tool Kit: Tips and Tactics for Effective Workplace Teams*. New York: AMACOM, 2007.

Focus. A basic, yet comprehensive, guide to all aspects of team development, organization, and management.

Approach. An instructional guide that includes questions, charts, checklists, guidelines, suggestions, tips, and tactics for effective workplace teams. This book can be easily used at all levels of the organization.

Relevance to strategic management. Topics of importance include team accountability, decision making, a problem solving process and tools, team scoreboards and performance assessments, and the teaming road map. The coverage, albeit basic, constitutes a basis for an audit of the operation of any team.

Recommended readership. While not specifically written for use in top management and/or strategic management teams, this book is useful at all levels of the organization by all managers and team members that need a comprehensive operational guide to the efficient and effective teamwork.

Appendix 2

7. MacMillan, Pat. *The Performance Factor: Unlocking the Secrets of Teamwork*. Nashville, TN: Broadman and Holman Publishers, 2001.

   Focus. Identification and discussion of six characteristics of high-performance teams. These are common purpose, clear roles, accepted leadership, effective team processes, solid relationships, and excellent communication. Secondly, the book addresses these principles in practice.

   Approach. Principles and practices presented are based on tested and proven results in real organizations. Each chapter ends with a summary of big ideas, key concepts, and a message to team leaders. In the final chapter presented ideas and concepts are applied to the development and maintenance of high-performance teams. Appendices include FAQs and a team evaluation survey based on the six performance factors.

   Relevance to strategic management. A new paradigm of leadership that outlines a new set of management responsibilities for leading, listening, asking questions, discussing, facilitating, coaching, and releasing initiative and creativity in others. These are in stark contrast to traditional leadership based on managing, telling, directing, convincing, deciding/providing answers, controlling, and supervising.

   Recommended readership. Executives and senior managers intent on incorporating a team-based management style in their organizations and for management teams intent on high performance.

8. Maxwell, John C. *The 17 Indisputable Laws of Teamwork Workbook: Embrace Them and Empower Your Team*. Nashville, TN: Nelson Impact, A Division of Thomas Nelson Publishers, 2003.

Focus. Seventeen principles of effective teams, team leadership, and team operations are identified as laws. These include, for example, the law of the big picture (the goal is more important than the role), the law of the compass (vision gives team members direction and confidence), the law of the scoreboard (the team needs to know where it stands), and the law of identify (shared values define the team).

Approach. A chapter is devoted to each law and includes the following six parts: a short reading, observations with illustrative questions, a learning section pertaining to the law being discussed, an evaluation section pertaining to your own teamwork abilities, a discussion section with suggested questions, and finally a take-action section outlining a project to be done.

Relevance to strategic management. These laws are easily applied to strategic management teams because they include the critical dimensions of team organization and operation. They form an excellent guide to top management for analyzing and evaluating team operations and identifying the root causes of success (or failure).

Recommended readership. The book-based exercises are useful for established teams that are committed to upgrading their performance to the next level. As such, they can be used by strategic management teams at any level of sophistication and complexity.

9. Parker, Glenn M. *Team Players and Teamwork: The New Competitive Business Strategy*. San Francisco: Jossey-Bass Publishers, 1990.

Focus. The central focus is on *team players* and what makes them effective or ineffective, team players as team leaders, and developing a team player culture. Team player styles are identified as contributors, collaborators, communicators, and challengers.

Approach. Drawing on the experience of more than 50 organizations, the author shows how team player styles can be integrated in a complementary manner to enhance team outcomes. Appendices are included containing tools for developing teams and team players including surveys, action planning guides, and team player styles.

Relevance to strategic management. The four roles of team players identified by the author are all critical to the success of strategic management teams. The cited roles are not usually identified and clearly understood nor are the concepts and techniques for their most effective use.

Recommended readership. Executives and senior managers that use, or plan to use, strategic management teams will find this book helpful in determining team membership, evaluating team processes, and improving team outputs.

10. Senge, Peter M. *The Fifth Discipline: The Art and Practice of the Learning Organization*. New York: Doubleday, 1990.

   Focus. Five disciplines are identified as being necessary for the development of a learning organization; they include systems thinking (the fifth dimension), mental modeling, having a shared vision, *team learning*, and personal mastery.

   Approach. An integrated development of the five disciplines and how they combine to create a learning organization. The book is based on theory and practice, especially the experience of the author in introducing the concept to thousands of employees in Fortune 500 firms.

Relevance to strategic management. The attributes of a learning organization are basic to a successfully operating strategic management system. The importance of being responsive to its threats and opportunities requires learning how to respond quickly and effectively. The section on team learning as a core competency is not covered significantly in any of the other references.

Recommended readership. Executives, senior managers, and top management team leaders that want to adopt "learning organization" principles and practices. This book is highly recommended for management teams in large organizations that are often mired in outmoded processes and technology.

11. Strauss, David. *How to Make Collaboration Work: Powerful Ways to Build Consensus, Solve Problems, and Make Decisions.* San Francisco: Berrett-Koehler Publishers, Inc., 2002.

Focus. Five principles of collaborative action are postulated and developed. These are as follows: involve relevant stakeholders, build consensus phase by phase, design a process map, designate a process facilitator, and harness the power of group memory.

Approach. The author draws on his own experience and that of his colleagues, using examples and proven concepts to develop and apply the five principles. These principles are then integrated in a model to develop facilitative leadership and collaborative organizations.

Relevance to strategic management. The principles of collaborative action underlie the development and management of team-based strategic management. Explicit knowledge of these principles and how to apply them are

Appendix 2

critical in the design and effective management of strategic management systems.

Recommended readership. All members of a management team committed to the development of a collaborative approach to strategic management, whether the team is confronting this challenge for the first time or well along in its strategic management journey.

APPENDIX 3

Internal Analysis/ Audit Checklist

Assess the internal performance of your organization using a six-point *Strength to Weakness* rating scale.

Functional Analysis

	S W
1. Management prepares a formal business plan or strategic plan annually.	1 2 3 4 5 6
2. The organization has an established strategy and direction that will keep it competitive in the future.	1 2 3 4 5 6
3. The organization uses a mission statement to guide the direction of the organization.	1 2 3 4 5 6
4. The values of the organization are clearly communicated to all employees.	1 2 3 4 5 6
5. Management decisions are based on long-term strategy rather than short-term results.	1 2 3 4 5 6

	S W
6. The organization uses strategic alliances when appropriate.	1 2 3 4 5 6
7. Management uses predefined "performance measures" on a regular basis to monitor and control progress.	1 2 3 4 5 6
8. Results are honestly reported without distortion or rationalization.	1 2 3 4 5 6
9. Management measures productivity on a regular basis.	1 2 3 4 5 6
10. Management measures customer satisfaction on a regular basis.	1 2 3 4 5 6
11. Management measures quality on a regular basis.	1 2 3 4 5 6
12. Management measures cost on a regular basis.	1 2 3 4 5 6
13. Management prepares budgets and uses them to guide decision making.	1 2 3 4 5 6
14. The organization maintains up-to-date information technology that meets the needs of all employees and stakeholders.	1 2 3 4 5 6
15. Record keeping is up-to-date in key areas.	1 2 3 4 5 6
16. The organization possesses good team problem-solving methods and skills.	1 2 3 4 5 6

Appendix 3

	S W
17. Effective leadership is exhibited on a regular basis.	1 2 3 4 5 6
18. Management is effective in dealing with professionals.	1 2 3 4 5 6
19. Management can delegate effectively and efficiently.	1 2 3 4 5 6
20. Employees have a great deal of confidence in the organization judgment of the management team.	1 2 3 4 5 6
21. Collaboration is encouraged at all levels and success is recognized.	1 2 3 4 5 6
22. Management culture encourages reasoned risk taking.	1 2 3 4 5 6
23. The organization adapts well to changing circumstances.	1 2 3 4 5 6
24. The correct mix of people is in place and functioning as a team.	1 2 3 4 5 6
25. Employees receive the appropriate training to take on their position.	1 2 3 4 5 6
26. Cross functional training occurs as needed.	1 2 3 4 5 6
27. Employees appear to enjoy what they are doing.	1 2 3 4 5 6
28. Job descriptions are in place for all employees.	1 2 3 4 5 6

	S W
29. Performance evaluations are conducted on a regular basis.	1 2 3 4 5 6
30. Employees are informed and involved in the decision-making process.	1 2 3 4 5 6
31. Management encourages employees to set their own goals.	1 2 3 4 5 6
32. An employee manual spells out benefits and policies.	1 2 3 4 5 6
33. A formal reporting hierarchy exists and is known to all employees.	1 2 3 4 5 6
34. All employees understand what is expected of them in order to accomplish their objectives.	1 2 3 4 5 6
35. Circumstances of employees are considered when decisions are made that directly affect them.	1 2 3 4 5 6
36. Employees are encouraged to express their ideas and innovate.	1 2 3 4 5 6
37. Employees are provided opportunities to grow and excel.	1 2 3 4 5 6
38. Open and honest expression, without fear of retaliation, is the norm in the organization.	1 2 3 4 5 6
39. Documented policies and procedures exist and are followed.	1 2 3 4 5 6

	S W
40. Quality control is a primary focus of the organization.	1 2 3 4 5 6
41. Adequate capacity exists to grow the organization to the next level.	1 2 3 4 5 6
42. A "continuous improvement" culture exists at all levels of the organization.	1 2 3 4 5 6
43. Organizational design is appropriate.	1 2 3 4 5 6
44. Established work units have a clear direction and purpose.	1 2 3 4 5 6
45. Company information systems support operations effectively and efficiently.	1 2 3 4 5 6
46. Measurement of performance is deliberate.	1 2 3 4 5 6
47. Supervisors know how to organize resources and get things done.	1 2 3 4 5 6

Core Process Analysis

Core Process:
☐ Product Design and Development
☐ Order Generation
☐ Order Fulfillment
☐ Customer Service

	S W
1. The entire process is defined, detailed, and communicated to all employees.	1 2 3 4 5 6
2. A baseline of performance is established against which improvement can be measured.	1 2 3 4 5 6
3. Total cycle time is within appropriate limits.	1 2 3 4 5 6
4. The process is consistent, and outputs are regular.	1 2 3 4 5 6
5. Work flows in unison between the external suppliers, the internal providers of the product or service, and the targeted customers.	1 2 3 4 5 6
6. The process can quickly produce work outputs in response to changing customer needs.	1 2 3 4 5 6
7. The process produces what is needed when it is needed.	1 2 3 4 5 6

	S　　　　　　W
8. The process is flexible and responsive and readily accommodates changes while remaining in balance.	1　2　3　4　5　6
9. Problems are identified on a systematic basis and eliminated.	1　2　3　4　5　6
10. Problems identified with the process get solved on the first attempt.	1　2　3　4　5　6
11. Changes to the process are well thought out and carefully implemented.	1　2　3　4　5　6
12. Managers of the process correct problems instead of rationalizing them away or blaming others.	1　2　3　4　5　6
13. Providing value to the customer is the overriding reason for the process.	1　2　3　4　5　6
14. Employees have a thorough understanding of the process and are committed to meeting performance standards.	1　2　3　4　5　6

APPENDIX 4

The Nominal Group Technique to Clarify and Prioritize an OTSW Evaluation

The nominal group technique is used after organization Opportunities, Threats, Strengths, and Weaknesses have been identified and a list of same constructed. This work gets done through a highly structured process requiring the participation of the planning team to the fullest extent possible. It is a nonthreatening because it maintains anonymity for those who participate. Here are the steps:

STEP 1: Silent Generation of Ideas

Give each participant time to silently think about the organization in terms of Opportunities and Threats they believe exist within the operating environment and the Strengths and Weaknesses the organization has in going about its work. Each person is directed to collect his/her thoughts on paper attending to each area (OTSW) separately. A second option is to have team members fill out these worksheets in advance of the meeting.

STEP 2: Round Robin Reporting of Ideas

Begin the round robin reporting of ideas using individuals' notes made in Step 1. For the sake of example we will use the Strengths category here. Ask for a volunteer to offer *one* Strength from his/her list and record it on the flip chart. Then ask the next person for *one* from his/her list and add it to the flip chart. Continue this process until everyone has made a contribution or, at the very least, has had sufficient opportunity to contribute.

The round robin process of collecting ideas and recording them on the flip chart continues as long as people have new things to contribute. No critical discussion of the individual Strengths is done during this step. When all of the Strengths are recorded, assign/label each one with a number or a letter. Repeat this process for each category (OTSW).

STEP 3: Discussion: Looking for Clarification and Duplication

Open up the discussion for the purpose of clarifying any of the ideas that were contributed. Team members are encouraged to ask each other the meaning of words and phrases that were recorded on the flip chart and move toward group understanding on ideas being brought forward.

The purpose of this step is to provide individuals the opportunity to give fuller explanations of their ideas and foster group recognition and consolidation of like-minded expressions. Doing this will keep the finalized choices clear cut and prevent confusion as to the choices and the watering down of the point totals/results of the ranking. Also, it is very important to make sure that ideas are not evaluated as to their merit at this time—do not allow arguments to develop.

Appendix 4

STEP 4: Ranking of Opportunities, Threats, Strengths, and Weaknesses

Give each team member a set of OTSW priority sheets, one each for Opportunities, Threats, Strengths, and Weaknesses. Each person is to write on the appropriate sheet the number (or letter) for each of the Opportunities, Threats, Strengths, and Weaknesses he/she believes important enough to be recognized as a high priority.

For example: On the "Opportunity" priority sheet each person will write the number (or letter) of the Opportunity he/she feels is of highest priority ("1st Priority" box), the second highest ("2nd Priority" box), the third highest ("3rd Priority" box), continuing down through, and including, the fifth highest priority.

Once this task is completed by the participants, collect the individual ranking sheets and do the following:

- Tally the results by ranked priority level and transfer the totals onto a master sheet.
- Take the tally total by priority level for each item and multiply it by the point value for that level ranking For instance, a given opportunity is ranked 10 times with a priority level of either 1st, 2nd, 3rd, 4th, or 5th. Multiply the total number of tallies for each given ranking by the point value assigned to that level of priority (that is, 4 rankings as the 1st priority where 1st priority = 5 points *means* calculate 4 tallies x 5 points = 20 points)
- Add up the individual results of each multiplication action for tally totals by level of priority. This will give you the total number of points for the entire priority ranking activity for a given OTSW item.

The items that end up with the highest aggregate scores are those that received the most attention by the team as priorities. There are usually three to six items that rise to the top as the highest priorities within each of the four areas. Write the number or letter of the highest priorities at the bottom of each tally sheet.

Note: Prioritize in the following order: (a) Opportunities, (b) Threats, (c) Strengths, and (d) Weaknesses.

Appendix 4

OTSW Ranking Ballot

OTSW Category ☐ Opportunities ☐ Threats ☐ Strengths ☐ Weaknesses **Review the master list (by category) and select five that you feel are the highest priority.** Write the number of each one in the appropriate box. Example: The most important opportunity goes in the 1st priority box; the second most important goes in 2nd priority box and so forth. **Identify each OTSW by the number or letter listed on the flip chart.**	**1st Priority** 5 points
2nd Priority 4 points	**3rd Priority** 3 points
4th Priority 2 points	**5th Priority** 1 point

Strategy in the 21st Century

OTSW Scoring Sheet

OTSW Category ☐ Opportunities ☐ Threats ☐ Strengths ☐ Weaknesses		
Tally each ballot by placing the point total next to the corresponding number. Add up the totals and enter the highest totals by rank at the bottom of the page.		
1		16
2		17
3		18
4		19
5		20
6		21
7		22
8		23
9		24
10		25
11		26
12		27
13		28
14		29
15		30
1st 2nd 3rd	4th	5th

Appendix 4

OTSW Priorities

Five highest ranked priorities: Opportunities, Threats, Strengths and Weaknesses

Opportunities	Threats
1st	1st
2nd	2nd
3rd	3rd
4th	4th
5th	5th

Strengths	Weaknesses
1st	1st
2nd	2nd
3rd	3rd
4th	4th
5th	5th

Glossary of Strategic Management Terms

Activity
One of the steps required to complete a process.

Analysis
The examination and close scrutiny of data and information without the introduction of opinions, biased perceptions of the data and information, or evaluative statements.

Balanced Scorecard
A Balanced Scorecard bridges the gap between vision and strategy and execution, based on the premise that financial performance depends on satisfying customers, which results from having effective business processes, which in turn requires necessary organizational competencies. It includes a set of linked and aligned and deployed performance measurements that are deployed across four organizational dimensions: financial, customer, internal processes, and learning and growth. Their primary purpose is to provide management with an integrated and comprehensive approach to the implementation of a given set of strategies and derived operational objectives.

Benchmark

The process of comparing an organization, its operations, or processes to those of an organization that is superior in regard to some metric(s). These comparisons need not be in the same industry.

Change management

The process of moving an organization, function, or process through a transformation process to a new and/or improved level of performance.

Consensus

A group decision or action that all members agree to support, even though it may not exactly reflect an individual's preferred choice. Consensus is possible when diverse points of view have been heard thoroughly and openly.

Cross-functional

A process or activity that includes portions of the process or activity from two or more functions within an organization.

Current operations

The organization's day-to-day activities with respect to all functions, processes, and departments of the organization.

Customer

The person(s) or organizations who use your output—the next in line to receive it. Whether your customers are internal or external to your organization, they use your output as an input to their work processes.

Customer requirements

What a customer needs, wants, and expects of an organization's output. Customers generally express requirements around the characteristics of timeliness, quantity, fitness for use, ease of use, expectations, and perceptions of value.

Delta

The delta is where change occurs, It is where people stop operating in the old way, learn new ways, make mistakes, mourn the loss of the old and test and integrate the new way into ongoing operations.

Development

The results of systematic efforts to bring about structural, operational, and performance improvements in a set of capabilities in order to enhance and/or increase outputs.

Distinctive/core competency

A unique capability that provide a competitive advantage over the competition.

Double loop learning

The process of questioning and subjecting to scrutiny the variables themselves that are used to operationalize (but not question) goals and plans (single-loop learning) as a basis for future action (double loop learning).

Environmental influences

Internal and external factors that have an impact on an industry and/or an organization.

Environmental scan

A systematic review of current and/or emerging trends, events, situations, problems, and issues that are or might impact the organization, its operation, and/or its performance. A scan may be focused on either external or internal factors.

Evaluation

The process of comparing and assessing some entity or attribute using a specific criterion (or criteria), that is, a norm, standard, regulation, or expectation.

External analyses

An examination of the dimensions of an organization's external environment, including the close scrutiny of those trends, events that are having or might have an impact on the performance capabilities of the management, resources, structure, processes, and operation of an organization.

Focused mission

The purpose or reason the organization exists, that is, who will be served, what services will be provided (generally), and where geographically the organization will target its efforts.

Function

Specialized area of related activities within an organization that are grouped together in order to manage them effectively and efficiently, for example, finance, marketing, and operations.

Functional management

A level of management below general management that is in charge of a given function.

Globalization

A process of interaction and integration among the people, companies, and governments of different nations, driven by international trade and investment and aided by information technology. This process also impacts the environment, culture, political systems, economic development and prosperity, and human well-being in societies around the world. It includes investing, managing, organizing, and operating on a worldwide scale, that is, across national boundaries and in different cultures and societies.

Goals

A generally stated long-term target or fixed purpose to be achieved in accordance with the organization's vision and mission.

Growth

The measurable increase in the input, throughput, or output of an organization, process, or activity.

Implementation

The set of management and operational processes required to add to, or modify, an existing strategy, organization structure, process or operating system, such that the change is accepted by the organization as the new strategic and operational norm.

Improvement

The enhanced capability and/or performance of an organization, its functions, processes, or activities made possible by changes in their design, management, and/or operation.

Innovation

Introduction and adaptation of a new idea, concept, or invention to an activity or process.

Input

The materials, equipment, information, people, money, or environmental conditions that are needed beforehand.

Internal analyses

Critical examination of the internal dimensions and performance capabilities of the management, resources, structure, processes, and operation of an organization.

Key performance indicator

A measure for which the organization has data that help quantify the achievement of a desired strategic objective. Key performance indicators give an "indication" as to whether a particular objective is being achieved *and* help to answer the question: "How would we know a result if we achieved it?"

Key result area

An explicitly stated area of concern or discipline (either externally or internally) where tangible results must be realized in order for the shared vision to be realized.

Lagging indicator

A measurable economic activity that changes *after* the economy has established a pattern or trend. They have no predictive value, but they are useful in confirming changes that have taken place in economic activity.

Leading indicator

A measurable economic activity that changes *before* the economy has established a pattern or trend. Useful in predicting changes in economic activity.

Line Manager

Person who heads a department or sub-function and is responsible for collaborating with his team to achieve a specific objective(s) via listening, learning, policy making, target setting, decision making.

Macro environment

Forces at work in the external operating environment that can affect an organization's ability to serve its customers and make a profit, for example, demographic changes and economic trends.

MAPP®

An acronym standing for Management through Applied Planning Process®. It is the planning methodology that defines and directs the use of MAPPware®.

MAPPware®

An easy to use online strategic management tool that integrates strategic planning, execution and performance measurement.

MAPPware® Guest

A person who can access the tool to read reports and participate in the Forum but who does not contribute directly to the planning process.

MAPPware® Team Manager

The person responsible for directing the strategic planning process and information management within the tool.

MAPPware® Team Member

A person who is participating and directly contributing in the strategic planning process.

Market positioning

The process of identifying and occupying a distinct niche or place in the market for products and services in order to achieve an advantage over competing products and services.

Micro environment

Forces close to an organization that affect its ability to serve its customers and make a profit, for example, regulatory changes and stakeholder perceptions.

Milestone

A key activity, whether a deliverable or a decision, being completed in a project or in the development or in the operations of the organization.

Mission

An organization's purpose—-the basic rationale for the existence of the organization. It defines *who we are, what we do, and how (in very general terms) we do it.* While a vision alludes to the future, the mission statement deals with the here and now—what we are currently doing. However, the two are not unrelated. A mission statement should describe activities that will lead to the fulfillment of the organization's vision.

Objectives

Outcomes the organization wishes to accomplish over a specific period of time.

Operating plan

A balanced set of objectives and related projects designed to meet the organization's primary goals.

Organization culture

The specific collection of values and norms that are shared by people and groups in an organization and that control the way they interact with each other and with stakeholders outside the organization.

OTSW evaluation (sometimes known as SWOT)

An evaluation of the external environmental scan to determine opportunities or threats, followed by an evaluation of internal scan to determine strengths and weaknesses. The result of this evaluation will be the development a comprehensive understanding of the current environment and context of the organization. This, in turn, will provide the foundation for strategic thinking and planning.

Performance evaluation

Tracking and analysis of key performance indicators linked to specific objectives of the strategic operating plan, in order to measure success or failure in achieving stated outcomes and evaluate how successful the organization is in achieving its goals and objectives.

Performance measures

Key performance indicators comprised of variables configured into formulas to calculate and report measureable results used to help an organization define and evaluate how successful it is in achieving its goals and objectives.

Policies

Guidelines developed to influence/instruct/specify how members of an organization should make decisions or act in given circumstances.

Process

A sequence of steps, tasks, or activities that converts inputs to outputs. A work process adds value to the inputs by changing them or using them to produce something new. Some processes may be contained wholly within a department or function (that is, accounting, marketing). However, the critical areas of work performed by an organization usually involve processes that cross functional or departmental boundaries. These are cross-functional processes. Processes are composed of sub processes that in turn consist of a group of related activities (for example, order entry). Activities consist of groups of related tasks (for example, writing an order). Tasks are elementary actions of work (for example, time stamping an invoice).

Project

An undertaking with a defined starting point and ending point. It includes significant allocation of resources and has defined parameters that determine completion of the project, A project has finite or limited resources assigned to it. In the case of a new projects it includes increased levels of risk and uncertainty.

SBU

A Strategic Business Unit of an organization. An internal profit center composed of discrete and independent product or market segments. An SBU may be any size, but it must have a unique mission, identifiable competitors, an external market focus, and significant control over its business functions and processes.

Scenario planning

The process of visualizing what future conditions or events are probable, what their consequences or effects are likely to be, and how to respond to, or benefit from, them.

Shared vision

A desired future state that a team shares and attempts to realize.

Stakeholder

Individual person, group, association, or external organization that has a significant interest in and/or impact on an organization.

Standard

Rule, norm, regulation, custom, or principle that is used as a basis for measurement, evaluation, comparison, or judgment.

Strategic alternatives

Potentially actionable options for achieving the direction of the organization. Options should be consistent with the external and internal dimensions of the organization to leverage its strengths and exploit available opportunities.

Strategic development program

What is to be undertaken (scope and extent) based on an understanding of the current situation with respect to strategy, organizational capabilities, and resources.

Strategic direction

The vision, mission, values, policies, and primary goal statements of a strategic plan.

Strategic information system

The system established to maintain an organization's strategic focus through ongoing management and communication of information related to the development, implementation, and performance evaluation of strategy.

Strategic management

Managerial decisions and actions that determine the long-run performance of a business, This philosophy of management focuses on positioning the organization for success—both now and in the future. It integrates analysis, planning, implementation, and assessment and incorporates concepts from strategic planning, operational planning, quality improvement (continuous improvement), and organizational effectiveness.

Strategic operating plan

The blueprint for strategy implementation linking long-term goals with a balanced set of objectives and projects.

Strategic performance

Assessing outcomes at the objective level through the analysis of key performance indicators in order to keep the organization on track or to take corrective action.

Strategic planning

The process by which an organization defines and articulates its vision, mission, values, goals, strategies, and strategic operating for an identified period of time.

Strategic thinking

Analytic, creative, and critical thought processes that produce the ideas and insights that drive the strategic management process from formulation, to planning, and through implementation.

Strategy

A plan of action to achieve a goal(s) that aligns capabilities, competencies, and resources to take advantage of opportunities and counter threats. A complete statement of strategy must include *what* is to be accomplished and *how* to accomplish it.

Strategy deployment

Cascading an organizational strategy through linked initiatives/projects in all functional areas and their derived objectives, down to the lowest operating level of the organization.

Strategy deployment map

Graphical representation of the deployment of a strategy to provide a comprehensive overview of the strategy to facilitate implementation and management of the strategy.

Strategy formulation

The processes required to articulate the overall strategic direction of the organization, to compile a set of feasible strategies, and to evaluate and select those strategic options that are to be included in the strategic plan.

Strategy implementation

The management and operational processes required to add, modify, expand, delete an organizational strategy or functional component of strategy. It inculdes all ancillary changes in structure, management, and operations required to incorporate the strategy, or component of a strategy, as the new and accepted mode of managing, organizing, and operating.

Sub process

Group of related tasks that are designed to accomplish a significant portion or stage of a process.

Sub task

Activity required to carry out a particular task.

Supplier

The people (functions, departments, or organizations) who supply a process with its necessary inputs.

SWOT

(See OTSW)

System administrator

Person responsible for creating a new business unit in the MAPPware® tool, assigning a team manager to it, and providing high level technical support to the team manager.

Tactics

Actions taken by line management to deploy and implement corporate strategy throughout all levels and functions of the organization, These actions are constrained by strategic policies and goals, At the same time line managers are allowed to improvise and use their own initiative in achieving the desired outcomes.

Task

One of the steps required to accomplish a particular process or project.

Value administrator

Person responsible for customizing some of the list options and, if necessary, deleting data from the MAPPware® database.

Values

Belief, preference, or philosophy held by members of an organization that is a primary determinant of an organization's culture and ethical behavior.

Vision

The extrapolation of a current organizational state to a *desired future state*. It is a summary and succinct visualization of that future state and includes the key dimensions that are to be achieved in order to realize the vision.

Bibliography

Andrews, Kenneth. *The Concept of Corporate Strategy.* 2d ed. Homewood, IL: Dow-Jones Irwin Inc., 1980.

Ansoff, Igor H. *Corporate Strategy.* New York: McGraw Hill, 1965.

Argyris, Chris. *Knowledge for Action: A Guide to Overcoming Barriers to Organizational Change.* San Francisco: Jossey Bass, 1993.

Below, Patrick J., George L. Morrisey, and Betty L. Acomb. *The Executive Guide to Strategic Planning.* San Francisco: Jossey-Bass, 1987.

Bossidy, Larry, and Ram Charan with Charles Burck. *Execution: The Discipline of Getting Things Done.* New York: Crown Business, 2002.

Chandler, Alfred. *Strategy and Structure.* Cambridge, MA: MIT Press, 1962.

Collins, Jim. *Good to Great: Why Some Companies Make the Leap...and Others Don't.* New York: Harper Collins Publishers, 2001.

Drucker, Peter. *Management for Results.* New York: Harper Collins Publishers, 1964.

Drucker, Peter. *The Practice of Management.* New York: Harper Collins Publishers, 1954.

Farneworth, Ellis. *The Art of War by Niccolo Machiavelli*. Cambridge, MA: Da Capo Press, 2001.

Fry, Fred, and Charles Stoner. *Strategic Planning in the Small Business*, Chicago: Upstart Publishing, 1995.

Ghyczy, Tiha von, Christopher Bassford, and Bolko von Oetinger (ed.). *Clausewitz on Strategy: Inspiration and Insight from a Master Strategist*. New York: John Wiley and Sons, Inc., 2001.

Grundy, Tony. *Gurus on Business Strategy*. London: Thorogood, 2004.

Hackman, J. Richard, ed. *Groups That Work (and Those that Don't). Creating Conditions for Effective Teamwork)*. San Francisco: Jossey-Bass, 1990.

Hamel, Gary, and C.K. Prahalad. *Competing for the Future*. Boston: Harvard Business School Press, 1994.

Hamel, Gary, and C.K. Prahalad. "The Core Competence of the Organization." *Harvard Business Review* 68, no. 3 (1990): 79-91.

Hamel, Gary, and C.K. Prahalad. "Strategic Intent." *Harvard Business Review* 67, no. 3 (1989): 63-76.

Hamel, Gary, and C.K. Prahalad. "Strategy as Stretch and Leverage." *Harvard Business Review* 71, no. 2 (1993): 75-84.

Horwath, Rich. *Storm Rider: Becoming a Strategic Thinker*. Chicago: Sculptura Consulting, Inc., 2004.

Hoskin, Keith, Richard Macve, and John Stone. "The Historical Genesis of Modern Business and Military Strategy: 1850-1950." Paper, UMIST, LSE and University of Wales, Aberystwyth. As submitted to Interdisciplinary Perspectives on Accounting Conference, Manchester, 7-9 July, 1997.

Hughes, Marcia, and James Bradford Terrell. *The Emotionally Intelligent Team: Understanding and Developing the Behaviors of Success*. San Francisco: Jossey-Bass, A Wiley Imprint, 2007.

Humphrey, Albert. T*he Origins of the SWOT Analysis Model*, Stanford Research Institute, 1960–1970, summarized at http://www.businessballs.com/swotanalysisfreetemplate.htm

Kanter, Rosabeth M. *The Change Masters: Innovation for Productivity in the American Corporation*. New York: Simon & Schuster, 1983.

Kanter, Rosabeth M. "Collaborative Advantage: The Art of Alliances." *Harvard Business Review* 72, no. 4 (July-August 1994): 96-108.

Kanter, Rosabeth M. *When Giants Learn to Dance: Mastering the Challenges of Strategy, Management, and Careers in the 1990s*. New York: Simon & Schuster, 1989.

Kaplan, Robert S., and David Norton. "The Balanced Scorecard: Measures that Drive Performance." *Harvard Business Review* 70, no.1 (January-February 1992): 71-79.

Kaplan, Robert S., and David Norton. *The Balanced Scorecard: Translating Strategy into Action*. Boston: Harvard Business School Press, 1996.

Kaplan, Robert S., and D. P. Norton. *The Strategy-Focused Organization: How Balanced Scorecard Companies Thrive in the New Business Environment*. Boston: Harvard Business School Press, 2000.

Katzenbach, Jon R. *The Discipline of Teams: A Mindbook-Workbook for Delivering Small Group Performance*. New York: John Wiley and Sons, Inc., 2001.

Katzenbach, Jon R. *Teams at the Top: Unleashing the Potential of Both Teams and Individual Leaders.* Boston: Harvard Business School Press, 1998.

Katzenbach, Jon R., and Douglas K. Smith. *The Wisdom of Teams: Creating the High Performance Organization.* New York: Harper Business: A Division of Harper Collins Publishers, 1993.

Kim, W.C., and Renee Mauborgne. *Blue Ocean Strategy: How to Create Uncontested Market Space and Make the Competition Irrelevant.* Boston: Harvard Business School Publishing Corporation, 2005.

Kippenberger, T. "Do Value Constellations Supersede Value Chains?" *The Antidote* 2 (Issue 5 1997): 29-32.

Kippenberger, T. "Strategy according to Michael Porter." *The Antidote* 3 (Issue 6 1998): 24-25.

LaMarsh, Jeanenne. *Changing the Way We Change: Gaining Control of Major Operational Change.* Reading, MA: Addison-Wesley Publishing Company, 1995.

Learned, Edmund Phillip, C. Roland Christiansen, Kenneth Andrews, and William D. Guth. *Business Policy: Text and Cases.* Homewood, IL: Richard D. Irwin, 1969.

Mackin, Deborah. *The Team Building Tool Kit: Tips and Tactics for Effective Workplace Teams.* Chicago: American Management Association, 2007.

MacMillan, Pat. *The Performance Factor: Unlocking the Secrets of Teamwork.* Nashville, TN: Broadman and Holman Publishers, 2001.

Bibliography

Malcolm Baldrige Criteria. *2009-2010 Criteria for Performance Excellence,* the Baldrige National Quality Program at the National Institute of Standards and Technology in Gaithersburg, MD.

Maxwell, John C. *The 17 Indisputable Laws of Teamwork Workbook: Embrace Them and Empower Your Team*. Nashville, TN: Nelson Impact, A Division of Thomas Nelson Publishers, 2003.

McNeilly, M.R. *Sun Tzu and the Art of Business: Six Strategic Principles for Managers.* New York: Oxford University Press, 1996.

Michealson, Gerald A. *Sun Tzu—The Art of War for Managers: Fifty Strategic Rules*. Avon, MA: Adams Media Corporation, 2001.

Mintzberg, Henry. *The Nature of Management Work*. New York: Harper and Row, 1973.

Mintzberg, Henry. *The Rise and Fall of Strategic Planning*. London: Prentice Hall, 1994.

Mintzberg, Henry. *The Structuring of Organizations*. Englewood Cliffs, NJ: Prentice Hall, 1979.

Mintzberg, Henry, J.B. Quinn, and Jon Voyer. *The Strategy Process*. Englewood Cliffs, NJ: Prentice Hall, 1995.

Paret, Peter, ed. *Makers of Modern Strategy, from Machiavelli to the Nuclear Age*. Princeton, NJ: Princeton University Press, 1986.

Parker, Glenn M. *Team Players and Teamwork: The New Competitive Business Strategy*. San Francisco: Jossey-Bass Publishers, 1990.

Peters, Tom, and R.H. Waterman. *In Search of Excellence: Lessons from America's Best-Run Companies.* New York: Harper and Row, 1982.

Porter, M. E. *The Competitive Advantage: Creating and Sustaining Superior Performance.* New York: Free Press, 1985.

Porter, M. E. *Competitive Strategy: Techniques for Analyzing Industries and Competitors.* New York: Free Press, 1980. (Republished with a new introduction 1998.)

Quinn, J.B. *Strategies for Change: Logical Incrementalism.* Homewood, IL: Richard D. Irwin Inc., 1980.

Sanderson, S. (1998) "New Approaches to Strategy: New Ways of Thinking for the Millennium." *Management Decision* 36 (Issue 1 1998): 9-13.

Senge, Peter. *The Fifth Discipline: The Art and Practice of the Learning Organization.* New York: Doubleday, 1990.

Stern, C.W., and M.S. Deimler (eds.), *The Boston Consulting Group on Strategy*: *Classic Concepts and New Perspectives.* Hoboken, NJ: John Wiley and Sons, Inc., 2006.

Strauss, David. *How to Make Collaboration Work: Powerful Ways to Build Consensus, Solve Problems, and Make Decisions.* San Francisco: Berrett-Koehler Publishers, Inc., 2002.

Tracy, Brian. *Victory! Applying the Proven Principles of Military Strategy to Achieve Greater Success in your Business and Personal Life.* New York: AMACOM, a division of American Management Association, 2002.

Index

The letter *t* following a page number denotes a table; the letter *f* following a page number denotes a figure.

activities underway with strategic impact, 176–178, 244–245
Alexander the Great: war strategy, 18, 19
alignment/linkage/synergy between core functions, 223–228
alternatives, strategic, 51, 179, 186–196, 200–210, 215, 216
analysis: defined, 69–70, 100; initial assessment, 71t; as part of assessment, 137, 138; of strategic environment, 99, 100, 101–137
Andrews approach to strategy, 26–27, 28
Andrews, Kenneth, 25, 26
Ansoff, Igor, 27–28
Ansoff's Grid, 27t, 28, 140, 141f
approval process of strategic operating plan, 295–296
Art of War: Machiavelli, 16; Sun Tzu, 17, 371
assessment: of current strategic direction, 72–77; defined, 69–71, 137; factors influencing strategic program, 81–82, 83–84t; of impact of strategic operating plan on organization, 354–355; as overview, 72; of strategic management capabilities, 5, 72–80, 137, 138. *See also* Step 1

Balanced Score Card model, 38–39f, 266–268; compared to traditional function approach, 268t
barriers to developing strategic operating plan, 366–368

baseline, as performance measure, 278
BCG. *See* Boston Consulting Group
BCG Growth Share Matrix, 30f
benchmark: as performance measure, 278–279
Berlin, Isaiah, 42
Blue Ocean Strategy, 40–42, 362, 363
Bossidy, Larry, 303, 304t, 307, 315
Boston Consulting Group, 30–32
BSC. *See* Balanced Score Card
budget: summary implementation, 294, 295
building block approach, 139
Business Policy, Text and Cases: SWOT analysis, 23

Caesar, Julius: war strategy, 18, 19
cash cow: as BCG unit, 30
Certificate in Strategic Management, 368
challenges to implementation of strategic operating plan, 341–344t
champion management role, 309–310, 352
Chandler, Alfred, 25
change agent management role, 310–311, 352
change management, 303, 305, 307, 311, 352
Changing the Way We Change: Gaining Control of Major Operational Changes, 303, 310
Charan, Ram, 303, 304t, 307, 315
Chief Strategy Officer, 94

427

Christensen, C. Roland, 23
city-state warfare model, 16, 17
Civil War: and West Point strategic management model, 19
classical strategic management, 22
Clausewitz: modern war strategy, 17
Collins, Jim, 42, 43, 44
commitment, from management leadership for strategic management program, 92–93
committee members in startup strategic management program, 94–95
comparative evaluation, 199
Competitive Advantage (Michael Porter), 36
Competitive Strategy (Michael Porter), 36
components of strategic direction, 74–77
comprehensive strategic plan, 9. *See also* Step 10
Concept of Corporate Strategy (Kenneth Andrews), 25
context of strategic management, 53–59
contextual/situational criteria as type of evaluation, 200, 202–210
contingency plans, 249
converting information into strategic intelligence, 50–51
core competencies, 49, 141, 142, 143
core criteria: in evaluation selection procedures, 215–232; as type of evaluation, 200–202
core organizational competencies, 49
core set of shared values, 48
core strategic management leadership team, 94
cost of maintaining and operating strategic information system, 130
CSM. *See* Certificate in Strategic Management

delta: defined, 305; features of, 305–306t
deployment map for strategic goals, 271–272
design approach to strategy, 27, 28
developing a strategic operating plan. *See* Step 11
developing a strategic plan. *See* Step 10
dimensions of implementation of strategic operating plan, 341–344t

distribution of strategic operating plan, 296–297
dog: as BCG unit, 31
dominant functional level of strategic management startup program, 88–90
double loop learning, 274–275
Drucker, Peter, 21–22

environmental analysis: external, 101f–109; internal, 110f
environmental variables: in external strategic analysis, 101f–109; in internal strategic analysis, 110f
evaluate/select strategies to include in strategic plan. *See* Step 9
evaluating results of strategic analysis. *See* Step 6
evaluation: based on strategic analysis, 137; defined, 70–71, 100, 198–199; comparative, 199; criteria, 200–210, 215–232; goal achievement expectations, 220–223; intrinsic, 199; premature, 121; of strategic activities underway, 176–178; 244–245; of strategic operating plan, 355–357t
evaluation criteria: for OTSW evaluation, 8, 137t, 138, 139, 140–145; for strategic alternatives, 188–191, 200–210
Execution: The Discipline of Getting Things Done, 303, 304
execution: as requirement of implementation of plan, 303–307
external scan, 137, 139, 140
external strategic analysis, 101–109; environmental variables, 101f–109; framework for, 101f; issues to address, 103–105t, 107–109t; questions to ask, 105–106. *See also* Step 3
external strategic information, 100

feedback: from management to SIS, 136
first generation snapshot: of organization's strategic environment, 99
first phase: of implementation of strategic management plan, 300–301
flow diagram of strategic management process, 11f
format of strategies: defined, 245–246

formatting new/revised strategies, 245–246
free-standing strategic information system, 125, 126–127
future state environments, 138

"gap" analysis, 28
generic strategies, 36
globalization, 54–56
goal achievement expectations: in evaluation of strategies, 220–223
goal setting, 167, 169t, 171–172
goal statements: characteristics, 168t; compared to vision and mission statements, 167; examples, 168t
goals: compared to term objectives, 167; as component of strategic direction, 51, 73t, 167–173; evaluating, 170t, 220–223; level of development, 76t; modifying, 171
good governance: and strategic management, 360–362
Good to Great (Jim Collins), 42
growth share matrix, 30–32
Guide to Project Management Body of Knowledge, 298

Hamel, Gary, 142. See also Hamel and Prahalad
Hamel and Prahalad, 39–40t
Harvard School of Business: and SWOT analysis, 22–23
Haupt, Herman: and application of West Point strategic management model, 18
Hedgehog Concept, 42f–46
history of strategic management, 14–46

identifying strategic activities underway, 176–178; 244–245
illustrative strategic plan, 254, 255–258t
impact activities underway, 177
implementation of strategic operating plan, 10, 273–293; alternative approaches, 318t–319; barriers to, 346–349t; dimensions/challenges of, 341–344t; factors impeding process, 307f, 331–337; formats, 285–287t; line management job descriptions, 351–353; line management skilled abilities, 350–351t;

managerial roles/responsibilities, 273, 308–317, 351–353; measurement, 325, 326–328f; plan budget, 294, 295; planning guidelines, 260–264; task characteristics, 344–346t; two-phase process, 300–301, 337, 339–340. See also Step 12
improving strategic operating plan, 355–357t
information: age, evaluation of, 70; base of facts, perceptions, attitudes, 68; collection for SIS, 132–136; gathering, 50–51; technology, 56–57
information base of facts, perceptions, attitudes, 68
information system, strategic. See strategic information system
initial assessment, 70, 71t, 72
initiatives, strategic, 210–232, 246
innovation: and strategic management, 360, 362–364
In Search of Excellence (Tom Peters and Robert Waterman), 37
intelligence, strategic, 50–51
internal Analysis/Audit Checklist, 121. See also Appendix 2
internal: environment scan, 143; key results areas, 181, 183–186t
internal strategic information, 100
internal strategy analysis, 6, 110–123; framework for, 111f; framework for environmental, 110f; issues to address, 112–120t; questions to ask, 122–123. See also Step 4
intrinsic evaluation, 199

Kantor, R.M., 38
key functional areas: for startup program, 89
key performance indicators, 274–279, 280t
key results areas: developing strategic alternatives, 196, 215, 216; external, 181, 182–183t; framework with typical strategies, 182–186; internal, 181, 183–186t; for new/revised alternative strategies, 179, 186–196; selecting strategies, 229–232
Kim, W.C., 40, 44, 363

knowledge gap: among management, 67–68
knowledge management, 57–58
KPI. *See* key performance indicators

LaMarsh, Jeanenne, 303, 305–307, 310
leadership: assessment for startup strategic management program, 93–96; in evaluation of strategies, 215–219; perceptions of capabilities/resources of organization, 189–190; in strategic management, 78, 79–80t; team, 174–176
levels of development of components of strategic direction, 74–77
line management skills: for implementation of strategic operating plan, 350–351t; job description, 351–353
linkage/synergy/alignment: between core functions, 223–228
logical incrementalism, 44–45
long-run strategic planning, 237, 238–243
long-term set of strategies, 233
long-term strategic plan: accountability linkages with strategic operating plan, 264–268

Machiavelli, 16
macro-environment variables: in external analysis, 101f, 102, 103t–106
Malcolm Baldridge Quality Award for Performance Excellence, 144
management: responsibility for managing SIS, 128, 129, 130, 131
management capabilities: assessment of, 77–80; in developing strategic information system, 130
Management for Results (Peter Drucker), 22
management roles: to implement formats, 285–287t, 288–294; to implement strategic operating plan, 273, 308–317, 351–353
MAPP, xxiii
MAPPware, 368
Mauborgne, Renee, 40, 44, 363
Measurement Calendar, 326–328f

measuring: implementation performance, 325, 326–328f
meta-model of strategic management: West Point, 18–19
micro-environment variables: in external strategic analysis, 101f, 106–109
military: origins of strategy, 16–19, 20, 315; strategy organization, 58–59; after World War II, 19–22
Mintzberg, Henry, 44, 45
mission: compared to vision, 157; as component of strategic direction, 73t, 151, 157–159; level of development, 76t
mission statement: characteristics of, 158t; compared to vision and goal statements, 167; examples, 160t

Napoleon: modern war strategy, 17, 19
National Food Service Association, 154, 172–173t; as example, 173, 220–223; illustrative strategic plan, 254–258
nominal group technique, 143
Nominal Group Techinque to Prioritize an OTSW Evaluation. *See* Appendix 4
nonproject formats: implementation plans, 284, 287

objective setting, 168–169
ongoing process, strategic management, 10. *See also* Step 13
online learning: integrating with strategic management, 360, 368–369
operational analysis: as complement to strategic analysis, 121
operational information: compared to strategic information, 126; defined, 126
organizational: building blocks, 179f; core competency, 49
organization-wide: leadership assignments, 93–96; level of strategic management startup program 90–91
OTSW: analysis, 24f, 28; criteria for, 138; evaluation, 8, 137f, 138, 139, 140–145, 397–403; Priorities Sheet, 403; Ranking Ballot, 401; Scoring Sheet, 402; technique to clarify and prioritize, 397–403

outside help: in organizing startup strategic management program, 96–97
overview: initial assessment, 72

Pennsylvania Railroad, 18
Performance Measurement Exercise, 278f
performance measures, 275–279
Peters, Tom, 37
planning: approach to strategy, 27; framework, 246
policies: as component of strategic direction, 73t, 151, 163–167; examples, 164t; impact, 165t, 166t; level of development, 76t
Porter, Michael, 36. *See also* Porter's Five Forces
Porter's Five Forces, 32f–37
Practice of Management (Peter Drucker), 21–22
Prahalad, C.K., 142. *See also* Hamel and Prahalad
process capabilities: in assessing leadership capabilities, 78, 79–80t
process design: and SIS, 132–137
project management, 285, 298; approach for startup program, 87, 88, 89
Project Management Institute, 298

question mark: as BCG unit, 31
Quinn, James Brian, 44, 45

Red Ocean and Blue Ocean Strategy, 41f
resources: needed for implementation of strategic operating plan, 293–294

Scenario Planning, 188, 363; in contrast to SWOT analysis, 138
scope of strategic management program. *See* Step 1 and Step 2
second phase: of implementating strategic operating plan, 301
selection/evaluation criteria for strategy alternatives: types, 200–210
Senge, Peter, 38
senior facilitator: in organizing startup strategic management program, 96, 97
Seven S Model, 37–38
shared values, 48

short-term strategic planning, 233, 237–238, 243–244
SIS. *See* strategic information system
Smith, George Albert, 23
software: strategic management, 368–369
SOP. *See* strategic operating plan
spokes of change management, 305, 307
sponsor management role, 309, 352
Springfield Armory, 18
staffing: for SIS, 131
staff level communication plan, 296–297
Stanford Research Institute: SWOT analysis, 22–23
star: as BCG unit, 31
startup program, 6, 85–97; based on initial assessment. *See* Step 2; design, 85–92; leadership assessment, 93–96; modify design, 91–92; organize, 92–97; select level and scope, 86, 88–90
Step 1, 5, 68–85, 92, 110, 150
Step 2, 6, 85–97
Step 3, 6, 100, 101–109, 125, 137, 186
Step 4, 6, 100, 101, 110–123, 125, 137, 186
Step 5, 123–137
Step 6, 100, 137–147, 150, 186
Step 7, 8, 69, 74, 150–173, 186, 215, 220, 251, 363
Step 8, 8, 149, 173–196, 198, 212, 230, 363
Step 9, 8, 148, 188, 197–232
Step 10, 9, 214, 215, 215, 229, 233, 234–258
Step 11, 9, 214, 233, 243, 246, 249, 252, 258–274
Step 12, 10, 233, 243, 251, 300, 301–337, 338, 352, 353
Step 13, 10, 243, 251, 301, 337–357
Stewart, Robert E., 22–23
strategic activities underway, 176–178, 244–245
strategic alternatives, 51, 179, 186–196; evaluation criteria, 188–191, 200–210; in set of key results areas, 196, 215, 216
strategic analysis: evaluation, 137; external, 101–109; internal, 110f–123
strategic change, 302
strategic development champion, 93–94

strategic direction: analysis, 137, 139; assessment of, 72–77; components of, 51, 73t, 74–77, 151t–173; defined, 69; levels of components of, 74–77; sample, 172t. *See also* Step 7
strategic external information, 100
strategic impact of activities underway, 176–178, 244–245
strategic information: compared to operational information, 126; sources of, 134–136
strategic information system (SIS), 7, 99, 100, 123–137, 360, 364–36; basic features of, 131–137; control of, 125; cost of maintaining, 130; designing, 124, 125, 127–130; free-standing SIS, 125, 126–127; management responsibilities, 128, 129, 130, 131; process design, 132–137; staffing, 131; team-based approach, 127. *See also* Step 5
strategic initiatives: defined, 246; evaluate/classify/select, 212–232; evaluate/select/modify, 210–212
strategic intelligence, 50–51
strategic internal information, 100
strategic leadership team, 174–176
strategic management: as academic discipline, 29; assessment of, 79t; capabilities of management, 77–80, 130; characteristics of effective systems, 59–65; competencies, 46–53; considerations for establishing new system, 191–196; context of, 53–59; defined, 13–14, 128; development of strategic information system, 130, 360, 364–366; discipline of, 58–59; good governance, 360–362; history of, 14–46; innovation, 360, 362–364; leadership in, 78, 79–80t; misconceptions, 46t–48; as ongoing process, 10; online learning and software, 360, 368–369; team-based approach, 359; tools and techniques for execution, 360, 366–368; after World War II, 19–22; West Point model, 18–19
strategic management plan: approval process, 253–254; bridging to strategic operating plan, 266–268; functional linkages for one goal, 265–266f; illustrative strategic plan, 254, 255–258t
strategic management process: flow diagram, 11f; overview, 3–5
strategic objectives: in core functions, 269–271; defined, 270; implementation in nonprofit format, 284, 287
strategic operating plan, 9, 246, 247t–249; approval process, 295–296; assessing impact on organization, 354–355; budget, summary implementation, 294, 295; challenge to implementing, 341–344t; distribution, 296–297; evaluation, 355–357t; implementing, 10, 273–293, 308–319, 325, 326–328f, 337, 339–340, 341–344t, 346–349t, 350–353; improving, 355–357t; line management skills, 350–351t; long-term, 264–268; reconciling plan requirements with resources, 293–294; relationship with strategic planning, 247–248f; samples, 283–284t; summary budget, 294; tactics of implementing, 279–282; two-phase, 236–238, 249–253, 300–301, 337, 339–340
strategic planning, 3; compared with strategic thinking, 235–236; comprehensive framework, 246; importance of, 234; long-run, 233, 237, 238–243; short-term, 233, 237–238, 243–244; two-phase process, 236–238, 249–253
strategic thinking, 49; compared with strategic planning, 235–236; for establishing new strategy management, 191–196; of military commander, 18
strategies for arriving at desired destination. *See* Step 8
strategy: defined, 13, 26f; deployment map, 271–272; design approach, 27, 28; evaluation and selection process, 198; formulation, 3, 7, 235–236; implementation, 3, 260–264, 294–295, 307f, 331–337; management capabilities review, 77–80; origin of word, 16; selection by key results, 229–232; support processes, 177–178; timeline, 14, 15f, 16

Index

Strategy and Structure (Alfred Chandler), 25
stretch and leverage, 40
Sun Tzu: war strategy, 17–18, 371–375
SWOT analysis, 22–25, 28, 138
synergy/linkage/alignment: between core functions, 223–228

tactics: implementing strategic plan, 279–282
target of change management role, 311, 352
task characteristics: of implementing strategic operating plan, 344–346
Taylor, Daniel: application of West Point strategic management model, 18
team-based: approach to strategic management, 359; consensus in developing strategic information system, 127
team building, 51–53
team leaders: compared to all-knowing leader, 4
teams: strategic leadership, 174–176
team work, 51–53
Thayer, Sylvanus: application of West Point strategic management model, 18
timeline, strategy, 14, 15f, 16
tools/techniques: for execution of plan, 360, 366–368

two-phase based strategic operating plan, 236–238, 249–253, 300–301, 337, 339–340

umbrella spokes of change management, 305, 307

values: characteristics, 161t; as component of strategic direction, 73t, 151, 159, 161–163; core, 162; examples, 162t; level of development, 76t
variable: environmental, 101–110; as performance measure, 278
vision: compared to mission, 157; as component of strategic direction, 73t, 151, 152–157; level of development, 76t
vision statement: characteristics, 153t; compared to mission and goal statements, 167; development process, 155t; examples, 154t
visioning, 48

war strategy, 16–19, 20; Sun Tzu, 17–18, 375; after World War II, 19–22
Waterman, Robert, 37
Western Railroad, 18
West Point Military Academy: meta-model of strategic management, 18–19
Whistler, George: application of West Point strategic management model, 18

About the Authors

Randall Rollinson, left, is President of LBL Strategies, Ltd., a full service strategic management education, consulting, and software development firm (www.mappware.com). He is a certified Strategic Management Professional.

His work includes the *Certificate in Strategic Management Program*, which won the 2001 Exemplar Award from the International Association for Continuing Education and Training as an "exemplary, outstanding results-oriented program." He co-designed and developed an award winning *Certificate in Business Administration Program* offered at DePaul University from 1985 to 1988 and at the University of Illinois at Chicago from 1988 to 1999. As an adjunct faculty member, he periodically teaches strategic management in the MBA Program at University of Illinois at Chicago.

He has an MBA in Management from DePaul University, a Master's degree in Rehabilitating Counseling and a Bachelor's degree in Psychology from Southern Illinois University.

Since 1985, LBL has served more than 2600 organizations in a wide range of industries with practical strategy facilitation, development, and execution services. LBL is now partnering with the Strategic Management Association and the Association for Strategic Planning - Chicago Chapter to offer a blended online version of the CSM Program (www.csmlearning.com).

Earl Young, right, is Professor Emeritus at DePaul University, where he taught in the Department of Management. Prior to that he taught in the Departments of Management at the Illinois Institute of Technology and the University of New York at Albany.

His primary teaching and consulting activities have been in operations management, strategic management, and international development. In these areas he also designed and administered programs in continuing and professional education and small business management and entrepreneurship.

He conducted research on the technological development of firms in Mexico and on small business development in both the United States and Mexico.

He received his MBA from the University of Chicago and his PhD in Industrial Engineering and Management Sciences from Northwestern University.